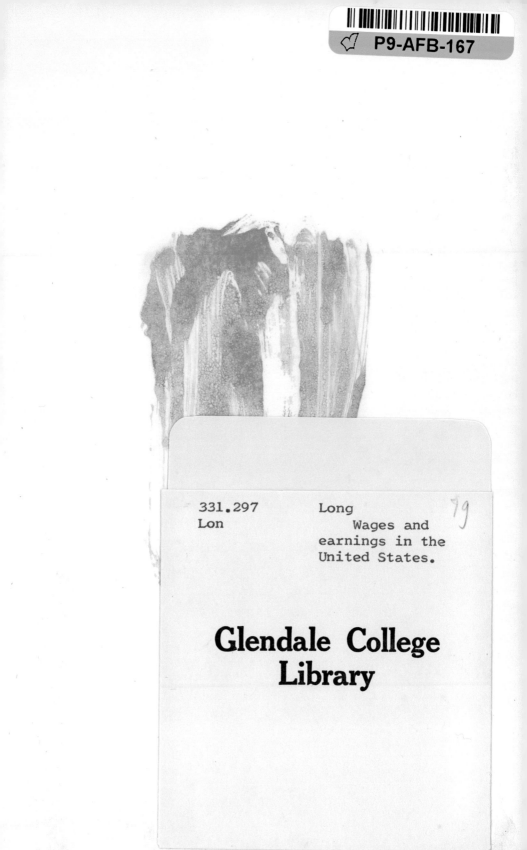

WAGES AND EARNINGS
IN THE UNITED STATES
1860-1890

NATIONAL BUREAU OF ECONOMIC RESEARCH

NUMBER 67, GENERAL SERIES

Wages and Earnings in the United States 1860-1890

BY CLARENCE D. LONG

The Johns Hopkins University

A STUDY BY THE

NATIONAL BUREAU OF ECONOMIC RESEARCH, NEW YORK

PUBLISHED BY

PRINCETON UNIVERSITY PRESS, PRINCETON

1960

FOREWORD

This monograph by Professor Clarence D. Long is one of several reports[1] on the history of wage rates and of changes in productivity in the United States over the past century which were made possible by a grant to the National Bureau from the Alfred P. Sloan Foundation. (The Foundation, of course, is not to be held responsible for the conclusions.) The period, 1860-1890, covered by Mr. Long's study is most interesting, for it included a great civil war followed by years of rapid industrialization, and saw a long decline in prices. Intensive study of the period was possible because of the availability for these years of the wage and price data of the Aldrich and Weeks reports, earnings data of the Census, and various collections of wage data by individual states and by the United States Department of Labor.

In reconstructing the wage history of this important segment in American economic development, Mr. Long shows the difficulties encountered in arriving at any single, most acceptable measure of money wages, prices, and real wages for a remote historical period in which the available data were sparse and of doubtful quality. He therefore places before the reader alternative bodies of data, discusses their respective virtues and defects, and finally chooses the series which, for the reasons he gives, appear most satisfactorily to depict the course of events he is engaged in describing.

A major finding is, first, that the money daily wage rate of factory employees in the United States, 1860-1890, increased about 50 per cent. Since hours of work declined during this period, money hourly earnings are found to have risen 60 per cent. By constructing a new index number of the cost of living, based on the index of Miss Ethel D. Hoover of the U.S. Department of Labor for the period 1860-1880 and on retail prices collected by himself for the decade 1880-1890, Mr. Long finds that cost of living in 1890 was 2 per cent less than in 1860. It follows, then, that real daily wages of factory employees, 1860-1890, rose by 50 per cent, and that real hourly earnings increased 60 per cent, or 1.6 per cent a year.

[1] John W. Kendrick, *Productivity Trends: Capital and Labor*, Occasional Paper 53, New York, NBER, 1956, and *Productivity Trends in the United States* (in preparation); Solomon Fabricant, *Basic Facts on Productivity Change*, Occasional Paper 63, New York, NBER, 1959; Albert Rees, *Real Wages in Manufacturing, 1890-1914* (in preparation), and a forthcoming paper presenting some revised statistics of real wages since 1914.

In addition, Mr. Long throws fresh light on changes in wage differentials—between regions, industries, occupations, and other classes of workers; and, during his discussion, suggests some of the important factors that played a significant role in accounting for the changes in wages and wage structure that he finds.

Everyone interested in the economic history of the United States and in the rate of development—past and future—in this and other countries will be influenced in his thinking by the combinations of data set forth and documented in Mr. Long's study.

LEO WOLMAN

ACKNOWLEDGMENTS

THE present work was begun at the suggestion of Leo Wolman, who turned over to me some files which had earlier been compiled under his direction. The study has benefited from the critical comments of Gerhard Bry, Richard A. Easterlin, Solomon Fabricant, Geoffrey H. Moore, Albert Rees, George Soule, and Leo Wolman. Much of any merit it possesses was made possible through the careful research assistance of Margaret Chen. H. Irving Forman drew the charts.

CLARENCE D. LONG

Baltimore, Maryland

CONTENTS

TABLES

Text tables show data at five- or ten-year intervals through the period (unless otherwise stated). Annual series are given in the appendixes.

APPENDIX TABLES

CHARTS

WAGES AND EARNINGS
IN THE UNITED STATES
1860-1890

CHAPTER 1

Introduction

The Time and the Questions

This monograph examines the changing level and structure of industrial wages in the United States between 1860 and 1890. Both of these years falling in a time of peace and at business peaks,[1] the wage comparisons between them benefit from comparable cyclical conditions; but otherwise the economy of the nation had changed markedly during the intervening thirty years. Indeed, these years rank among the most turbulent and dynamic in the nation's history, for they included one of its greatest wars, one of its sharpest inflations, one of its most protracted deflations,[2] and one of its longest and most widespread depressions.[3] They also bore witness to enormous economic growth. Clark has observed, perhaps with some exaggeration, that there was "a greater expansion of industry during 1860-1914 than in all the previous history of the race";[4] and the portion of time under review here could surely claim its share in that development. Employment in manufacturing and construction tripled, and Persons' index of physical output in manufacturing rose six times.[5] The iron and steel industry starting at almost scratch in 1860, had by 1890 become the largest producer in the world.[6]

Part of the economic growth was due to an enormous population addition, equal to the entire number of inhabitants in 1860. A third of the addition stemmed from a net immigration of about 10 million, mainly unskilled workers from Britain and northwestern and central Europe, rising to a flood in the decade of the 1880's. It was associated with an internal migration on a "previously unknown scale," as

---

[1] Arthur F. Burns and Wesley C. Mitchell, *Measuring Business Cycles*, National Bureau of Economic Research, 1946, p. 78.

In 1893 the Commissioner of the Bureau of Labor wrote: "The year 1860 represents, more nearly than any other year during this half-century, normal economic conditions." Carroll D. Wright, "Cheaper Living and the Rise of Wages," *Forum*, October 1893, p. 223.

[2] "Seldom has a highly organized business community carried on its transactions for 17 years on the basis of such unstable prices." Wesley C. Mitchell, *Gold, Prices, and Wages under the Greenback Standard*, 1908, p. 249.

[3] Rendigs Fels has characterized the decline from 1873 to 1878 as our longest and second most severe contraction, though he points out that it was a mild contraction so far as production was concerned. "American Business Cycles, 1865-79," *American Economic Review*, June 1951, pp. 344-345.

[4] Victor S. Clark, *History of Manufactures in the United States*, Vol. II, 1929 edn., p. 6.

[5] *Historical Statistics of the United States, 1789-1945*, Bureau of the Census, 1949, p. 179. The initial date of the index was 1863.

[6] Clark, *op.cit.*, p. 250. Actually Clark uses 1893 as the date.

3

Union and Confederate veterans and the surplus populations of the eastern farms took up the western lands. The North gained nearly two million persons at the expense of the South, while the West beyond the Mississippi gained, at the expense of the East, a number equal to the net immigration from abroad.[7] The westward migration was aided by a more than fivefold increase in railroad mileage[8] as numerous companies raced to tie the nation together with an iron network, stimulating, and stimulated by, the start of many new manufacturing industries in both South and West.

Thus the period—no longer than a generation—provides every major variety of experience for a study of wage behavior. It also furnishes an opportunity—which we shall not exploit fully—to see how wages behave in the absence of strong unions. The national trade-union movement put down many of its roots in this period; severe strikes were called; and unions no doubt exercised marked influence in some industries and occupations. But it is highly questionable whether, up to at least 1880, most firms in manufacturing were either touched directly by unions, or obliged in setting wage rates to take the threat of unionization very strongly into account.[9]

What questions then do we ask concerning wage behavior in these three decades of war and peace, inflation and deflation, boom and depression, immigration and migration, industrial expansion and consolidation, and transition from weak unionism to the early beginnings of a firmly established national trade-union movement?

Can we arrive statistically at a true average dollar wage level for workers in manufacturing and building?

Did money wages rise slowly or rapidly? Can we construct a wage index which reflects the true relative advance in the price of labor? Or, are the changes hopelessly obscured by shifts of workers between occupations, and by varying practices with respect to hours worked, overtime premium payments, bonuses, deductions, fringe benefits, and payments in kind?

Did wages rise slowly or rapidly in dollars of constant value—that is, adjusted to retail prices of cost-of-living items?

How did wages respond to the turbulence during the years between 1860 and 1890? To the Civil War? To the great depression of the 1870's? To the prolonged and almost uninterrupted deflation of prices from the end of the Civil War to 1890—a quarter of a century?

[7] *Historical Statistics*, pp. 30, 33-34.

[8] *Ibid.*, p. 200.

[9] *Report on the Statistics of Wages in Manufacturing Industries* . . . , by Joseph D. Weeks, *1880 Census*, Vol. xx, pp. xv, 3-563. However, the *Report on Trade Societies in the United States* indicates "marvelous development of organization during the years 1879 and 1880." (Vol. xx, p. 3.)

How did wages compare at a given time among different regions, industries, and occupations? Did these relationships vary as between East and West and South? Between metals and cotton? Between skilled and unskilled, males and females, adults and youths? Did the consolidation of the nations' internal economy through the construction of the rail network, and the vast movement of population tend noticeably to make wages in different regions, industries, and occupations more alike?

Finally, how did wages and earnings respond to such influences as labor supply, employment, productivity, and unionization?

These are the questions. How far we can answer them depends on the amount and quality of the statistics.

The Kind of Wage Statistics Needed

An effective study of the wage rate requires a good deal of knowledge about the firm paying it, the worker receiving it, and the service for which it is paid. Ideally, an average wage for the nation's manufacturing and building industries should rest on the wage received by every worker, classified by his personal characteristics and his precise occupational job description, as well as by the nature of his firm and its industrial classification. Such information would earmark variations in the price of a given quantity and quality of labor, as industries and occupations alter in character, as workers grow older and become more or less skillful, as women supplant men or children and immigrants the native-born in industrial jobs.

It would also be desirable to know how many hours the worker puts in as straight-time and as overtime; the rate for overtime; the prevalence of bonuses, tips, or gratuities in addition to the quoted wage; the nature of allowances in the form of reduced rent, firewood, garden privileges, or merchandise at discount prices; the amount of deferred compensation in the form of retirement pensions, paid vacations, and sick benefits; the extent of wage deductions through a worker's being charged for tools and materials used or for damages to equipment or product; the amount of his out-of-pocket payments to underhands; and the loss for workers paid in merchandise instead of cash.

Such wage statistics would be the ideal; we now consider the actual data.

Sources and Coverage of Data

Our wage statistics as distinguished from annual earnings data derive from three principal sources: the Aldrich Report, covering our full period, the Weeks Report, covering all except the last decade; and Bulletin 18 of the Department of Labor, covering all except the first decade. There are also wage statistics from the *First Annual Report of the Commissioner of Labor* for 1885, and from the 1900 census report by Davis R. Dewey for 1890, but these surveys give information for only a single year, and are used here mainly to test the levels of the Aldrich Report data.[10]

This section examines the content, coverage, and reliability of these data. It compares the methods used in this and other studies to combine the data of different occupations, firms, and industries into averages. In addition, it analyzes the data on average annual earnings from the decennial censuses for 1860, 1870, 1880, and 1890. The annual earnings data are full of pitfalls but they offer an additional check on the trend of wages during this period.

THE ALDRICH REPORT

The wage data are stated to have been taken by investigators of the Department of Labor "from actual payrolls" of business firms[11] (Appendix Table A-1), gathered in such a way that we have for the period 1860-90 from 78 firms, about 500 continuous series of occupational wage-quotations, each "showing the pay received by persons of one sex employed at one kind of work on one establishment," the great majority daily wage-rates, given for January and July.[12] On the average, wage data were reported for over 5,000

[10] Still other series might have been compiled in this study from the reports of various state departments of labor; but most of the state collections do not begin until late, are seldom continuous, and seem largely noncomparable. See Carroll D. Wright: "Nearly every one of the other bureaus in the country has at times published fragmentary wage and cost-of-living statistics; but the attempt of the student of real wages to ascertain from any single report, successive rates of wages and successive prices of commodities for a long period of years has either met with comparative failure or involved a labor which discouraged him almost at the start." From "Cheaper Living and the Rise of Wages," *Forum*, October 1893, p. 222.

[11] Carroll D. Wright, *loc.cit.*

The statistics of the Aldrich Report were collected under the direction of Wright, then Commissioner of the United States Bureau of Labor; Nelson W. Aldrich was chairman of the Senate Committee which made the report: *Wholesale Prices, Wages, and Transportation*, Report by Mr. Aldrich from the Committee on Finance, March 3, 1893, 52nd Congress, 2nd Session, Senate Report 1394.

[12] Little is known about the collection aside from this. The courtesy of Harry Douty and Richard Jones, in making possible an exploration of the archives of the Department of Labor resulted in the discovery of the wage schedule used by the investigators. The schedule was skimpy and included no instructions, but it did reveal *that a separate schedule was filled out for each employee*, with the firm's name, business, post office, street number, and state, and the employee's name, sex, and occupation. Space was provided for the payroll date of January and July for each year during 1840-91; also provided were columns for the industry, the unit of payment, and the wage rate. Although in the Aldrich Report the hours worked are indicated in detail for January and July of each year, the actual schedule provided only a single box for this entry at the top of the form. An exhaustive search of government archives and the private papers of Senator Aldrich and Carroll Wright—in the hope of discovering the original schedules as they were filled out for the individual workers and information about the sources and methods—was completely without result.

earners; the number varied widely over the period. Most were skilled and semiskilled manual workers; some unskilled manual laborers were among them also. A few (not included in this study) were sales clerks in two New Hampshire stores or worked on railroads or on city works. Clerical and managerial employees were entirely omitted; also piece-workers, as far as can be told. The original wage data covered about a score of industries, of which about three-fourths were manufacturing; the rest were miscellaneous nonmanufacturing, and—except for the building industry—were not analyzed in this investigation.[13] The industries varied widely in their importance in the economy and in the number of firms and employees represented.[14] In no sense was the sample a true cross section of the nation's firms, industries, or employees. The number of establishments on which most industries rested was small. Twenty-five were reported for the building trades and twenty-two for metals; but only one was reported for each of six of the industries used in this study, and we rely for the remaining industries on the records of two to four firms. Nearly two-thirds of the employees, in fact, were in less than a fourth of the establishments. Less than half of the industries included were represented by 100 or more employees. The Aldrich Report covered only the New England and Middle Atlantic states, and tells us nothing about the South and West.

THE WEEKS REPORT

Weeks, like the Aldrich Committee, gathered his data from payroll records so as to give a continuous wage history of the same occupations in the same firms for some one date each year over a considerable period.[15] (See Appendix Table A-3.) In each of the more

---

[13] The Aldrich Report also contained supplementary series on wages in the coal, iron, glass, and pottery industries, as well as on salaries of public schoolteachers, by rank, in large cities, but the series were not accompanied by data on the number of persons employed at these wages.

[14] The manufacturing industries together with the number of firms and the average number of employees represented during 1860-90 were: agricultural implements (1 firm; 21 employees); ale, beer, porter (1; 43); books and newspapers (3; 120); carriages and wagons (1: 22); cotton goods (4; 715); ginghams, included in cotton goods in this study (1; 707); illuminating gas (4; 394); leather (2; 61); lumber (2; 34); metals and metallic goods (19; 1,094); paper (1; 33); spices, excluded from this analysis (1; 19); stone (6; 488); white lead (1; 10); woolen goods (3; 283). Building trades were represented by 21 establishments with 436 earners. The nonmanufacturing industries, not analyzed in this study, were: sidewalks (1; 17); railroads (1; 269); city public works (4; 953); dry goods stores (1; 10); grocery stores (1; 4).

[15] *Report on the Statistics of Wages in the Manufacturing Industries with Supplementary Reports on the Average Retail Prices of Necessaries of Life and on Trade Societies, and Strikes and Lockouts,* by Joseph D. Weeks, *1880 Census,* Vol. xx, pp. ix-xi. The Weeks investigation could obtain no useful wage data from employees (p. xvi).

prominent manufacturing, mechanical, and mining industries in various sections of the country, "typical" establishments were selected, based on their age, standing, productive capacity, and general reputation. From these firms were secured "the most complete and accurate returns practicable." The mailing list of firms was said to be prepared after much correspondence with experts in each industry and recourse to trade directories and publications. No important branch of manufacturing was overlooked, but the information on some was not returned or was unsatisfactory. Moreover, of the more than fifty industries with satisfactory returns, less than a score could be used in the present investigation, for only that many had wage data covering the entire period 1860-80.

Views differ as to adequacy of methods and accuracy of results. Carroll D. Wright, who may have felt some need to justify his Aldrich investigation, declared that the Weeks statistics of wages "were averages [rather than actual payments] in nearly every instance, made up in counting rooms of manufacturing concerns, the method of arriving at the average, the elements entering into it . . . not being known to the officers in charge of the work."[16] The report itself, conceding that the first returns were unsatisfactory, indicated that they were checked over carefully by the investigators and "Not infrequently . . . were passed backward and forward several times before a final adjustment was reached."[17]

It is probably not possible to decide which data are best. The Weeks data span fewer years, give almost no employment information nor wage data for males and females, report wages for only once a year, and do not always refer to the same month (indeed, they do not even indicate the month). On the other hand, they embrace more establishments, industries,[18] and states—for they also include wages paid by many establishments in the South and West (we follow Mitchell in classifying the western states as those beginning with Ohio). In addition, the Weeks Report tells more about how the data were gathered and offers possibly better information on methods of paying wages. It states that the data do not usually cover overtime, holiday and Sunday work, and other extra earnings, and that it has deducted any payments to helpers and underhands, so that the worker's wage

[16] Wright, *op.cit.*, p. 221.
[17] Weeks Report, p. xv.
[18] The Weeks Report covers over 600 establishments in over fifty industries; the establishments were probably better distributed among industries than was the case in the Aldrich Report. On the other hand, much of the Weeks data were fragmentary. From that source, the present investigation makes its fullest reliance on 67 establishments in 18 manufacturing industries; from the Aldrich data, on 49 establishments for the 13 manufacturing industries, and 21 establishments for the building trades.

covers what he receives only for his own work. Finally, Weeks attempted to convert piece rates into daily wages, wherever the firms could furnish information on time put in by piece workers.

BULLETIN 18 OF THE DEPARTMENT OF LABOR[19]

If the Aldrich and Weeks Reports are reticent as to sources and methods, Bulletin 18 is virtually silent (Appendix Table A-4). It provides no separate data by firm or industry, but merely wage quotations for each of 14 occupations in each of twelve large cities in the East, West, and South—quotations that in most instances were taken directly from payrolls, in each city, of at least two establishments that had existed and done business continuously since 1870.[20]

The Labor Department regarded these wage levels as being higher than the average in the specified occupation for the entire country, because they were drawn only from the larger industrial centers. The report converted the wages for 1870-78 into equivalents in gold, but for present purposes, they were reconverted into currency on the basis of the greenback price of gold which the Department of Labor showed on the tables.

THE FIRST ANNUAL REPORT OF THE COMMISSIONER OF LABOR[21]

The data in this report were gathered by fifteen agents who worked with "faithfulness and assiduity" for 10 months on all aspects of the depression including the collection of wage data.[22] "The wages in nearly all cases were taken direct from the payrolls."[23] The report covered well over 500 establishments in 36 manufacturing industries in the United States and provided daily average wage rates classified by occupation, industry, and state. It furnished separate wage rates for adult males, adult females, and children and youths, and additional information on hours and days of work (Appendix Table A-7). The

[19] September 1898; edited by Carroll D. Wright.
[20] "Thus continuous and accurate returns for the period covered have been made possible, greatly enhancing the value of the tables." The Department gathered a great deal of information which it did not publish, including data on "number of employees working on full time and receiving each specified rate of pay. This information in its detail is extremely interesting, but almost 400 pages of the Bulletin would have been required for its publication...." Bulletin 18, pp. 666-667, 670-693.
[21] *The First Annual Report of the Commissioner of Labor*, March 1886, "Industrial Depressions," pp. 143-226.
[22] "The agents of the Bureau have, as a rule, been met with courtesy and a desire to furnish the information sought; yet it should be distinctly understood that if the manufacturers of any locality miss comparative data in the construction of tables ... the lack of completeness is due entirely to the apprehension of manufacturers that the information required would do them some harm, or to their positive refusal to furnish the information," p. 6.
[23] P. 141.

data, gathered for only 1885,[24] can tell us nothing about wage behavior over time; but since the survey was based on twenty-five times as many employees as the Aldrich Report, it may be useful as a bench mark in testing the level of the Aldrich wages and as an indication of whether the level was higher or lower than that of all workers in 1885.

THE DEWEY CENSUS REPORT

The Dewey Report for 1890, collected in connection with the census of 1900 (Appendix Table A-8, below), restricted inquiry "to a few stable and normal industries." When collected, the data for 1890 were twelve years old. Many records had been destroyed or left with previous owners of firms that had changed hands. Others could not be used because they were obscure, especially where child labor was concerned. The data do not all refer to the same month, but rather to a full-time payroll during a normal period, thus avoiding periods characterized either by overtime or by slackness, holidays, and short time. (The census year included the twelve months ending May 31, 1890.)

The Dewey Report data do have certain advantages. They were extracted from actual records of employers; were based insofar as possible on wage rates rather than earnings; and were classified by industry, occupation, sex, and broad age groups—under 16, and 16 and older. Efforts were made to take account of allowances and deductions, and to exclude the wages of nonproduction workers—supervisors, officials, and office workers. Though far from complete, the figures compiled were nevertheless comprehensive by the standards of our Weeks and Aldrich data, covering over thirty industries and more than 100,000 workers. "On the whole, the Dewey Report was probably the most important and most reliable report on wages which had, up to that time, been published in the United States."[25]

IN SUMMARY

It will be appreciated that the statistics of this period are far short of ideal. First, some industries were not covered in the original reports and others could not for various reasons be used in this analysis.[26] The number of firms reported was very small and almost

[24] The report does not indicate what month of 1885 the wage data refer to, or even whether the wage data of all the establishments refer to the same month.

[25] Paul F. Brissenden, *Earnings of Factory Workers 1899 to 1927; An Analysis of Payroll Statistics*, Census Monographs x, 1929, p. 261.

[26] Of the 21 two-digit manufacturing industries which exist at present, all but one—electrical machinery—had some operation in 1860-90. In the main, these industry groups were fairly well represented. The Aldrich Report represented 13 of them, omitting ordnance, furniture, instruments, miscellaneous, tobacco, apparel, and rubber products; Weeks also represented 13, omitting printing, chemicals, petroleum and coal products, and rubber products, as well as ordnance, instruments, and miscellaneous. The First Annual Report represented all 20 of the existing two-digit industries.

certainly unrepresentative, for it is the superior employers who tend to survive for long periods, or to keep records if they do survive, and to furnish data if they were kept—firms were not reported if they went out of business before 1880 or 1890, and new firms were not covered because they had too brief a wage history or escaped notice.

Second, the number of employees covered, while presenting a considerable task in manipulation of data, was tiny compared to total employment in manufacturing and building.

Third, none of the published reports identified the workers individually, and it was therefore impossible to tell, when a given wage-rate fell, whether the actual wage-rate schedule had fallen or whether, merely, a high-wage worker had quit and had been replaced by a new worker at a beginner's rate. Data on the number and sex of the workers were given only by the Aldrich, First Annual, and Dewey Reports; information on age was confined to some occupational classifications for "children or youths" or "boys" or "girls."

Fourth, the data were confined almost entirely to daily rates and gave only small representation to piece-rate earnings (which may advance more rapidly than time rates, as methods and machinery improve). Little or no wage representation was given to sales, clerical, supervisory, or managerial employees.

Fifth, the occupational classifications were rather general and—in a period of great technological change when new machinery and methods were breaking down old jobs and creating new skills—did not necessarily reflect actual developments in the quality and intensity of effort of the workers.

Sixth, most of the data seemed to come closer to measuring wage rates than earnings, but some of the data were based on the latter and no explicit indication was given as to which data are which. Except possibly for the Aldrich data, the reports were obscure as to what month the data refer to, or even to whether they always refer to the same month.

Seventh, while the Weeks Report attempted to eliminate overtime and other premium payments so as to express wages in the price of a regular workday, and to take account of allowances and deductions so as to make the daily wage reflect the actual rather than the nominal wage, it could scarcely do so adequately; the other reports make no mention of an attempt.

Eighth, none of the wage reports taken separately provided a continuous wage series for the whole nation and the entire period. The Aldrich Report covered manufacturing and building for 1860-90, but only for the Northeast. The Weeks Report gave some coverage to all regions but only for 1860-80 and only for manufacturing. Bulletin

18 also covered all major regions but only for selected large cities and selected occupations during 1870-90. However, the average annual earnings data of the decennial censuses while they do not provide reliable indication of how wage rates were moving in the nation as a whole, or even perhaps how average earnings were behaving, may furnish an independent check on the change in the industrial and regional structure of earnings over time.

Finally, the quality of both collection and tabulation was uncertain in view of the small size of the statistical staffs, the skimpiness of the descriptions, and the delay in gathering the data—from old records, years after the wages were earned.

Are the wage materials useless, then, for study of wage behavior during these years?

A principal advantage is their continuousness over a long period for the same nominal occupations, firms, and industry; we are not in the position, as are students of wages in some nations or periods, of having to patch our series together from smaller series, sometimes covering different periods and sometimes relating to different concerns or parts of the industry.[27] Another advantage is their variety of classification, by sex, occupation, firm, industry, and locality: we are not forced to say, "as almost always in regard to historical wage statistics, it has been practically impossible to compile averages for different groups of workmen, which can be compared with each other for the same year."[28] A third advantage is that the data are based—so far as we can tell—on actual business records and, while subject to clerical or other technical error, do not depend for their accuracy on the memory, truthfulness, or knowledge of an employee or some member of his family. And a fourth advantage is that the data come in independent sets, each taken by different investigators or staffs from the records of entirely different firms, but often duplicating the same occupation, industry, and locality; thus we can test for accuracy through comparison of the levels and rates of change. All in all, while much inferior to the wage data of the present day, the materials for 1860-90 are very likely as good as, or superior to, those of many other nations.

[27] Gösta Bagge, Erik Lundberg, and Ingvar Svennilson, *Wages in Sweden, 1860-1930*, Vol. II, Part 1, 1933: "The work of patching together all these different sources of Swedish wage statistics has not only been laborious and lengthy but has also entailed many risks of errors and mistakes. ... As is so often the case in regard to wage statistics, our problems have been mainly problems of finding and turning to useful account different and often defective sources." (Pp. 10-11.)

[28] P. 11. "We have been reduced to ... studying not the wages themselves, but their rates of change." See also Arthur L. Bowley, *Wages and Income in the United Kingdom since 1860*, 1937, p. 3.

CHAPTER 2

The Course of Money Wages
during 1860-1890

Daily Wages in Manufacturing and Building

The average daily wage made an estimated net over-all advance between 1860 and 1890 of roughly 50 percent for manufacturing and 60 percent for building trades workers (Tables 1 and 2). We have some confidence in these estimates, at least in the one for manufacturing which rests on three independent estimates from four sets of basic data: the Weeks and the Bulletin 18 data, which combine to form one estimate; the Aldrich data; and the census decennial average annual earnings. Still, it would be well to disclaim any precision for these materials. The Weeks Report ends in 1880, covers only manufacturing, and has sparse representation from the South. The Bulletin 18 Report begins in 1870, and provides wage data for mainly skilled occupations in large cities—only two of them southern. The Aldrich Report gives no wages for the South and West. And the censuses, though they undertake to cover all manufacturing for the whole nation, report only decennial years and annual earnings, which can be compared with daily wages only under comparable employment conditions. All the estimates refer to manual workers.

The 50 percent increase for daily wages in manufacturing is supported by all three independent estimates: The Aldrich data yield a rise over the thirty years of 48 percent. The Weeks and Bulletin 18 data, in combination, yield a rise of 50 percent (the former indicating a rise of 34 percent from 1860 to 1880 and the latter 12 percent from 1880 to 1890. And the average annual earnings in manufacturing, derived from the decennial censuses and described in Chapter 3, yield a 44 percent rise for all manufacturing and 49 percent for 17 industries that come closest to comparability with those in the Weeks and Aldrich Reports. These increases are a fifth less than those found by Mitchell and Falkner from weighted means of Aldrich data.[1]

The advance of approximately 60 percent for building trades daily wages was, by necessity, derived almost entirely from Aldrich data. These data are confined to the eastern states, but they cover the entire thirty years. The Weeks Report contains no information on building, and the Bulletin 18 data cover only four skilled building occupations

---

[1] Falkner obtained an increase of nearly 60 percent in his simple mean and nearly 70 percent in his weighted mean. Mitchell obtained an increase of close to 60 percent in both his simple and weighted means, but only 53 percent in his weighted median.

MONEY WAGES, 1860-1890

TABLE 1

Money Average Daily Wages in Manufacturing Industries, Based on Aldrich, Weeks, and Bulletin 18 Reports, Compared with Census-Reported Average Annual Earnings in Manufacturing: 1860-1890

Year	Aldrich Report	Weeks Report	Bulletin 18	Weeks– Bulletin 18	Census: Average Annual Earnings All manufactures	17 Industries[a]
			CURRENT DOLLARS			
1860	1.19	1.32			297	277
1865	1.64	1.82				
1870	1.79	1.92	2.05		384	363
1875	1.72	1.84	1.93			
1880	1.54	1.77	1.72		345	325
1885	1.61		1.87			
1890	1.75		1.93		427	412
			RELATIVES: 1860 = 100			
1860	100	100		100	100	100
1865	138	138		138		
1870	151	146		146	129	131
1875	145	139		139		
1880	130	134		134	116	117
1885	136			146		
1890	148			150	144	149
			PERCENTAGE CHANGES			
1860-1880	+30	+34		+34	+16	+17
1880-1890	+14		+12	+12	+24	+27
1860-1890	+48			+50	+44	+49

Source and explanation: Text of Chapter 2; Appendix Tables A-1, A-3, A-4, A-9.
[a] Adjusted to exclude, in 1890, earnings of officers, firm members, and clerks, and in all census years, the following: wage earners in hand trades; two industries, boots and shoes and men's clothing, dominated by custom and repair shops; nonmanufacturing industries; and intermittently reported manufacturing industries. For detailed listing of the excluded earnings, see Table 14; for a listing of the 17 industries, Appendix Table C-2.

beginning in 1870. Unlike our results for manufacturing, the building wages from these two sources were not in close agreement, the Aldrich data showing a larger net decline between 1870 and 1890 and fluctuating more in the 1870's and 1880's. Again, our rise for the thirty years was about one-sixth smaller than that found by Mitchell—apparently because of our using census-reported employment weights for different states and our averaging dollar instead of relative wages.

TABLE 2

Money Average Daily Wages in the Building Trades, Aldrich and
Bulletin 18 Reports, 1860-1890

Year	Aldrich Report	Bulletin 18	Census: Average Annual Earnings, Construction
	CURRENT DOLLARS		
1860	1.69		412
1865	2.55		
1870	3.06	2.97	423
1875	2.69	2.78	
1880	2.14	2.55	453
1885	2.56	2.89	
1890	2.68	2.94	620
	RELATIVES: 1860 = 100		
1860	100		100
1865	151		
1870	181		103
1875	159		
1880	127		110
1885	151		
1890	159		151
	PERCENTAGE CHANGES		
1860-1880	+27		+10
1880-1890	+25	+15	+37
1860-1890	+59		+51

Source and explanation: Text of Chapter 2; Table 14; Appendix Tables A-1 and A-4.

The Method Used in This Study

Our investigation of wages differs from others of this period in a number of features. First, the use of dollar wages enables us to study the absolute wage level, the absolute variations in wages over time, and the structure of wages among different occupations, industries, regions, or type of worker at a given time. Other investigators have studied only the relative changes in wages, and only changes in the relationship compared to the base date.

Second, our analysis is confined to manufacturing and building industries, and eliminates railroads, sidewalks, city public works, dry goods, and grocery stores. Moreover, it keeps building trades separate from manufacturing.

Third, it relies mainly on those firms, industries, and occupations

15

with wage data covering the entire period 1860-80 or 1860-90, and excludes data beginning after 1860 or having substantial gaps during 1860-90. This means that our average wages based on the Aldrich Report were for only 49 firms in manufacturing and 21 in building, instead of a somewhat larger number, and that our average based on the Weeks Report was for only 69 firms instead of over 200 firms with more or less continuous data that begin after 1860, and more than 600 for which some wage information has been issued.

Fourth, the wage averages in this study are weighted averages, based at the establishment level on the number of persons employed at the various wage rates, and at the state and industry levels on the number of persons that the decennial censuses reported as gainfully occupied. The averages for the Aldrich and Weeks data were computed in five steps:

Step one. Establishments were classified by industry and state, e.g., cotton goods in Massachusetts.

Step two. An average wage was computed for each establishment from the wages for each occupation. For the Aldrich data, the occupational wage rates could be weighted by the number employed in that occupation. For the Weeks data, the lack of necessary employment information obliged us to compute an unweighted average of these occupational wage rates within a firm.

Step three. An average wage was computed for each industry in each state for which wage data were available. For the Aldrich data, the average wage of each establishment could be weighted by its employment, to arrive at a weighted average wage for all the establishments in the industry in that state. For the Weeks data, the state-industry average could not be weighted, owing to the lack of employment data for the firms. Where there was only one firm, its wages data had to represent the industry in the state and in the nation.

Step four. For both Aldrich and Weeks data the state wage for each industry was weighted by the number gainfully occupied in that industry in that state, using decennial census data for 1860, 1870, 1880, and 1890, and linear interpolations between censuses. The result was the weighted average wage for an industry, covering all the states in which that industry was reported. Separate averages were computed for eastern states, western states, and southern states.

Step five. The wage for each industry was combined into the wage for all manufacturing industries. This was done for the Aldrich Report by means of weighting by the gainfully occupied in each of its industries, to obtain national and regional weighted average wages for all the 13 industries in that report. The same was done for the 18 industries of the Weeks Report.

Bulletin 18 did not report on an establishment or industry basis; rather, it reported on only 14 occupations. Four of these—bricklayers and masons, carpenters and joiners, house painters, and plumbers— were of the kind found in the building trades and were therefore averaged to obtain a so-called national wage for building, despite the fact that some persons in these occupations are also employed in most manufacturing industries. The remaining ten—blacksmiths, boilermakers, cabinetmakers, compositors, iron-molders, laborers (nonstreet), machinists, patternmakers, stonecutters, and teamsters— might be called manufacturing occupations, though many of them are also found in industries like transportation, construction, or repair service. Since Bulletin 18 did not furnish employment data, the occupations were weighted by the number gainfully occupied at the decennial census in the states in which the cities reported on in the bulletin were located.

Methods Used by Others

Almost every analyst of these materials has resorted to a different system for combining the relative wage rates of the various occupations into an average for the industry and the nation. The principal analysts have been Roland P. Falkner, Wesley C. Mitchell, Alvin Hansen, and E. H. Phelps Brown with Sheila V. Hopkins.

Falkner, who wrote the Aldrich analysis, used two kinds of averages. One was a simple average of relatives, with each occupational series having equal weight within the industry, regardless of wage and number of employees, and each industry also having equal weight, regardless of the number of firms and employees in the industry. The other was a weighted average, constructed in the same way up to the industry level, but differing in that the average wage of each industry was weighted by the number of persons attached to that industry at the decennial population censuses.[2]

Mitchell criticized the weighting methods employed by Falkner

[2] Aldrich Report, Part 1, p. 176. Falkner reduced the number of industry groupings from 22 to 17, sidewalks and spices not having been important enough for separate classifications, gingham having been included under cotton mills, and dry goods and groceries having been combined under the census term dry goods (stores). Since census designations did not always cover exactly the categories for which wage data were reported, Falkner let white lead stand for chemical manufactures, and city public works for government. He used the census number of gainful workers (say for 1860) for the first five years of the decade (say 1860-64), and used the average of the numbers reported at the two censuses (say 1860 and 1870) for the last five years of the decade (say 1865-69). Since the 1890 census had not yet been tabulated, Falkner used the 1880 data for the period 1880-90.

as "so faulty that I have thought it necessary to do the whole work over again."[3] His chief criticism of Falkner's averages was that —weighted or unweighted on the national level—they both rested within an industry on simple averages of the relative wages of the different occupational series. Instead, Mitchell constructed two sets of averages.[4] One set for the Aldrich data consisted of means— weighted and simple. His weighted mean was constructed by multiplying each relative wage quotation by the number of employees receiving that wage, summing the products, and dividing by the number of employees.

His second set consisted of medians—again simple and weighted. The simple median was constructed by ranking the relative wage quotations at any given time from lowest to highest, without regard to number of employees receiving them, then choosing the middle-most wage as median. This method, for lack of employment data, was the sole one applied to the Weeks data. His weighted median was constructed from the Aldrich data by ranking the relative wage quotations at any given month from lowest to highest alongside the number of employees receiving them and then choosing the wage quotation as median which belonged to the middle-most worker. At the same time he also constructed the deciles. Mitchell confined his analysis of Aldrich data to the median weighted by employment.

Hansen's study was part of a "long-run view of the course of real wages" for the period 1820-1923. He used two indexes of *money* wages for this period. Curve A was constructed by joining (1) Mitchell's weighted average daily wage index for the period 1860-80 (which he described as more scientifically constructed than Falkner's index), and (2) Falkner's unweighted index for 1880-90. Curve B was an average of the index numbers of the weekly wages of laborers and artisans compiled by the Russell Sage Foundation from "governmental" sources, including the Massachusetts, Weeks, and Aldrich (Falkner) Reports, and Bulletin 18 of the Bureau of Labor Statistics.[5] Hansen did not describe the data further, and he made no analysis of money wages, proceeding immediately to his adjustment for price level changes and his discussion of real wage behavior.

In a recent, comparative study of wage rates in a number of countries, E. H. Phelps Brown and Sheila V. Hopkins also relied upon the Aldrich materials for the American experience during

[3] Wesley C. Mitchell, *Gold, Prices, and Wages under the Greenback Standard*, p. 92.
[4] Mitchell's entire analysis was of wages expressed in relatives of 1860.
[5] Alvin H. Hansen, "Factors Affecting the Trend of Real Wages," *American Economic Review*, Vol. xv, 1925, p. 27. The B series he obtained directly from Ralph G. Hurlin.

1860-89, and have put together an index which combines, with modifications, the methods of Mitchell and Falkner. They followed Mitchell in weighting the wages of the occupations by the number of employees receiving these wages in order to obtain the weighted average for the industry, but deviated in using the average employment for 1870-79 rather than for each individual date. They followed Falkner in using as weights the total numbers occupied in the several industries, but again deviated in using as constant weights throughout the number of persons occupied in the several industries in 1870.[6]

Comparison of Average Wages Obtained in This and Other Investigations Using Aldrich Data

Relative wages obtained by this and other investigations from the Aldrich data are compared for quinquennial dates in Table 3. Several features are worth noting.[7]

There was very little difference in relative change between the mean and the median—whether Mitchell's simple mean is compared with his simple median or his weighted mean with his weighted median. The median is laborious to compute and, though free of the randomness that derives from the influence of extreme values, is subject to the randomness that derives from gaps in the distribution of the values in a smaller number of observations. Since wage data of manual workers are free of really extreme values, it seemed easier, and at least as safe, to use the mean.

It did make a difference whether the average was weighted or unweighted by employment. Mitchell's weighted mean rose substantially more than his unweighted mean during and after the Civil War, stood relatively about 10 percent higher in 1870, then fell proportionately more to 1875. The same may be said for the comparison of weighted and unweighted medians. However, the over-all advance between 1860 and 1880 or 1891 was much the same whether the relative wages were weighted or unweighted. Falkner's weighted means also advanced more than his unweighted means during and after the Civil War. This difference had disappeared by 1875 and 1880, but it reappeared during the 1880's, making the net advance between 1860 and 1890 greater for his weighted average. The reason

[6] E. H. Phelps Brown with Sheila V. Hopkins, "The Course of Wage-Rates in Five Countries, 1860-1939," *Oxford Economic Papers*, New Series Vol. 2, June 1950, pp. 267-269.

[7] The averages presented by Hansen do not merit separate comment, since they were derived by merely splicing the indexes of Mitchell for 1860-80 and of Falkner for 1880-90. The average presented by Phelps Brown and Hopkins, since their chief distinction of method was in using fixed instead of variable weights, will be discussed in a later chapter in connection with that question.

TABLE 3

Relatives of Average Daily Wage-Rates, Computed from the Aldrich Report in This
and Other Investigations: 1860-1890

(Basic Data, Average of January and July; 1860 = 100)

	This Study 13 Manufacturing Industries, Weighted Mean[a] (1)	Falkner		Mitchell 21 Industries				Hansen Series A (8)	Phelps Brown (9)
		21 Industries, Simple Mean[a] (2)	17 Industries, Weighted Mean[a] (3)	Simple Mean[a] (4)	Weighted Mean[a] (5)	Simple Median[a] (6)	Weighted Median[a] (7)		
1860	100	100	100	100	100	100	100	100	100
1865	138	143	149	144	154	144	151	153	158
1870	151	162	167	162	180	162	180	179	182
1875	145	158	158	158	165	158	163	164	170
1880	130	142	143	143	143	138	139	140	151
1885	136	151	156	n.c.	n.c.	n.c.	n.c.	149	170
1890	148	159	168	161[b]	158[b]	n.c.	153[b]	157	174

n.c. Not computed.

Source: Table 2, above; Falkner, Aldrich Report, Vol. 3, Part 1, pp. 173-176; Wesley C. Mitchell, *Gold, Prices, and Wages under the Greenback Standard*, pp. 105-118, 120, 169-170, 173-174, 204-206; Alvin H. Hansen, "Factors Affecting the Trend of Real Wages," *American Economic Review*, Vol. x (1925), p. 32; E. H. Phelps Brown with Sheila V. Hopkins, "The Course of Wage-Rates in Five Countries, 1860-1939," *Oxford Economic Papers*, New Series, Vol. 2, June 1950, p. 277.

[a] Computed from occupational wage quotations, not from wages of individual persons.
[b] January 1891.

for this greater fluctuation of the average, Mitchell felt, was that the more widely fluctuating wages were those of the relatively numerous unskilled and semiskilled workers and that the larger establishments had a stronger tendency than the smaller firms to advance wages more rapidly during the general rise and reduce them more sharply during the general fall.[8]

Third, Mitchell's weighted mean fluctuated more widely than Falkner's, rising relatively more during and after the Civil War and falling relatively more during the 1870's, but it lost ground during the 1880's and realized a smaller net advance between 1860 and 1890. In commenting on these differences, Mitchell remarked that Falkner, in his method of weighting the wages of the 17 industries by the census returns for the numbers gainfully occupied in these industries, "kept his old errors of method, and added new ones to them."[9] This was because the Falkner method retained the faulty technique

[8] Mitchell, *Gold, Prices, and Wages*, p. 171-172.
[9] *Loc.cit.* Before making his comparison, Mitchell recomputed Falkner's simple or unweighted average (in order to make sure that the disparity of movement was not caused by Mitchell's omission of a few series which Falkner used), made separate series for males and females in occupations in which both sexes are employed, and computed relative wages always on the basis July 1860 = 100.

of arriving at the average for each industry by giving each occupational series equal weight, and numbers reported gainfully occupied by the census "do not give weights properly applicable to industries." We shall say something about these "errors" presently, since they bear on the accuracy of the method of weighting used in this study.

Fourth, the weighted averages of wages derived in this study for the 13 manufacturing industries and for building (Tables 3 and 4) differ somewhat from the averages obtained in all the other investigations—showing less fluctuation during the 1860's and 1870's and less net advance between 1860 and 1880 or 1890.

What is the explanation of this smaller fluctuation and advance? In the case of manufacturing, about two-thirds of the disparity seems to be due to my use of census-reported, instead of Aldrich-reported, employment weights for averaging the wage rates of firms in different states and for computing the wages of different industries (Table 5, line 5). This is brought out most clearly in that Falkner's weighted mean which relied on census-reported employment, was substantially lower in 1865, 1870, and 1875 and therefore closer to my averages than Mitchell's weighted mean which used Aldrich-reported employment. On the other hand, Falkner's index was substantially higher than Mitchell's index in 1890 and therefore not so close to my average in that year. Mitchell, as we have seen, felt that the Falkner method was in error, but after all, the purpose of the average should be to give most weight to industries that employ the most workers in the nation as a whole and not to the ones that happened, through accident of selection and reporting, to be the largest employers in the Aldrich sample.[10] Mitchell is on firm ground in stating that census weights give excessive importance to some industries for which his data were too scanty to give reliable averages. However, his chief examples of this were dry goods (stores) and railroads, which we exclude from our average of wages in the 13 manufacturing industry average.

Much of the remaining difference is provided by the exclusion of nonmanufacturing industries; of these, public works, railroads, and building have much the most of the weight (Table 5, line 4). The final source of measurable difference is in computing my average from dollar rather than relative wages. The effect was tested by comparing for 13 individual industries my index computed from dollar wages with Mitchell's computed from relative wages. On the whole the effect was very small (see Table 5, line 6).

[10] Albert Rees is in disagreement with me on this method of weights. However, he suggests that he is willing to yield the point if the census annual earnings data should turn out to move more closely with my daily wage data than with those of Mitchell as between decennial dates 1860-90. This proves to be the case (Table 15).

21

TABLE 4

Relatives of Average Daily Wage-Rates in the Building Trades; Computed
from the Aldrich Report in This and Other Investigations: 1860-1890
(Basic Data, Averages of January and July; 1860 = 100)

	This Study Weighted Mean	Falkner Simple Mean	Mitchell	
			Weighted Mean	Weighted Median
1860	100	100	100	100
1865	151	161	150	148
1870	181	186	188	182
1875	159	169	167	168
1880	127	143	141	144
1885	151	170	n.c.	–
1890	159	173	169	175

Source: See Table 3.

TABLE 5

Factors Explaining the Discrepancy in Relative Behavior between the
Weighted Mean of Dollar Wage-Rates in Manufacturing Derived in
This Study from the Aldrich Report, and the Weighted Mean of Relative
Wage-Rates, Derived from It by Wesley Mitchell for the Manufacturing
Industries along with Others: 1860-1890
(Basic Data, Averages of January and July; 1860 = 100)

	1860	1865	1870	1875	1880	1885	1890
1. Mitchell: 21 industries[a]	100	154	180	165	143	n.c.	158[b]
2. This study: 13 manufacturing industries	100	138	151	145	130	136	148
3. Excess of line 1 over line 2	–	16	29	20	13	–	10
Estimated discrepancy due to fact that this study:							
4. Excludes city public works, railroads, building[c]	–	4	10	4	0	–	1
5. Uses census- instead of Aldrich-employment weights on industry and state levels[d]	–	14	20	10	8	–	9
6. Computes dollar averages before converting to relatives[e]	–	−1	1	1	3	–	0
7. Sum of lines 4-6	–	17	31	15	11	–	10
8. Remaining discrepancy[f] (line 3 minus line 7)	–	−1	−2	5	2	–	0

n.c. Not computed by Mitchell.
Source and explanation: Mitchell, *Gold, Prices, and Wages*, pp. 94, 95, 120, 173;
this study, Appendix Table A-1, and text of this chapter. (Notes continue on p. 23.)

In the case of building wages, however, the reason for most of the excess of Mitchell's index over mine is that his was computed from relative wages whereas mine was computed from dollar wages. My use of census-reported employment in weighting occupational wages on the state level was accountable for only a minor part of the difference. (Table 6.)

In sum, the smaller rise in my averages of manufacturing and building wages between 1860 and 1870, or between 1860 and 1890, has been due almost entirely to three factors: First, dollar wages give more weight to high-wage occupations in which wages typically advanced relatively less during this period. Second, census-reported weights happen to give greater weight to certain industries whose average wages showed smaller advance. Third, the 13-industry average excludes certain nonmanufacturing industries whose wages rose substantially more than those in manufacturing. If these differences in method are justifiable, the restrained fluctuation and smaller over-all advance of my wage-averages represent more accurately the true wage behavior of this period.

---

[a] The industries include—besides manufacturing—railroads, building, dry goods, and others.

[b] January 1891.

[c] Line 4 was computed as the difference between Mitchell's index of relative wages with and without building, city public works, and railroads.

[d] Line 5 was computed by subtracting for each quinquennial year my 13-industry average of wages weighted by census-reported employment in each industry, from a 13-industry average of wages weighted by Aldrich-reported employment in each industry.

[e] Line 6 was computed by: (a) taking the difference in each of the 13 industries for quinquennial years between my weighted average wage, derived by averaging dollar wages in the various occupations, and Mitchell's weighted average wage derived by averaging relative wages in the various occupations; (b) weighting these differences by the Aldrich-reported employment in each of the industries to obtain the weighted average differences given on line 6. In order to lighten the heavy burden of computation, this was done only for July of each quinquennial year. Presumably, the average of January and July would have yielded somewhat different results.

[f] The remaining discrepancy could be due to several factors: (a) Mitchell includes several other industries which have only small weight in his result, but nevertheless they have some effect in causing his index to deviate from mine; (b) the discrepancies in lines 4-6 have been weighted by Aldrich-reported employment instead of census-reported employment; neither set of weights can yield a complete account of the discrepancy; (c) this study builds its averages up, for certain industries, by first computing state averages and then combining these state averages on the basis of the importance of the industry in those states as reflected in census-reported employment, whereas Mitchell combines his establishments wages directly by means of Aldrich-reported employment without regard to states. These differences are significant for a few industries such as cotton, woolens, and metals; (d) Mitchell includes a number of occupations for which wage data are missing during certain years; this study includes only those occupational wage series for which the data are almost completely continuous; (e) Mitchell's 1890 figure really refers to January 1891 whereas mine is the average of January and July 1890.

TABLE 6

Factors Explaining the Discrepancy in Relative Behavior between the
Weighted Mean of Dollar Wages in Building Derived in This Study from
the Aldrich Report, and the Weighted Mean of Relative Wages Derived
from It by Wesley Mitchell: 1860-1890
(Basic Data, Averages of January and July; 1860 = 100)

	1860	1865	1870	1875	1880	1885	1890
1. Mitchell	100	150	188	167	141	n.c.	169[a]
2. This study	100	151	181	159	127	151	159
3. Excess of line 1 over line 2	–	−1	7	8	14	–	10
Estimated discrepancy due to fact that this study:							
4. Uses census weights on state level instead of averaging directly with Aldrich weights[b]	–	0	2	2	3	–	1
5. Computes dollar averages before converting to relatives[c]	–	−1	4	7	8	–	8
6. Sum of lines 4 and 5	–	−1	6	9	11	–	9
7. Remaining discrepancy[d]	–	0	1	−1	3	–	1

n.c. Not computed by Mitchell.
Source and explanation: Mitchell, *Gold, Prices, and Wages*, pp. 94, 95, 120, 173;
this study, Appendix Table A-1.

[a] January 1891.

[b] Line 4 was computed by subtracting (a) my average of dollar wages for building
trades occupations, weighted by Aldrich-reported employment on the occupational
and firm level and by census-reported employment on the state level, from (b) my
average of dollar wages for building trades weighted by Aldrich-reported employment
on all levels.

[c] Line 5 was computed by substituting my average of *dollar* wages for building
trades occupations weighted by Aldrich-reported employment, from Mitchell's average
of *relative* wages similarly weighted.

[d] The remaining discrepancy is explained by: (a) This study does not use occupational wage series with substantial gaps between 1860 and 1890; (b) Mitchell's figure
for 1890 is really for January 1891, whereas mine is the average for January and July
1890. (c) In order to lighten the heavy burden of computation, lines 4 and 5 were
computed for only July. If the differences for January had been included, the average
for each quinquennial year would have been somewhat different.

Comparison of Average Wages Obtained in This and Other Investigations Using Weeks Data

My wage series and that prepared by Mitchell are the only two Weeks
series which, so far as I am aware, have been constructed in any
systematic way, the Weeks Report not furnishing an analysis of its
own wage materials.[11]

[11] Hansen makes some use of the Weeks data in his series B, but tells nothing about
his method (*op.cit.*).

TABLE 7

Relatives of Average Daily Wage-Rates Computed in This and
Mitchell's Investigations from the Weeks Report: 1860-1880

	This Study: 18 *Manufacturing* *Industries,* *Weighted Means*[a]	*Mitchell:* 30 *Manufacturing* *Industries,* *Unweighted Medians*[b]
1860	100	100
1865	138	139
1870	146	155
1875	139	145
1880	134	138

Source: Appendix Table A-3; Mitchell, *Gold, Prices, and Wages*, pp. 176-177.
[a] 67 establishments.
[b] 144 establishments, p. 176.

The two studies differ markedly in coverage and method. The present study relies on 67 establishments in 18 industries for which data cover the period 1860-80 without serious gap. It computes unweighted means on the occupational and establishment level, and means weighted by census-reported employment on the state and industry levels. And it derives weighted averages of dollar wages before converting them into relatives. Mitchell covered 144 establishments in 30 industries. He computed unweighted medians of occupational series. And he converted his occupational wage data into relatives before computing his unweighted medians.

The two series based on Weeks and presented in Table 7 for quinquennial years reveal comparative behavior analogous to that for the Aldrich Report: my series rising relatively less than Mitchell's during and after the Civil War, and advancing less between 1860 and 1880. The explanation is no doubt largely the same as that for the Aldrich data, with the added fact that my average was a mean and Mitchell's was a median; but the labor involved in testing the source of the differences was so great that the test was not repeated in the case of the Weeks data.

Comparison of Average Wages from the Several Sources of Wage Data

The results derived from Aldrich and Weeks have not yet been compared with each other or with the data derived from other sources described earlier in the book, namely; Bulletin 18 of the Department of Labor covering 1870-90, the First Annual Report of the Commissioner of Labor for 1885, or the Dewey Report for 1890.

ALDRICH AND WEEKS

The averages from these two, during the two decades between 1860 and 1880, on the whole manifested similar patterns of behavior. Both showed a rapid rise during and after the Civil War to a peak in the early 1870's, a marked decline to a low point in the late 1870's and a net advance from 1860 to 1880. However, two differences are noted. The Aldrich daily wage (as computed in this study) was substantially lower throughout than the Weeks average: in 1860, $1.19 compared with $1.32; in 1880, $1.54 compared with $1.77. And the Aldrich average fluctuated a bit more than the Weeks average during the Civil War boom and the deflation of the 1870's.

It will be remembered that the Aldrich Report covered industries located entirely in eastern states, whereas the Weeks Report had representation in the West and South also. Were the lower level of wages and the higher relative fluctuation of the Aldrich data due to those differences? To test the possibility, the Aldrich average was compared with the Weeks average for the eastern states—but without significantly different results.

Could the explanation lie in the industries covered? Separate averages were computed for wages in the six industries common to the two reports—cotton goods, woolen goods, lumber, paper, breweries, and metals. There was no certainty that industries called by the same names produced the same commodities. For example, it was necessary to assume that saw and planing mills in the Weeks Report were the same as lumber in the Aldrich Report, and that the three metal industries—iron blast furnaces, rolling mills, and nail factories; machinery; and stove foundries—in the Weeks Report correspond to the category called metals and metallic goods in the Aldrich Report. As before, my Aldrich wage average was lower than my Weeks average at each decennial date although the differences in level were smaller, but the fluctuations of the two six-industry averages were almost exactly the same. It would seem that although the lower absolute level of the Aldrich wage data was an inherent characteristic, the wider fluctuation was due to the differences in industrial coverage.[12]

During 1870-90 the data of the Aldrich Report for 13 manufacturing industries may be compared with those of Bulletin 18 of

[12] Wesley Mitchell made a similar finding as a result of his comparison for the three individual industries with substantial numbers of firms reporting in each set of data: cotton, woolens, and metals. In each case he used the unweighted median of relative occupational wage quotations. He concluded: "The general result of these comparisons is to strengthen the claim of both sets of figures to recognition as a reliable indication of the trend and, broadly speaking, the degree of variations in wage-rates in manufacturing industries from 1860 to 1880." Gold, Prices, and Wages, p. 217.

the Department of Labor for ten occupations more or less identifiable with manufacturing. This comparison for quinquennial dates. indicates again that the Aldrich average wages were lower in absolute level—roughly 10 percent—throughout the period, but that they manifested rather similar fluctuations: both declining by a sixth or a

TABLE 8

Daily Wage-Rates in Selected Occupations: Aldrich and Bulletin 18
Data Compared by States, 1870-1890

State, and number of establishments or city reported on	Current Dollars					Percentage Changes	
	1870[a]	1875[a]	1880	1885	1890	1870-1890	1880-1890
BLACKSMITHS							
Maryland							
Aldrich (1 est.)	2.59	2.42	2.09	2.35	2.38	−8	14
Bulletin 18 (Balt.)	2.38	2.09	2.21	2.24	2.12	−11	−4
New York							
Aldrich (4 est.[b])	2.84	3.06	2.42	2.55	2.89	2	19
Bulletin 18 (N.Y.C.)	2.73	2.67	2.68	2.63	2.83	4	6
Massachusetts							
Aldrich (1 est.)	3.00	3.50	2.75	3.25	3.25	8	18
Bulletin 18 (Boston)	3.64	3.02	2.94	3.02	2.80	−23	−5
Pennsylvania							
Aldrich (2 est.[b])	2.84	2.46	1.96	1.98	2.16	−24	10
Bulletin 18 (Phila. and Pittsburgh[c])	2.28	2.42	2.15	2.31	2.31	1	7
CARPENTERS							
Maryland							
Aldrich (1 est.)	2.72	2.33	2.00	2.59	2.59	−5	30
Bulletin 18 (Balt.)	2.57	2.09	2.15	2.42	2.43	−5	13
New York							
Aldrich (2 est.[b])	3.49	3.06	2.12	2.63	2.94	−16	39
Bulletin 18 (N.Y.C.)	3.49	3.43	3.41	3.49	3.48	0	2
Massachusetts							
Aldrich (1 est.)	2.50	2.29	1.69	1.95	2.20	−12	30
Bulletin 18 (Boston)	2.59	2.15	2.29	2.42	2.52	−3	10
Pennsylvania							
Aldrich (2 est.[b])	2.58	2.55	2.50	2.74	2.73	6	9
Bulletin 18 (Phila. and Pitts.[c])	2.87	2.62	2.16	2.72	2.72	−5	26

27

Table 8 (*continued*)

State, and number of establishments or city reported on	Current Dollars					Percentage Change	
	1870[a]	1875[a]	1880	1885	1890	1870-1890	1880-1890
COMPOSITORS							
New York							
Aldrich (2 est.[b])	3.00	3.00	2.52	2.43	2.50	−17	−1
Bulletin 18 (N.Y.C.)	3.07	2.90	2.98	3.03	3.06	0	3
MACHINISTS							
Maryland							
Aldrich (1 est.)	2.56	2.56	2.39	2.56	2.55	0	7
Bulletin 18 (Balt.)	2.26	2.31	2.29	2.31	2.32	3	1
New York							
Aldrich (5 est.[b])	2.50	2.72	2.10	2.44	2.38	−5	13
Bulletin 18 (N.Y.C.)	2.75	2.62	2.53	2.50	2.70	−2	7
Massachusetts							
Aldrich (4 est.[b])	2.77	2.44	2.12	2.45	2.31	−17	9
Bulletin 18 (Boston)	3.00	2.67	2.43	2.53	2.58	−14	6
Pennsylvania							
Aldrich (2 est.[b])	2.78	2.37	2.11	2.28	2.60	−6	23
Bulletin 18 (Phila. and Pittsburgh[c])	2.17	2.22	2.03	2.29	2.24	3	10
PAINTERS							
Maryland							
Aldrich (1 est.)	3.00	2.50	1.75	2.50	2.50	−17	43
Bulletin 18 (Balt.)	2.50	2.50	2.50	2.50	2.50	0	0
New York							
Aldrich (2 est.[b])	4.50	3.42	2.85	3.00	3.50	−22	23
Bulletin 18 (N.Y.C.)	2.97	3.27	3.15	3.38	3.55	20	13
Massachusetts							
Aldrich (2 est.[b])	2.15	2.15	1.75	2.41	1.89	−12	8
Bulletin 18 (Boston)	4.25	3.97	2.98	2.48	3.10	−27	4
Pennsylvania							
Aldrich (1 est.)	–	2.94	2.35	2.57	2.74	–	17
Bulletin 18 (Phila. and Pitts.[c])	2.81	2.80	2.45	2.78	2.78	−1	13

[a] Converted from gold to currency by multiplying the gold wages during 1870-79 by the following ratios: for 1870, 1.213; 1871, 1.107; 1872, 1.091; 1873, 1.127; 1874, 1.114; 1875, 1.125; 1876, 1.128; 1877, 1.062; 1878, 1.014. (The wage data, originally expressed in currency, were converted into gold in Bulletin 18.) Multiplying by the above ratios has reconverted them into the original currency.

[b] Mean, weighted by employment.

[c] Mean, weighted by numbers reported by the census for these occupations.

seventh from 1870 to 1880, and both recovering most of this during 1880-90, with a net decline over the twenty years of a few percent.

Bulletin 18 covered mainly skilled occupations in large cities in all sections of the nation; the Aldrich data skilled and semiskilled occupations in communities of unknown but widely varying size, located in eastern states only. What happens if we compare only occupations of the same names in the same states? This we do in Table 8 for blacksmiths, carpenters, compositors, machinists, and painters in Maryland, New York, Massachusetts, and Pennsylvania. The results were not encouraging. There was fairly close agreement in net change between 1870 and 1890 in the case of blacksmiths in Maryland and New York, carpenters in Maryland, and machinists in Maryland, New York, and Massachusetts, but not much in the other occupational-state comparisons. There was also little agreement in fluctuation. The rather similar movement of the over-all averages thus seems to have been the result of the offsetting of differences in occupational, geographical, and even industrial coverage.[13]

THE ALDRICH, FIRST ANNUAL, AND DEWEY REPORTS

The First Annual Report of the Commissioner of Labor referred only to 1885 and could not reveal fluctuations in wages over time, but it covered about 130,000 workers in nearly 40 manufacturing industries. Its wage level was substantially lower: $1.44, in 1885 compared with $1.61 for the Aldrich Report and $1.87 for Bulletin 18 for that year. In an effort to reveal whether this discrepancy was due to differences in industrial and geographical or occupational coverage, the wages were compared, from the two reports, for the same industry, occupation, and states: e.g., male mule spinners in cotton goods in Massachusetts (Table 9). Even greater discrepancy was disclosed between the Aldrich and First Annual Reports, with the average for 12 occupations in seven states being about 28 percent higher in the Aldrich data. The discrepancy varied widely by occupation, but Aldrich wages were higher in two out of three of the comparisons.

The probability that the Aldrich wage level, though lower than the Weeks level, was inherently higher than the wage level of all manufacturing workers in the United States, was further supported by the Dewey-Census Report, based on 1890 wage data of many thousands of workers. Comparison of hourly wages for 10 industries

---

[13] The ten occupations included in the Bulletin 18 average, while presumed here to represent manufacturing, may also be found in nonmanufacturing industries such as transportation.

TABLE 9

Wage-Rates in Same Industry, Occupation, and State: Selected Data
Comparing Aldrich Report and First Annual Report, 1885
(wages and hours are weighted averages)

Industry and Occupation	Number Employed	Hours per Day	Daily Wage	Hourly Wage
MASSACHUSETTS				
Cotton goods				
Mule spinners, male				
Aldrich[a]	22	10.5	1.63	.155
First Annual	274	10	1.25	.125
Weavers, male				
Aldrich	292	11	1.20	.109
First Annual	390	10	1.13	.113
Weavers, female				
Aldrich	331	11	1.03	.094
First Annual	2,018	10	.94	.094
Laborers, male				
Aldrich	14	10	1.27	.127
First Annual	127	10	1.08	.108
Woolen and worsted goods				
Loom fixers, male				
Aldrich	7	10	1.93	.193
First Annual	10	10	1.90	.190
Carders, male				
Aldrich	7	10	1.15	.115
First Annual	18	10	1.18	.118
CONNECTICUT				
Woolen and worsted goods				
Loom fixers, male				
Aldrich	3	11	2.20	.200
First Annual	2	11	1.35	.123
Weavers, female				
Aldrich	15	11	1.40	.127
First Annual	61	11	1.05	.096
Burlers, female				
Aldrich	8	11	.82	.075
First Annual	13	11	.69	.063
NEW YORK STATE				
Cotton goods				
Mule spinners, male				
Aldrich	4	11	1.65	.150
First Annual	157	11	1.32	.120
Weavers, female				
Aldrich	57	11	.83	.076
First Annual	1,229	11	.90	.082

Table 9 (*continued*)

Industry and Occupation	Number Employed	Hours per Day	Daily Wage	Hourly Wage

NEW YORK STATE, (*continued*)

Industry and Occupation	Number Employed	Hours per Day	Daily Wage	Hourly Wage
Metals and metallic goods				
Machinists, male				
Aldrich	132	10	2.26	.226
First Annual	281	10.1	1.93	.191
Pattern makers, male				
Aldrich	21	10	2.80	.280
First Annual	12	10	2.28	.228
Molders, male				
Aldrich	45	10	2.37	.237
First Annual	7	10	2.50	.250
Blacksmiths, male				
Aldrich	23	10	2.60	.260
First Annual	35	11	2.25	.204

PENNSYLVANIA

Industry and Occupation	Number Employed	Hours per Day	Daily Wage	Hourly Wage
Metals and metallic goods				
Machinists, male				
Aldrich	68	10	2.28	.228
First Annual	181	10.4	2.35	.226
Laborers, male				
Aldrich	90	10	1.23	.123
First Annual	1,934	10.3	1.20	.117
Pattern makers, male				
Aldrich	10	10	2.24	.224
First Annual	2	10	3.00	.300
Molders, male				
Aldrich	42	10	2.28	.228
First Annual	135	10	2.28	.228
Blacksmiths, male				
Aldrich	9	10	2.00	.200
First Annual	240	10.1	1.84	.183

MARYLAND

Industry and Occupation	Number Employed	Hours per Day	Daily Wage	Hourly Wage
Metals and metallic goods				
Machinists, male				
Aldrich	23	10	2.53	.253
First Annual	1	12	2.30	.192
Laborers, male				
Aldrich	16	10	1.22	.122
First Annual	25	12	1.25	.104

NEW JERSEY

Industry and Occupation	Number Employed	Hours per Day	Daily Wage	Hourly Wage
Metals and metallic goods				
Machinists, male				
Aldrich	5	10	2.55	.255
First Annual	4	9	2.00	.222

Table 9 (*concluded*)

Industry and Occupation	Number Employed	Hours per Day	Daily Wage	Hourly Wage
	NEW JERSEY, (*continued*)			
Laborers, male				
Aldrich	6	10	1.59	.159
First Annual	12	9	1.35	.150
Pattern makers, male				
Aldrich	3	10	3.15	.315
First Annual	4	9	2.40	.267
	NEW HAMPSHIRE			
Metals and metallic goods				
Machinists, male				
Aldrich	6	10	1.75	.175
First Annual	5	10	2.25	.225
Moiders, male				
Aldrich	15	12	2.13	.177
First Annual	25	10	2.00	.200
	12 OCCUPATIONS IN 7 STATES			
Aldrich	1,274	10.6	1.51	.143
First Annual	7,202	10.4	1.18	.113

Source: Aldrich Report, Vol. 3, Parts 2-4, Table XII; *First Annual Report of the Commissioner of Labor*, 1886, Appendix A.

[a] The Aldrich data throughout are for July.

(Table 10) once more suggests a higher general level for Aldrich wage rates, though again there were exceptions.

Averages of Wages from a Constant List versus an Increasing List of Occupations or Establishments

The main analysis has rested on those occupations, establishments, and industries for which wage data were available throughout 1860-80 in the Weeks Report, or throughout 1860-90 in the Aldrich Report, thus leaving out many for which fragmentary wage data were available after 1860. Doesn't this omission introduce bias? After all, a continuous wage history over a long period can come only from well-established firms in older industries. Not all of the firms and occupations whose data began later than 1860 were new; the lack of early data was often due to lost records or a change of ownership. But in a rapidly growing nation would not the proportion

TABLE 10

Comparison of Hourly Wages from the Aldrich Report and the Dewey
Report, Ten Manufacturing Industries, 1890

| | Number of Employees for Whom Wages Were Reported | | Hourly Wage Rates | | |
| | | | Median of Occupations,[a] | Median of Individual Workers, Dewey | Column 3 Minus Column 4 |
	Aldrich (1)	Dewey (2)	Aldrich (3)	(4)	(5)
Agricultural implements	51	4,134	.17	.16	.01
Ale, beer, porter (breweries)	64	3,434	.16	.20	−0.04
Books and newspapers (printing)	192	3,587	.25	.26	−0.01
Carriages and wagons	40	2,098	.25	.16	.09
Cotton textiles	1,079	6,757	.12	.10	.02
Leather (tanneries)	83	2,581	.16	.15	.01
Lumber and planing mills	23	2,307	.10	.14	−0.04
Metals and metallic goods (foundries and metal working)	1,810	24,266	.22	.16	.06
Paper	27	1,121	.08	.13	−0.05
Woolen textiles	595	7,995	.13	.10	.03
Ten industries: Employees reported on	3,964	58,280			
weighted median rate			.22	.16	.06
All industries:[b] Employees reported on		120,848			
weighted average rate			.17	.15	.02

[a] Weighted by employment in those occupations. The median daily wage in July
was divided by the mean hours in the workday from Table 13.

[b] Thirteen industries from the Aldrich Report; 31 industries from the Dewey Report,
listed in Appendix, Table A-8.

Source: Appendix Table A-1; Census of 1900, *Employees and Wages*, by Davis R.
Dewey.

of new firms and new occupations be higher among those which
furnished only recent data, and would not new firms, occupations,
and industries have to pay higher wages in order to attract labor?

Two complete sets of occupational wage averages were compared in
the Aldrich data: a list of wage series which remained constant over
the entire period, and a list which increased from 462 occupations
in 1860 to 675 in 1890. Comparison was made first for 12 industries,
including: agricultural implements; ale, beer, and porter; books and
newspapers; building trades; city public works; cotton goods; dry
goods; illuminating gas; leather; metals and metallic goods; white
lead; and woolen goods. Then comparison was made separately for
building trades and 8 manufacturing industries. The differences could

TABLE 11

Weighted Average Daily Wage-Rates for a Constant List of 69 Establishments, 1860-1880,
Compared with a List Including Establishments Newly Reporting during the Period;
from the Weeks Report

The varying list increased from 69 establishments in 1860 to 212 in 1875
Wages are weighted by given-year employment[a]

	United States			Eastern States			Western States		
	Varying List	Constant List	Effect of Additions to List	Varying List	Constant List	Effect of Additions to List	Varying List	Constant List	Effect of Additions to List
1860	1.35	1.35	–	1.28	1.28	–	1.72	1.72	–
1865	1.96	1.96	0	1.90	1.88	0.02	2.32	2.37	−0.05
1870	2.07	2.13	−0.06	2.03	2.17	−0.14	2.18	2.34	−0.16
1875	1.86	1.89	−0.03	1.76	1.85	−0.09	2.17	2.20	−0.03
1880	1.81	1.88	−0.07	1.73	1.83	−0.10	2.13	2.21	−0.08

[a] Computed by taking the unweighted average of daily wages for appropriate occupations at the establishment level and averages weighted by census-reported employment at the state and industry levels. Employment in 1865 and 1875 was derived from the decennial censuses by linear interpolation.

less significant. The daily average wage for the list which increased differed from that for the constant list by two cents in 1890 and only one cent at the other five-year dates.

Instead of a higher wage, which might be expected, the addition of wage series yielded a slightly lower wage. Finally, the separate comparisons for building and manufacturing yielded similar differences—a trifle larger, but in no case exceeding a few cents a day.[14]

A more severe test can be administered through the Weeks data (Table 11). Of 212 establishments, only 69 had wage data covering the entire period of 1860-80.[15] Again the differences were slight. True, many manufacturing industries, especially new ones, were not covered by either the complete or the fragmentary sets of data, and those manufacturing industries not covered might have paid higher

[14] Conceivably, the insignificance of these differences has been due to the offsetting of wider differences for individual industries. In order to test this, a separate comparison was made for each industry. For example, the average daily wage for the 58 occupations in the woolens industry for the entire period 1860-90 is compared with that for the 102 occupations which include the above 58 plus the 44 with wage data becoming available at five-year intervals during 1860-90. These differences were larger than those for the industry groups (understandably, from randomness), but they were nevertheless small in all cases. The largest effect of increasing the list of occupations was 15 cents a day for agricultural implements in 1875 and 12-13 cents for ale and beer and for city public works in 1885 and 1890. The rest of the differences were under 10 cents, most of them under 5 cents.

[15] This was so not only for the United States, but also for eastern and western states considered separately.

hardly be wages or advanced them more than the industries studied here. This is not a problem that can be solved satisfactorily; completely new industries can probably never be adequately represented in any statistical sample.

Trends in Length of Workday

The analysis has so far ignored length of workday. Would hourly wages have behaved differently from daily wages?

Weeks asked establishments to indicate the number of hours in a day's work at quinquennial dates between 1860 and 1880. He presented the replies in a frequency distribution, without regard to industry classification or employment, each item being a statement concerning hours; some establishments returned several statements for different classes of workers (Table 12).

TABLE 12

Hours per Day: Distribution of Manufacturers' Statements Concerning
Length of Workday, Weeks Report, 1860-1880
(Percent)

Workday (hours)	1860	1865	1870	1875	1880
8 and less than 9	3.7	4.0	5.0	5.3	5.1
9-10	6.3	6.9	7.8	8.3	8.8
10-11	57.1	58.5	60.1	60.3	59.6
11-12	14.0	13.0	10.8	9.5	9.6
12-13	16.6	15.6	14.1	14.6	14.6
13-14	2.3	2.0	2.2	2.0	2.3
All statements	100.0	100.0	100.0	100.0	100.0
Number of statements[a]	350	496	744	930	1,039
Average hours per day[b]	10.9	10.9	10.8	10.8	10.8

Source and explanation: Text of this chapter; Weeks Report, p. xxviii.

[a] A number of firms returned several statements about hours worked by different classes of workers.

[b] The average for each interval had to be taken arbitrarily as the midpoint of that interval. This arbitrary midpoint may have concealed some drift within the intervals.

The replies indicated that:

1. The average workday in 1880, 10.8 hours, was almost the same as it had been in 1860, 10.9 hours.
2. The most common workday (about 60 percent of the statements) at all five-year dates was 10 hours; the next in frequency (about 15 percent) was 12 hours (owing to the prevalence of the two-shift system); the one after that (10-15 percent) was 11

hours. Only a small percentage of statements indicated less than 10 or more than 12 hours. The longest were 15.5 hours, in breweries.[16] There were frequent reports of shorter workdays in the winter months and longer ones for the rest of the year—because of seasonal differences in daylight, temperature, and demand for goods.[17]

3. More substantial decreases occurred during 1860-80 for occasional establishments, e.g., in cotton and woolen manufactures, but increases occurred in others, e.g., in a saw and planing mill, and temporary reductions occurred during the 1870's depression in a very few, e.g., in a firm producing machinery.

What trend in hours is found in the Aldrich data? A weighted average for the 13 manufacturing industries (Table 13, Part A) indicated a workday of 10.9 hours in 1860, the same as in Weeks', but a somewhat shorter day in 1880.[18] A drop of four-tenths of an hour appears, compared to only one-tenth for the Weeks data. The latter might very well have concealed a greater downward drift within the class-interval distribution, but unfortunately there was no way of measuring such a drift. For the decade 1881-90, the Aldrich Report data show a further drop in the workday, to 10.1 hours. All of the decline for 1860-1890 was due to 4 industries: cotton, woolens, leather, and lumber; 8 industries showed almost no change and white lead actually manifested a rise. Even the larger decline in the Aldrich data suggests that the shrinkage in the workday in manufacturing would have been only 3.5 percent in the twenty years between 1860 and 1880, and only 7 percent by 1890. However, the Aldrich group of firms is not necessarily representative of manufacturing in general; the report itself states: "The reduction in the number of hours seems hardly so considerable as might have been expected. It must be remembered that our figures refer to certain picked establishments, where, in view of the complete organization at an early date, it is probable that shorter hours made an earlier appearance than in the mass of work shops."[19]

Despite these cautionary remarks, the Aldrich and Weeks data may not greatly misrepresent the length of the workday. The result

[16] In some of the very long-hour industries constant work was not performed during the whole number of reported hours e.g., puddlers in rolling mills and blacksmiths in hardware supply.

[17] A number of establishments reported a shorter day on Saturday, with the time made up by a slightly longer day during the week.

[18] In averaging the Weeks distribution, the mid-interval figure was chosen: for instance, 8 hours and less than 9 was given an arbitrary value of 8.5 hours.

[19] Pp. 179-180.

obtained from the very comprehensive data of the First Annual Report for 1885—whether for the entire 35 industries covered in that report, for the 12 of the 13 industries covered in the Aldrich

TABLE 13

Hours per Day in Manufacturing Industries, Based on Aldrich Report
Hours Data; Annually 1860-1890

	1860	1870	1880	1890
A. THIRTEEN INDUSTRIES; DECENNIAL YEARS[a]				
Agricultural implements	10.0	10.0	10.0	10.0
Ale, beer, porter	12.0	12.0	12.0	12.0
Books and newspapers	10.0	10.0	10.0	10.0
Carriages and wagons	10.0	10.0	10.0	10.0
Cotton goods	12.2	11.0	10.3	10.0
Illuminating gas	10.4	10.0	10.0	10.0
Leather	11.0	10.0	10.0	10.0
Lumber	10.8	10.8	10.8	10.0
Metals	10.1	10.1	10.1	10.1
Paper	12.0	12.0	12.0	12.0
Stone	10.0	10.0	10.0	9.8
White lead	9.3	10.5	10.5	10.7
Woolen goods	12.7	11.5	11.4	10.0
Weighted average[b]	10.9	10.6	10.5	10.1

B. THIRTEEN INDUSTRIES COMBINED; ANNUAL;
ADJUSTED TO 1890 AVERAGE OF 10 HOURS
FOR ALL MANUFACTURING

1860	10.8	1870	10.5	1880	10.4
1861	10.7	1871	10.5	1881	10.4
1862	10.7	1872	10.5	1882	10.4
1863	10.7	1873	10.5	1883	10.3
1864	10.7	1874	10.5	1884	10.3
1865	10.6	1875	10.4	1885	10.3
1866	10.7	1876	10.4	1886	10.2
1867	10.7	1877	10.4	1887	10.0
1868	10.6	1878	10.4	1888	10.0
1869	10.6	1879	10.4	1889	10.0
				1890	10.0

Source: Aldrich Report, pp. 178-179; 1890 average for all manufacturing, see text note 20.

[a] The hours worked per day are indicated in detail for January and July of each year for each occupation. However, the schedule provided only a single box for hours at the top of the form. An exhaustive search was made of the archives of the various government agencies, in the hope of finding the original schedules filled out for the individual workers, but the search was completely without result.

[b] Weighted according to census-reported employment.

Report, or the 18 industries covered in the Weeks Report—was almost the same:

Aldrich Report	
13 Industries	10⅓ hours
First Annual Report[a]	
35 industries	10⅓ hours
12 of the 13 industries covered in the Aldrich Report	10½ hours
18 industries covered in the Weeks Report	10½ hours

[a] Computations made in this study.

Finally, the 1890 estimate of the Department of Commerce and Labor for 456 occupations in 48 industries, weighted by employment, yielded 10.0 hours a day,[20] compared with 10.1 hours computed from the Aldrich Report for that year.

Until better evidence is adduced, we judge that average hourly wages rose about 11 percent more than average daily wages during 1860-90: 61 percent compared with 50 percent (Appendix Table A-11).

[20] Actually 59.9 hours per week. Computed by Leo Wolman from the *Nineteenth Annual Report of the Commissioner of Labor* 1904; Wolman, *Hours of Work in American Industry*, National Bureau of Economic Research, Bulletin 71, 1938, p. 2.

CHAPTER 3

Annual Earnings

CLOSE agreement has been found between the over-all increases of the two series on daily wages in manufacturing developed in this study—the one from Aldrich data, the other from the Weeks–Bulletin 18 data. Both series increased much less than those of the other investigators developed from the same materials. The smallness of these increases has been traced to the exclusion of wages in nonmanufacturing industries and to the use of industry-employment weights (from the census) instead of firm-employment weights or no weights at all. It would seem more logical to weight the wage data by industry- instead of by company-employment, since the size of the reporting firm is largely accidental and bears no necessary relation to the importance of its industry. But which yields better measures of final wage behavior? For a test, we turn to the annual earnings from the Census of Manufactures.

Sources and Nature of the Earnings Data

Annual earnings per wage-earner are based on the Censuses of Manufactures for years ending on May 31, 1860, 1870, 1880, and 1890. These censuses have been criticized as lacking in continuity of organization and method. No permanent organization existed until after this period. In 1860 and 1870, the enumerations were made by United States marshals, who were not under the discipline of the directors of the census and were paid at low rates even for those days: in 1870, fifteen cents per factory establishment, with no extra compensation for extra visits. The "marshals did their ... work as carelessly and hastily as possible," and in both 1860 and 1870 the results were obviously defective, though less defective in the latter than in the former census.[1] In 1880 the census, under Francis Walker, an eminent economist, provided for the appointment of special agents, but they were assigned only to the 279 principal cities and towns, so that the rural areas were not so well enumerated.[2]

[1] Charles J. Bullock, "Wage Statistics and the Federal Census," *Publications of the American Economic Association*, New Series No. 2, March 1899, pp. 343-346. Approximately one-fifth of the sums of money owing to marshals and their deputies in connection with the enumeration of the 1860 Census was "suspended on account of the presumed or known disloyalty of officers or the existence of some good reason for suspending payments." *Preliminary Report on the Eighth Census*, 1860, H.R. Doc. 116, 37th Congress 2nd Session, p. 1. This statement is partially contradicted on the same page: "... the marshals were generally faithful to their trusts and manifested an anxious desire for the proper completion of their duties."

[2] Bullock, *op.cit.*, p. 347.

Although in 1890 the census was still more thorough, its director, Carroll D. Wright, issued a warning concerning its misleading character.[3] There seemed to be agreement among the late nineteenth century critics of the census that each successive enumeration had improved in accuracy and coverage.[4]

It is possible that the average annual earnings were more accurate than the other data gathered by the Census of Manufactures—say, value of output or horsepower. Average earnings equal the total payroll for the census year, divided by the number of wage-earners employed; omission of an establishment would not affect average earnings as much as the total wage or total employment from which they were derived, since the errors would partially cancel out. Nevertheless, the average earnings materials have been subjected to plenty of criticism as to their meaning, completeness, representativeness, and comparability from one census to the next.

First there was no means of separating earnings of workers of different sex or age, except for 1890, and skill classifications of the workers were usually lacking; thus average annual earnings could vary from census to census merely because the proportion of workers at different earning levels changed, even if none of the levels altered.

Second, no data were available from the census telling directly the number of days worked per year by persons reported as employed in manufacturing establishments. Average annual earnings could change from census to census partly because of changes in the number of days of employment. The same could be said for changes in the length of the workday.

Third, the census of 1890 counted not only wage-earners or "hands," but also higher paid officers and members of firms.[5] The 1890 average earnings were therefore biased upward; when the non–wage-earners are excluded for comparability with the earlier years, average annual earnings in 1890 are reduced from $485 to $445 (Table 14).

Fourth, there was considerable variation in industry coverage. The 1860 census included numerous mining, fishery, agricultural processing, and forestry establishments; the 1870 and 1890 censuses included some manufacturing industries not covered in the other two censuses, for example car and railroad shop construction; and all

[3] H. L. Bliss, "Eccentric Official Statistics," *American Journal of Sociology*, Vol. III, July 1897–May 1898, p. 96.

[4] "Defective as they are, our manufacturing statistics are the best produced in any country . . . since 1860 they have improved steadily from decade to decade." S.N.D. North, "Manufactures in the Federal Census," *Publications of the American Economic Association*, New Series No. 2, 1899, pp. 257-258.

[5] The census of 1880 probably lumped some of these persons in the employment data, but did not include their salaries "except in exceedingly few cases." Bliss, *op.cit.*, pp. 360-361.

four censuses included varying numbers of construction and other hand-trade establishments which tend to employ mainly adult males in skilled occupations—painters, paperhangers, carpenters, blacksmiths, wheelwrights, and others. These skilled workers often had relatively high earnings, so that an enumeration (such as the 1890 census) which included many of them in relation to previous censuses would be biased upward in its average annual earnings. There is logical force in the position of a census official that hand trades do not belong with manufacturing anyway. "Many handicraftsmen carry on business without any shop or paraphernalia which can be identified or enumerated as a manufacturing establishment. It would seem to be plain than industrialism pursued under such conditions ought not to be confused, for census purposes, with factory manufacture, and that the two classes of data cannot be mingled and combined, in the consolidation of manufacturing statistics, without affecting the exactness of the results."[6]

In addition to the pure hand trades, large numbers of custom and repair shops were included in two manufacturing industries: boots and shoes, and men's clothing.[7] These were not separated in the statistics from the factories. Comparability was best served by excluding these two industries altogether.

Deduction of the nonmanufacturing industries, the hand trades, the intermittently covered industries, and the industries biased with repair shops, has the effect of raising the annual earnings of the average worker by $8 in 1860 and $6 in 1870, and of lowering them by $2 in 1880 and $18 in 1890 (Table 14). The adjusted figures of 1870-90 are very close to those arrived at by Richard A. Easterlin of the University of Pennsylvania, and the adjusted figure for 1890—the only one significantly altered—is close to both his estimate and that of William M. Stuart, an official of the 1890 census:

	1860	1870	1880	1890
Reported by the census	289	378	347	445
Adjusted in this study	297	384	345	427
Adjusted by Easterlin[a]	–	378	343	425
Estimated by Stuart[b]	–	–	–	429

[a] Computed from Table 3.1, p. 636 on his work cited in Table 14. Easterlin did not construct an estimate for 1860.

[b] "Official Statistics," *American Journal of Sociology*, Vol. 3, July 1897-May 1898, pp. 626-627.

[6] North, *op.cit.*, p. 271.

[7] The custom and repair work could be separated for both industries in 1890 and for boots and shoes in 1880, but it could not be separated at all in 1860 or 1870. Some evidence of the inclusion of many small shoe repair and tailoring establishments may be adduced from the fact that these two industries included about 12.5 percent of all establishments listed by the 1860 Census of Manufactures, but had only about 4 percent of the capital. Approximately the same was true for 1870.

41

TABLE 14

Adjustments to Data on Wage-Earners and Earnings as Reported by the Census of Manufactures, in Order to Exclude Nonmanufacturing Industries, Hand Trades, and Intermittently Reported Manufacturing Industries, 1860-1890
(number of wage earners in thousands; total earnings in millions of dollars)

	1860		1870		1880		1890	
	Wage-Earners	Earnings	Wage-Earners	Earnings	Wage-Earners	Earnings	Wage-Earners	Earnings
Reported by census	1,311.2	378.9	2,054.0	775.6	2,732.6	948.0	4,251.5	1,891.2
Deduct:								
Mining	107.5	42.3						
Fisheries	30.6	6.1						
Agric. processing	0.4	0.I						
Forestry	1.6	0.5						
Hand trades[a]	35.5	10.7	67.2	12.5	63.5	21.5	147.2	51.8
Boots and shoes, including custom and repair	123.0	30.9	135.9	52.0	133.8	51.0	150.7	68.0
Men's clothing, including custom and repair	114.8	19.9	108.1	30.7	160.8	45.9	217.3	87.7
Building	13.1	5.4	99.7	42.2	104.9	47.5	355.4	220.3
Intermittently reported manufactures:								
Cars and general shop construction (railroad and streetcar)			15.9	9.7			108.6	61.6
Smelting and refining							13.2	6.8
Flax and hemp, dressed			0.8	0.2	1.0	0.3	0.5	0.2
Gas, illuminating and heating			8.7	6.5			13.0	8.5
Grindstones and millstones			0.5	0.3	0.4	0.2	0.1	0.1
Adjusted manufacturing	884.7	263.0	1,617.2	621.5	2,268.2	781.6	3,245.5	1,386.2

AVERAGE ANNUAL EARNINGS

	1860	1870	1880	1890
All industries included by census	289	378	347	445
Hand trades	301	186	339	352
Building	412	423	453	620
Adjusted manufacturing	297	384	345	427

Data are for year ending May 31.
[a] Exclusive of construction and of custom and repair shops in men's clothing and boots and shoes.
Source: For 1860 and 1870, Census of 1870, *Manufacturing*, Vol. 3, pp. 394-405; 1880 and 1890, Census of 1890, *Report on Manufacturing Industries in the U.S.*, Part 1, Tables 2, 5. For suggestions concerning adjustments during 1870-90 the author is indebted to Richard A. Easterlin (see his "Estimates of Manufacturing Activity," *Population Redistribution and Economic Growth, United States, 1870-1950*, American Philosophical Society, 1957). For suggestions concerning adjustments in 1860, I am indebted to Robert Gallman.

The shortcomings of the census earnings data ought not be taken lightly. Even present-day censuses—conducted at great expense and after long preparation, with modern methods, ingenious equipment, trained personnel, and carefully devised mailing texts— are plagued with undercounts and incomparabilities. The earlier censuses must have been still less satisfactory, from every point of view.

On the other hand, the shortcomings need not be critical for this investigation. The objection that separate earnings are not provided for persons of different age, sex, and job classification would be serious only if the census earnings were the sole source of information about wages. Since rather detailed wage-rate classifications are available from the other sources, we need the census earnings mainly to test the over-all accuracy and comprehensiveness of the average wage of all workers. This service the census earnings provide, for the numbers of establishments and employees represented in these statistics, if not complete, are very great, and the census earnings cover an entire twelve months, whereas the wage data usually refer to one or two dates that might not be representative of the other seasons of the year, especially if economic conditions change rapidly.

In sum, the census earnings must be judged by their accuracy and completeness relative to other wage information. None of the statistics were reliable enough to stand alone. But if very different data show basic agreement, we should have much more confidence in our results than if we relied on one set alone.

Comparison of Census Average Annual Earnings and the Daily Wage Data of the Aldrich and Weeks Reports

Which estimates find strongest support from the census data on annual earnings—the wage series of this study, manifesting increases between 1860 and 1890 of 48 to 50 percent, or those of other investigators, suggesting increases of 58 to 74 percent? We seek the answer in the comparison in Table 15. Three features are worth noting.

First, the census earnings do not support the larger increases shown by the other studies. They do confirm the indications in the foregoing chapter that wages did not rise more than 50 percent during the thirty-year period and suggest that, if anything, they rose less than 50 percent.

Second, the census earnings do not move closely with the daily wage data so far as the increases to 1870 or to 1880 are concerned, but the disparities of movement give no support to the other investigations, since annual earnings rise even less than daily wages during intervening decades.

43

TABLE 15

Index of Average Annual Earnings in Manufacturing from the Census
Compared with Wage Indexes for Manufacturing Computed in This
Study and with Wage Indexes for Mixed Industries by Other Investigators:
1860-1890

	1860	1870	1880	1890
AVERAGE ANNUAL EARNINGS (CENSUS)				
All manufacturing industries[a]	100	129	116	144
17 manufacturing industries[b]	100	131	117	149
AVERAGE DAILY WAGES[c]				
This study				
Aldrich Report	100	151	130	148
Weeks–Bulletin 18 Reports	100	146	134	150
Mitchell				
Aldrich Report, 21 industries	100	180	143	158
Weeks Report, 30 industries	100	155	138	–
Falkner				
Aldrich Report, 17 industries	100	167	143	168
Hansen				
Aldrich Report; Series A[d]	100	179	140	157
Phelps Brown				
Aldrich Report	100	182	151	174

  [a] Computed from Table 14, adjusted manufacturing.
  [b] Computed from sources of Table 14, for the industries listed in Appendix Table C-2.
  [c] From Tables 3 and 4.
  [d] Same industries as Mitchell for 1860-80; same industries as Falkner for 1880-90.
(unweighted).

Third, the 17 manufacturing industries—conforming as nearly
as the data permit to industries drawn from Aldrich and Weeks—
moved closely in average annual earnings with *all* manufacturing.
The narrower list of industries thus seems reasonably representative
of all manufacturing industries during these thirty years.

We now consider some objections to this comparison of over-all
movement between annual earnings and daily wages. A minor
objection—that boots and shoes and men's clothing ought to have
been retained despite the inclusion of custom and repair shops—may
be appraised by computing the average earnings with these industries
restored. The re-computation yields an increase of 51 percent
between 1860 and 1890, which is still very close to the increase in our
daily wage series.

A more important objection might be that other differences
between 1860 and 1890 could have held down the average earnings
increase. We can imagine three such possibilities.

Did the proportion of women and children differ in such a way that larger increases in wage rates were offset by growing proportions of these persons whose average earnings are always low? Relevant data, for women 16 or older and children under 16, at each of the four censuses are given in Table 16.

TABLE 16

Number of Men, Women, and Children Reported as Wage-Earners to the Census of
Manufactures, 1860-1890
(thousands)

	1860[a]		1870		1880		1890	
	Number	Percent	Number	Percent	Number	Percent	Number	Percent
Men 16 and older	988	75.4	1,616	78.6	2,019	73.9	3,327	78.3
Women 16 and older	257	19.6	324	15.8	532	19.4	804	18.9
Children under 16	66	5.0	115	5.6	182	6.7	121	2.8
Total	1,311	100.0	2,054	100.0	2,733	100.0	4,252	100.0

[a] Estimated.

The comparison shows that the proportion of men—the high earners—was, if anything, greater in 1890.[8] It certainly does not suggest that the changing age-sex composition could have offset a large basic wage increase over these thirty years.

Theoretically important, in comparing annual earnings with daily wages, is the number of days worked per year. Suppose, purely for illustration, that the average worker was employed fewer days in 1890 than in 1860: this could have offset a higher daily wage rate than was suggested by our figures. Such a hypothetical reduction in average days worked could have been due either to greater unemployment or labor turnover.

However, it does not seem likely that either of the two could have been materially greater in 1890 than in 1860, since both the 1890 and 1860 censuses occurred during business cycle peaks in the Burns-Mitchell chronology. Some difference in unemployment is possible as between two business cycle peaks but even a substantial difference—say, 5 percent of the labor force—would not in itself greatly alter our conclusions.

Concerning labor turnover, there seems no doubt that all four censuses reported more persons on the payroll for the average month than were at work on the average day. (This is true even now of census employment and earnings reporting.) But the four censuses of 1860-90 admittedly varied among each other as to what they

[8] Even if all the males reported as earners in 1860 were assumed to be 16 and older, the proportion of men in 1860 would have been only slightly above that in 1890.

included in the employment divisor.[9] The 1860, 1870, and 1880 censuses requested the average number of hands employed; the 1880 census asked, in addition, the greatest number of hands employed at any one time during the year. The 1890 census asked for the average number employed during the actual time the establishments were reported as being in operation. The first three censuses undoubtedly obtained an employment figure in excess of the average daily number employed throughout the year. The 1890 enumeration was believed by the officials of that census to have come as close as possible to the average number.[10] It is unlikely that all excess reporting could thus have been eliminated, even in 1890.[11] But if we assume that there was less excess reporting of employment in 1890 than earlier, the true increase in average earnings over the thirty-year period would have been not greater than our estimates, but less.

There remains the puzzling observation that although daily wages and annual earnings both rose by nearly the same percentage between 1860 and 1890, annual earnings lagged behind daily wages at 1870 and 1880. Why were they depressed by unemployment?

For an answer, two steps are necessary. One is to adjust our two daily wage series for the fact that both are undoubtedly on too high an absolute level, judged by the First Annual Report for 1885, the Dewey-Census report for 1890, and a number of state reports. The Dewey report, based on very large numbers of workers, indicated that the daily wage rates were $1.53 in 1890, about 13 percent below the $1.75 estimated from Aldrich data and 23 percent below the $1.98 estimated from the Weeks–Bulletin 18 data.[12] The wage level of the

[9] "The total amount of wages paid at each of the periods named is . . . one of the most certain elements of the industrial census, but the average is obtained by dividing the total wages paid by the average number of employees during the year." Carroll Wright, quoted in Bliss, *op.cit.*, p. 362.

[10] *Census of 1890, Report on Manufacturing Industries in the United States*, Vol. VI, Part I, p. 14.

[11] An employment figure in excess of the average daily number at work could still persist even if the 1890 census had succeeded in obtaining the average number employed during the actual time the establishments were reported as being in operation, or even if the establishments were in operation every working day of the year.

[12] The daily average of $1.53 in 1890 is reasonably close to the estimate of $1.46 derived by Albert Rees from estimates of annual earnings and days worked. ("Real Wages, 1890-1914," in the Thirty-Eighth Annual Report of the National Bureau of Economic Research, May 1958, pp. 59-60.) It happened to be the same as the median of the average daily wages reported to the labor bureaus of the following six important states for that year. In Maryland, the weighted average daily wage actually earned in 13 important manufacturing industries—including many in our lists from the Aldrich and Weeks Reports—was $1.58. In Maine, the average for a small number of workers in 12 manufacturing industries was $1.57. In Iowa, the average for nearly 30,000 workers including females and unskilled wage-earners in over two dozen important manufacturing

First Annual Report was below the wage levels of the two series by almost exactly the same respective percentage margins. On the rather bold assumption that a relationship which held constant between 1885 and 1890 would hold constant also during the earlier years, we reduce our entire Aldrich daily wage series by 13 percent and our entire Weeks–Bulletin 18 series by 23 percent.

The second step is to compute the average number of days of employment under the business-cycle-peak conditions of 1890, using the census, which gathered information on the number of workers attached to manufacturing industries (excluding hand and construction trades) who had been unemployed for various periods during the census year ended May 31, 1890:

		Workers idle		Number unemployed
Months	Average assumed by Census	Number	Man months	Equivalent full-time years
		000	000	000
1–3	2	268	536	
4–6	5	160	800	
7–12	9.5	50	475	
		478	1811	150

From Census of 1890, *Special Census Report on the Occupations of the Population of the United States*, pp. 25-26.

From this distribution, we estimate that 150,000 persons were unemployed an equivalent full-time year during the census year: 6.6 percent of the 2.3 million persons ten years of age and older reported by the 1890 population census as attached to these industries.[13] If we assume that a full-time year was 299 days (deducting Sundays and 14 days lost in holidays and illness), the average worker in manufacturing was unemployed 20 days and employed 279

---

industries was $1.49. In Wisconsin, the average for over 80,000 workers in over 1,300 factories was $1.43. In Ohio, the average for over 30,000 employees in 31 manufacturing occupations was $1.65. And in Missouri, the average for 3,820 workers in 10 manufacturing industries was $1.35. The median of the six averages, $1.53, was taken as lying halfway between the third- and fourth-ranking averages, $1.57 for Maine and $1.49 for Iowa.

(Sources: *Fourth Biennial Report of the Bureau of Industrial Statistics and Information of Maryland, 1890-91*, pp. 241-258. *Fifth Annual Report of the Bureau of Industrial and Labor Statistics, Maine, 1891*, pp. 122-125. *Fourth Biennial Report of the Bureau of Labor Statistics of Iowa, 1890-1891*, pp. 179-199. *Seventh Biennial Report of the* [Wisconsin] *Bureau of Labor, Census and Industrial Statistics, 1895-96*, pp. 339-341. *Fourteenth Annual Report of the* [Ohio] *Bureau of Labor Statistics for the Year 1890*, pp. 113-196. *Twelfth Annual Report, Bureau of Labor Statistics of Missouri, 1890*, pp. 220-394.

[13] The unemployment rate for gainful workers attached to all industries, computed on the same basis, was 5 percent.

days in 1890.[14] A daily wage of $1.53 for 279 days would yield annual earnings of $427 in 1890, the same as our adjusted average annual earnings figure for manufacturing wage-earners in the year ended May 31, 1890. Accordingly we next estimate the number of days worked for the other census years by dividing our adjusted-level daily wage from the Aldrich Report into the census average annual earnings:

	1860	1870	1880	1890
(1) Average daily wages (Aldrich data, corrected for level)	$1.04	1.56	1.34	1.53
(2) Average annual earnings (census)	$297	384	345	427
(3) Average employment days (line 1 divided by line 2)	286	246	257	279
(4) Full-employment days assumed	299	299	299	299
(5) Unemployment days (line 4 minus line 3)	13	53	42	20
(6) Percent of assumed full employment	4.3	17.7	14.0	6.6[a]

[a]The unemployment rate was based on actual census data.

This computation yields an estimated unemployment rate which was somewhat lower in 1860 than the rate computed from census data for 1890. The difference is comparable to economic conditions at the various dates. The 1860 and 1890 censuses were taken in years for which Burns and Mitchell report business-cycle peaks, and the unemployment rates of both years were low enough to be characteristic of years of full employment, considering that the actual peak of business cycle occurred each time one quarter after the end of the census year. Thus the census-year earnings and employment occurred during the expansion phase rather than at the actual peak of the cycle.

[14] This figure of 279 days does not seem to agree closely with the median of 260 days computed from weighted averages for four states. In Maine 462 workers reported an average of forty-eight days lost including illness, unemployment, and "other causes." If this figure is subtracted from 310 days (313 weekdays minus three holidays), the average number of days worked was 262. In Iowa, nearly 20,000 employees in 32 manufacturing occupations lost an average of 2.13 months or fifty-three workdays, from which we estimate an average of 257 days worked. In Maryland, workers in 13 manufacturing industries reported an average of 255 days worked. And in Ohio, over 30,000 employees in 31 manufacturing occupations reported an average of 275 days worked. (See footnote 12 for sources of state data.)

The smaller average for the four states may possibly represent the additional number of days lost by persons who were employed but were absent part of the payroll period because of illness, drunkenness, and "personal reasons," or by persons who joined late or left early in the payroll period. If 260 days should turn out to be the average actually worked by factory wage workers in the United States, dividing this figure into the average annual earnings of $427 would yield a somewhat higher average daily wage in 1890: $1.64. However, it would not be safe to rely on four states for an estimate of the national average of days worked.

The fact that the unemployment rates for 1870 and 1880 were higher than for either 1860 or 1890 was also compatible with the fact that the census year June 1, 1869 to May 31, 1870 occurred during the contraction phase of a cycle that started in the month the year began and reached its trough two quarters after the year was over, and that the census year June 1, 1879 to May 31, 1880 occurred during the expansion phase of a cycle that had reached its trough in early 1879 and was not to reach its peak until three years later. Nevertheless, the unemployment rates seem very much on the high side, even for manufacturing, since economic conditions were far from serious in these two census years.

It is much more likely that the relatively lower average number of days of employment in 1870 and 1880 may be due to the failure of the censuses of 1870 and 1880 to exclude persons who were on payrolls of firms for very short periods, because such persons may have been out of the labor force or on the payroll of another firm during the rest of the year. Overstatement of employment results in understatement of the average number of days employed. Whether this does explain the excessive gap between days employed and assumed days of full employment in 1870 and 1880 cannot be told with certainty from the information that has come down to us.[15]

[15] Some recognition should be paid to an apparent discrepancy for 1880 between our average employment of 257 days for the United States and the 296 days of actual working time reported for manufacturing establishments in Massachusetts, the latter tabulated from unpublished data of the 1880 Census of Manufactures. Part of this discrepancy may represent the difference in economic conditions between Massachusetts and the United States as a whole. But there is a better explanation. The average employee works fewer days for a given establishment than the establishment itself operates, because some workers join the payroll after the month begins or leave before it ends, and most workers are ill a few days or stay off the job for personal or family reasons. The number of such absences is probably much greater than the small number of workers, such as watchmen and maintenance staff, who work even though the establishment is closed down. Since the number of days an average establishment operates bears no close relation to the number of days worked by the average employee, these data cannot be used to compute average daily earnings from average annual earnings.

CHAPTER 4

The Buying Power of Wages and Earnings

The Previous Indexes of Living Cost

The index of cost of living used in this study (Tables 17 and A-10) was constructed by linking a new index for 1860-80, prepared by Ethel D. Hoover from retail price data gathered by the Weeks Report,[1] to a new index of retail prices for 1880-90, prepared by this writer from various documentary sources (Appendix Tables B-1, B-2, and B-3).

These indexes are definitely preferable to the indexes of essentially wholesale prices used by Falkner or Hansen, despite the fact that the wholesale prices apply to more commodities and were collected in greater abundance and possibly with more precision as to quality-grade and date. The prices used in this investigation were the prices presumably charged the working man. They could deviate widely from wholesale prices among different localities because of trans-portation cost from the wholesale markets, or differences in degree of competition among retail stores or differences in quality, in credit policy, and in delivery service. They could wander widely from the path followed by wholesale prices over time, because retail stores absorb wholesale price increases at some times or increase their margins at other times—depending on competition, store policy, and consumer resistance, on variations in wages of store and delivery clerks and cost of fuel, light, and heat, or on changes in the standards of cleanliness and attractiveness of packaging. Also, retail prices can be collected for finished goods and services of the kind not ordinarily reported in the nineteenth century sources on wholesale prices—confined as the latter usually were to basic or raw materials.

An alternative to the Hoover-Long index of living cost would have been the Mitchell index of retail prices for 1860-80 and the Burgess index of food prices for 1880-90. Mitchell constructed his index entirely from tables of retail prices published by the 1880 census, and gathered by investigators under the direction of Joseph D. Weeks, who had sent out schedules to shopkeepers of a large number of towns, asking them to enter the retail price of the product listed, for as many years as they could. The price asked for was the "fair average" for the year or the price for June 1 of each year.[2]

[1] Ethel D. Hoover, "Prices in the Nineteenth Century," *Trends in the American Economy in the Nineteenth Century*, Studies in Income and Wealth, Vol. 24 (in press).

[2] *Average Retail Prices of Necessaries of Life*, by Joseph D. Weeks, *1880 Census*, Vol. xx, Supplementary Report, pp. 1-111. The schedules were not reproduced.

The Weeks Report listed about 400 tabulations of retail prices of detailed items (such as "shirtings, brown, 4 × 4, standard quality") in the amount of each item that would be purchased for a family's use. It listed them under the name of the reporting firm, identified by town and state. It included only "what might be regarded as the chief necessaries of life," and all the detailed items tabulated belonged to the following categories: "plain" board, groceries, flour, meat, provisions, etc.; drygoods, men's heavy boots; coal, wood, and oil; house rent, generally for four- to six-room houses. The intention was to obtain price data covering the towns for which the wage schedules were drawn. These represented sixteen states in nearly all sections of the country; most of the tabulations, however, were drawn from a few cities or towns in Connecticut, New York, Pennsylvania, Illinois, Indiana, Missouri, and Ohio.[3]

From them, Mitchell rejected all series of quotations not expressly stated to show the "fair average" of prices and not approximately complete for the entire twenty years 1860-80. He converted each series he used to 1860 = 100, and computed unweighted averages of relative prices from different towns for the same commodity. This process resulted in 60 national series of relatives, many of which he then grouped together by computing simple averages for closely related commodities—reducing the number of series to 35.

Each of the 35 series of commodity price relatives was next weighted in accordance with its importance in the budget of a working-class family, taken from the expenditures of 2,567 families surveyed for 1901:

	Number of Retail Price Series Used by Mitchell[a] for 1860-1880	Percent of Average Family Budget Spent on Each Item[b] (2,567 families in 1901)
Food	24	31.6
Fuel	3	4.2
Lighting	1	.5
Clothing	4	3.1
Rent	1	16.0
Sundries	2	.3
Other items[c]	0	44.3
	35	100.0

[a] Mitchell, *Gold, Prices, and Wages*, p. 84-85.

[b] Average expenditure on each kind of goods for those families which bought the goods. *Eighteenth Annual Report of the Commissioner of Labor* (1903), pp. 510, 569.

[c] That is, items for which no prices are included in the Mitchell study: food, 10.9 percent; clothing, 11.9; miscellaneous (liquor, tobacco, insurance, religious and charitable expenditures, sickness, etc.), 21.5.

[3] *Ibid.*, p. 2.

Despite the care with which Mitchell constructed his cost-of-living index, his own appraisal of its accuracy was not high. Data were available for relatively few localities. Weights for some commodities were based on conjecture—family expenditures rested on a small sample of budgets collected after 1900, as a measure of importance of commodities bought and used twenty to forty years earlier. Since items totaling approximately 44 percent of the expenditures were unrepresented in the index, it involves the assumption that their prices moved in the same way as those for which Mitchell had price data. Specifications were necessarily loose; for instance, "the flour given in one table may be of a higher or lower grade than that in another." It was not certain as to what time of year the prices refer to. The sparseness of the returns did not allow him to match the price data by locality with the wage data. Finally, the deep South was not represented; his index covered only the East and West—typically only one or two cities in each of six to a dozen states.

The Burgess series for the decade 1881-90, was still less adequate, since it relied entirely upon the "retail prices of 10 staple articles of food which constituted the bulk of all goods purchased in the average wage earner family." Burgess felt that the index was a reasonably satisfactory indication of living cost, on the ground that food represents nearly half of the typical family budget, and that "the trends which it has been possible to construct for the retail price of clothing, the price of rent, and of fuel . . . show a remarkable resemblance to the food curve." However, he gave little information on sources beyond the fact that "from a number of different sources sufficient quotations were secured for each year to give a representative figure."[4]

The decision not to use the Mitchell and Burgess series in this study was based partly on the narrowness and the vagueness of the Burgess index, partly on our discovery of some new retail price series for 1880-90, and partly on the fact that Ethel D. Hoover of the Bureau of Labor Statistics had just made available a new series from 1860 to 1880—which rests, as did Mitchell's index, on Weeks Report data on retail prices, but makes use of modern statistical methods of the kind now employed by the Bureau of Labor Statistics in constructing its current consumer price index, and obtains strikingly different results from those of Mitchell.

[4] W. R. Burgess, *Trends of School Costs*, Russell Sage Foundation, 1920, pp. 51-53.

The New Consumer Price Index

THE HOOVER INDEX FOR 1860-80

Miss Hoover's method differs from Mitchell's in five important respects:

Data. She relies almost entirely on the Weeks data but makes much fuller use of them by including the price series which covered less than the whole period of twenty years—for example, 1869 to 1880 or 1875 to 1880—or which referred to only one month in the year. She found that the price data referring to the one month in the year conformed well in timing and degree of change to the average for the year.

Averaging of prices of the same commodity in different localities. Miss Hoover computed two averages of actual prices for each commodity in each year—one for firms in various localities reporting for both the given and preceding year, and one for firms reporting for the given and the following years. She then linked these together to form a continuous chain index with 1860 as 100. This index was multiplied by the average actual price in 1860 to obtain the average price for each year to 1880. Her use of link relatives enabled her to include several times as many series as Mitchell, and her averages of actual prices enabled her to avoid a serious upward bias which can result from averaging relatives. Such a bias will be found to be an important part of the explanation of the differences in results. Neither Mitchell nor Miss Hoover found it feasible to use weights in combining the series of different cities into an average.

Weights. Miss Hoover weighted the prices of the different groups of commodities such as food and rent by expenditures of families in Massachusetts in 1875, instead of the 2,567 families in 1901 used by Mitchell. The two sets of weights were very similar for food, but the Massachusetts expenditures gave greater percentage weight to clothing prices, which had a downward trend, and less to rent, which had an upward trend:

	Mitchell *2,567 U.S. Families, 1901*	*Hoover* *Massachusetts Families, 1875*
Food	56.7	57.4
Fuel	7.6	7.0
Lighting	0.9	–
Clothing	5.6	15.2
Rent	28.7	17.7
Other	0.5	2.7
Total	100.0	100.0

53

Miss Hoover allocated individual items within groups (e.g., butter and cheese within food) on the basis of the expenditure study of 232 families made for the Aldrich Commission in 1890-91. She assumed that items for which no prices could be obtained moved in the same way as all items other than food, in order to avoid adding to the very large weight already given to food. These expenditure values for 1875 were extrapolated back to 1860 by dividing 1875 values by price indexes for each item, on the 1860 basis. "This procedure (and the procedure used for calculating the index) assumes that the quantity purchased remains the same over the years. This assumption seems more reasonable than that implied by fixed percentage weights."[5]

The formula used,

$$I = \frac{\left[PoQo\left(\frac{Pi}{Po}\right) \right]}{\Sigma\, PoQo}$$

is equivalent to saying that the prices of each commodity and group were weighted by dollar expenditures at the base date.

Additional items. Miss Hoover included retail price data for a few items additional to those in the Weeks volume. These were shoe repair, medical care, and overalls in Vermont,[6] and newspapers and fruit.

The methodological differences between Mitchell and Hoover are reflected in large discrepancies in the major movements of their retail price indexes, even though they both move in the same direction in nineteen out of the twenty years.

The Hoover index showed the cost of living rising by almost the same amount as Mitchell's during the Civil War (though reaching a peak a year earlier), but declining much more rapidly, so that it was always lower after 1864. The gap was wide by 1866 and kept gradually growing. By 1875 the Hoover index was only 123, compared with 138 for the Mitchell index; and by 1880 it was only 110 compared with 128.

The upward bias in the Mitchell index was due to the following causes.

Mitchell gave inadequate weight—only 5.6 percent of family expenditures—to clothing, which, though rising more in price than

[5] Hoover, *op.cit.*, p. 50.

[6] T. M. Adams, *Prices Paid by Vermont Farmers for Goods and Services and Received by Them for Farm Products, 1790-1940: Wages of Vermont Farm Labor, 1780-1940*, Vermont Agricultural Experiment Station, Bulletin 507, February 1944.

any other group during the Civil War, declined so rapidly afterward that its price was lower in 1880 than twenty years earlier. He gave excessively large weight (28.7 percent of expenditure) to rent, which, rising less than other prices during the Civil War, continued high thereafter and had an upward trend for the whole twenty-year period. This maldistribution of weights occurred because Mitchell allowed items in certain clothing, food, and "other" groups for which he had no price data to fluctuate in accordance with all prices. The effect was to raise the weight of food from 42.5 percent of family expenditure, as reported from a study of 2,567 families in 1901, to 56.7 percent. This weight for food was much too high for 1901, but it was close to the percentage actually spent in 1875 according to the Massachusetts study which Miss Hoover relied on.[7]

Mitchell's redistribution of weights did no apparent harm so far as food was concerned, but its effect on clothing, rent, and "other items" was such as to bias his index upward somewhat. If Miss Hoover's prices for her major groups were reweighted by the expenditure distribution used by Mitchell, her cost-of-living relative in 1880 would be 113 instead of 110.

Most of the upward bias in Mitchell's index was imparted by his averaging relatives of prices of the same commodity in different localities, instead of averaging actual prices, as Miss Hoover did. This bias may be revealed by a very simple illustration. Let the average price of butter in Philadelphia, say, rise from 20 cents a pound in 1860 to 29 cents in 1880; at the same time let it fall in Lawrence, Indiana, from 30 cents in 1860 to 20 cents in 1880. A simple average of actual retail prices in the two communities would yield a *decline* from 25 cents in 1860 to 24.5 cents in 1880 or 2 percent. But a simple average of relatives would yield a price *rise* of 6 percent:

	1860		1880	
	Price	*Relative*	*Price*	*Relative*
Philadelphia	0.20	100	0.29	145
Lawrence	0.30	100	0.20	67
Average of prices	0.25	100	0.245	98
Average of relatives		100		106

When relatives are averaged for items of similar absolute size, of which some decline and others rise, there will be an upward bias.

[7] Engel's law, which was widely quoted in the late nineteenth century in state labor bureau documents, suggested that poorer families spend larger proportions of their incomes on food.

If the increases and decreases are only a few percent, the bias will be negligible. If they are very large, relative to differences in absolute size of the various items, the bias can be enormous. As Mitchell himself observed, the variation of prices of the same commodity among different localities was much greater in 1860 than in 1880.[8] The most extreme change occurred in Cedar Rapids, Iowa, where the prices reported for many commodities in 1860 were low relative to those in other communities in that year and where they rose by very large percentages to 1880—for some commodities by percentages in the hundreds. In order to determine the influence of the extreme Cedar Rapids prices, this writer examined the retail price indexes for the 58 commodities used by Mitchell (excluding the two board items). Of the 43 commodities for which Mitchell's 1880 price relatives were above Miss Hoover's, 25 included Cedar Rapids prices. Of the 15 commodities in which Mitchell's prices were the same or lower than Miss Hoover's, 11 did not include Cedar Rapids. In a large percentage of the first set of cases, the exclusion of Cedar Rapids from the Mitchell average brought the relative price of the commodity in 1880 closer to Miss Hoover's result; in a substantial proportion of these cases the discrepancy was largely eliminated.

It may be concluded that the principal reasons Miss Hoover obtained lower relative prices than Mitchell did are that (1) by averaging the actual prices of each commodity in different cities, she avoided the statistical bias caused by averaging relatives, and (2) by using price data for a much larger number of cities and towns than Mitchell did, she absorbed the accidental impact of a few communities—Cedar Rapids, New Cumberland, West Virginia, and Springfield, Ohio—which had relatively great net price increases during the twenty-year period.

THIS STUDY'S INDEX FOR 1880-90

This study's consumer price index for the 1880's differs markedly from that of Burgess, the only other one for this decade; whereas the Burgess index included only food, the present one includes food, shelter, fuel and light, clothing, house furnishings, and miscellaneous items.

The retail price data for these items are extremely thin and derive from a wide variety of sources. For many of the series on food, fuel, clothing, and house-furnishing items, retail prices were quoted

---

[8] Mitchell, *Gold, Prices, and Wages*. Mitchell was aware of the bias involved in constructing index numbers by simple arithmetic averages of relatives (see *ibid.*, p. 58). He therefore based much of his own analysis on medians of relatives, as well as on deciles that showed the entire distribution.

for each year 1880-90 by a small number of retail stores in New York City and Brooklyn, and two localities in Pennsylvania.[9]

In addition, annual prices were taken from T. M. Adams' original collection of prices paid by Vermont farmers for articles of food, clothing, fuel and light, as well as for miscellaneous items of family expenditure, such as tobacco, fire insurance, railroad passenger travel, and physician's services.[10] Retail price data in scattered years were obtained for a few states, including Iowa, Massachusetts, Ohio, Wisconsin, Missouri, and New Jersey, from a compilation by the Massachusetts Bureau of Statistics of Labor.[11] These data were especially spotty for the 1880's and their main contribution was a better bench mark for meats, wood, and a few clothing items. Data were most often available for only 1880 and 1885. For 1890 quotations for items answering similar description as to quality-grade had usually to be obtained from the extensive studies by the United States Department of Labor for that year and published in reports of the Aldrich Committee and of the Department of Labor itself.[12] Rents for four-room and six-room houses were obtained for each of three places: Leavenworth, Kansas, for 1880 and 1889, and Boston and St. Louis, for 1880 and 1890. Rents for 1880 were from the Weeks Report on retail prices;[13] those for 1889 and 1890 were from state reports.[14] Some rentals were based on sketchy reports, others on extensive returns, as in the case of Massachusetts.

[9] *Tenth Annual Report of the Bureau of Statistics of Labor of the State of New York* (for 1892), Part 1, pp. 277-284; *Annual Report of the Secretary of Internal Affairs of the Commonwealth of Pennsylvania* (for 1890), Part III, "Industrial Statistics," Vol. XVIII, pp. A-44 to -47. The New York stores, except for one whose prices were quoted for January and another whose prices were quoted for September, did not specify the time of year to which the prices referred. The Pennsylvania stores quoted their prices for four months each year—January, April, July, and October. These four months were combined into a year's average in the present study.

[10] T. M. Adams, *op.cit.*, Bulletin 507 Supplement, pp. 41-66.

[11] *Thirty-first Annual Report of the Massachusetts Bureau of Statistics of Labor*, Public Document No. 15, March 1901.

[12] Nelson W. Aldrich, *Retail Prices and Wages*, Report by Mr. Aldrich from the Committee on Finance, July 19, 1892, 52nd Congress, 1st Session, Senate Report 986, Parts I and III.

Eighteenth Annual Report of the Commissioner of Labor (for 1903), *Cost of Living and Retail Prices of Food*, Part II, Table I.

[13] Pp. 104-107.

[14] For Leavenworth, 1889: *Seventh Annual Report*, Kansas Bureau of Labor Statistics, p. 198. Computed on a per-room basis from rent expenditures where the number of rooms was stated.

For Boston, 1890: *Twenty-second Annual Report of the Massachusetts Bureau of Statistics of Labor*, March 1892, pp. 481, 491. Weighted average rents paid by 18,661 Boston families occupying four-room houses, and 7,965 occupying six-room houses; several thousand higher-bracket rents were excluded.

For St. Louis, 1890: *Twelfth Annual Report* ... Missouri Bureau of Labor Statistics, for the Year Ending November 5, 1890, "Family budgets," pp. 414-515.

In Massachusetts, comparisons of 1885 with 1880 and 1890 could be obtained from the *Thirty-first Annual Report*. This 1885 comparison was the sole basis for our assumption that United States rents during the 1880's could be interpolated linearly between 1880 and 1890. Prices of daily newspapers in eight cities were obtained from newspaper files at the Library of Congress.[15] Postage on first-class letters was obtained from a Post Office publication.[16]

These prices were compiled into the consumer price index in three steps.

First, the prices of the same commodity in different localities in each year were averaged together. Wherever the quality or grade was reasonably similar, actual prices were averaged to obtain the mean price for the United States—thus minimizing the bias described in connection with Mitchell's method. Wherever the items differed—for example, Rio green coffee and Rio roasted coffee—each year's price was first expressed as a relative of 1880 and these relatives were then averaged. Possibility of bias thus persisted, but since the average prices of commodities did not fluctuate anything like as widely as prices for the same commodity in different stores or localities, the bias was much reduced. This study follows the Mitchell and Hoover practice of not weighting the prices of the same commodity in different stores or localities, on the ground that there was no information on the relative expenditures at these different prices.

The second step was to combine the prices of the various commodities into an average for the major group: for example, eggs, butter, milk, and lard, within the food group. This was done by converting each price series into relatives on the basis of 1880 = 100, then weighting each relative by the importance of the commodity in the group. Eggs, for example, were assigned a weight of about 3.75 percent of food expenditure. These weights, following Hoover and Mitchell, were taken from the expenditures of 232 families as reported by the Aldrich Committee.[17]

The third step was to combine the major groups—food, rent, fuel

---

[15] I am indebted to my son, Clarence D. Long, III, for this compilation. The eight cities are Baltimore, Boston, Hartford, New York, Philadelphia, Chicago, Charleston, and Memphis. They were chosen as closely as possible in accordance with the list compiled by Miss Hoover, but some changes were forced by the fact that certain newspapers used by her in earlier years had discontinued in the 1880's.

[16] *United States Domestic Postage Rates, 1789-1956*, Post Office Department, Publication 15, pp. 22-23.

[17] *Retail Prices and Wages*, Senate Report 986, Part 1, p. XLII. The weights assigned here, however, differ from those assigned by Miss Hoover because her weights were readjusted for changes in prices between 1860 and 1890. They differ somewhat from those given in the Aldrich Report because the weights assigned there to items for which we have no price data were redistributed among the items for which we do have price data.

and light, clothing, house furnishings and miscellaneous—into the final consumer price index. The major groups were given the following percentage weights based on the expenditures of 2,567 United States families in 1901: food 42.5; rent 13.0; fuel and light 5.3; clothing 14.0; furniture and utensils 3.4; and miscellaneous 21.8.[18] This distribution assigned less weight to food, fuel and light, and rent, and more to miscellaneous items than was assigned by Miss Hoover. It also attached different weights than Mitchell, who relied on the same expenditure study but redistributed the expenditures for which he had no price series in such a way as to give more weight to food, fuel, and rent and much less to clothing and miscellaneous items. The distribution of weights in the present study seems closer to the expenditure patterns of the 1880's than to those of the earlier period, as might be expected in view of the fact that rising real incomes allow families to spend more on luxury and semiluxury items. The smaller proportion of expenditures on food seems to be generally borne out by the percentage distributions obtained in the following studies of expenditures in various states in the 1880's:

	Massa-chusetts	Illinois	St. Louis	Kansas		Mean	United States (2,567 families)
	1883	1884	1890	1886	1890		1901
Food	49.28	41.38	38.16	47.4	42.88	43.8	42.5
Rent	19.74	17.42	15.38	18.3	16.63	17.5	13.0
Fuel and light	4.30	5.63	a	a	a	–	5.3
Clothing	15.85	21.00	18.65	16.6	13.62	17.2	14.0
Miscellaneous	10.73	14.57	27.81	17.9	26.87	21.5	25.2
Total	100.0	100.0	100.0	100.0	100.0	100.0	100.0

a Fuel and light were probably included in miscellaneous.
State expenditure data: *Second Annual Report of the* [Kansas] *Bureau of Labor and Industrial Statistics*, January 1, 1887, p. 306; *Fifteenth Annual Report*, Massachusetts Bureau of Statistics of Labor, July 1884, p. 465.
United States: *Eighteenth Annual Report of the Commissioner of Labor*, p. 6480.

However, the state distributions seem to assign greater relative importance to rent and clothing.

The new consumer price index suggests a net decline in living costs during 1880-90 of about 11 percent, much more than the 3 percent manifested by the Burgess index. All of the decline occurred during 1883-86. All the major groups dropped, with clothing and "other" items falling the most, rents the least, and food about the same as the all-items index. The all-items index thus moved very similarly with food, as it did in Miss Hoover's indexes for the two previous

[18] *Eighteenth Annual Report of the Commissioner of Labor*, p. 648.

decades, despite the fact that food prices were given much less weight in this third decade.

When linked to the Hoover index, the result is a new series of consumer prices for 1860-90 which behaves very differently from the series of the Federal Reserve Board prepared by linking the Mitchell and the Burgess indexes (Table 17). If reliable, it shows that, except for a couple of Civil War years, living costs were lower, in relation to 1860, throughout the entire thirty years than previously suggested. The gap was small at the close of the Civil War; thereafter living costs fell much more rapidly to 1870. The gap gradually widened to 1885, then opened still wider in the last five years. As a result, 1890 living costs were 2 percent below—instead of 24 percent above—the level of thirty years before. The cost of living measured by the new index of living cost was relatively somewhat higher in 1890 than if it had been measured, as by Falkner and Hansen, in wholesale prices. It also manifested much less rise during the Civil War and less decline during the 1870's.

How accurately this new index measures the cost of living is probably impossible to say. It rests on more data and is less subject to bias than the Mitchell-Burgess index, and it is surely more representative than a wholesale price index for adjusting wages of working people. But it is undoubtedly inferior to modern indexes, and could surely be improved by an exhaustive examination of newspaper advertisements, store catalogues, and business and family records.

TABLE 17

Indexes of Cost of Living, Country-Wide, 1860-1890
(1860 = 100)

	1860	1865	1870	1875	1880	1885	1890
New index (Hoover-Long)	100	176	141	123	110	103	98
Mitchell[a]-Burgess	100	179	156	138	128	119	124
Burgess[b] (food)	100	172	147	129	111	103	107
Falkner[c] (also used by Hansen)	100	232	144	129	105	93	94

Source: This study, Appendix Tables B-1 and -2; Mitchell, *Gold, Prices, and Wages*, p. 91; Aldrich Report, Vol. 3, Part 1, p. 93; W. R. Burgess, *Trends of School Costs*, Russell Sage Foundation, 1920, p. 54.

[a] The Mitchell index is the mean of retail prices of necessities drawn from the Weeks Report and weighted according to importance in working class family expenditure as surveyed by the Department of Labor around 1900. See text.

[b] The Burgess index is the weighted mean of retail prices of ten articles of basic food (beef, pork, poultry, butter, eggs, milk, flour, sugar, lard, potatoes); weighted in accordance with the same family budget used by Mitchell.

[c] The Falkner index is based on the mean of wholesale prices drawn from the Aldrich Report and weighted in accordance with the same family budget study used by Mitchell.

Mitchell also computed separate indexes for eastern and western states. These behaved similarly, except that the eastern index rose somewhat less during the Civil War and fell somewhat more thereafter. Regional differences in retail-price fluctuations doubtless existed, and were possibly greater in the earlier decades, but the wide variations in retail prices of different qualities of the goods at different stores make it difficult to measure the price trends for the different regions with the sparse data at hand. We therefore present only one retail price index for the whole nation during this thirty-year period.

Real Wages in Manufacturing and Building

Real wages, if the Mitchell-Burgess cost-of-living index were used, would show an increase of about 20 percent from 1860 to 1890. The results of using the new consumer price index are dramatically different, for the thirty-year net rise in real wages was roughly the same as the rise in money wages—about 50 percent (Chart 1).

Real wages rose in every one of the three decades, but very unevenly. The Civil War inflation was such that real wages in 1870 were still only 3-7 percent above 1860—though the level of money wages in 1870 was almost at its peak for the next twenty years. During the 1870's, the cost of living fell greatly but a decline in money wages kept close pace, so that by 1880 real wages had gained only an additional 10-19 percent. Most of the over-all gain occurred in the third decade, when a substantial increase in money wages combined with a substantial decrease in the cost of living to give a real-wage increase of 25-28 percent for the ten-year period—more than in the previous two decades combined. The progress of real wages was still more uneven when observed over shorter intervals. During most of the Civil War, living costs outstripped money wages; the result was that in 1864 real wages were less than three-fourths their 1860 level. In every one of the nine post-Civil War years, living costs fell while money wages rose, with the result that by 1869 real wages had erased their war declines and by 1873 had reached a level 17 percent above 1860. After 1873 money wages reversed their trend and declined, but living costs continued their rapid drop to 1879, so that, in the Aldrich data, real wages declined in only one year—1877—and then by only 5 percent. Thereafter, real wages rose in two waves—1878-84 and 1886-90, interrupted by only an insignificant dip of 1 percent. In both waves money wages rose while prices fell, but the first wave of increase was due mainly to a decline in living costs, the second mainly to a rise in money wages.

61

We now compare changes in real wages found in this study with those found by Falkner, Hansen, Phelps Brown and Hopkins, and Wesley Mitchell (Table 18). All these investigators use Aldrich data,

CHART I

Daily Money and Real Wages in Manufacturing, Annually, 1860-1890

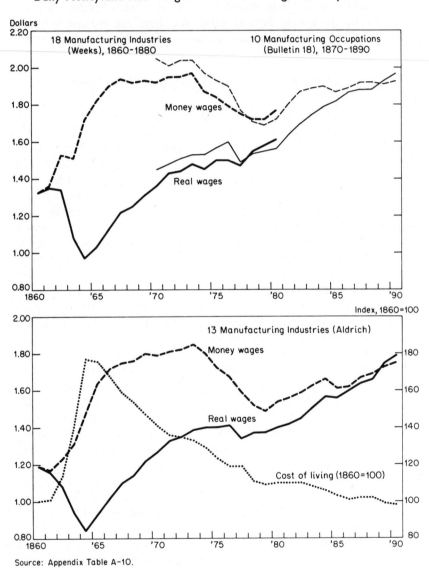

Source: Appendix Table A-10.

which cover only the eastern states, except that Mitchell also uses Weeks Report data which represent eastern and western states as well as a few southern states for a few industries.

Wide differences in the increase of real wages show up in the comparisons for the thirty-year period: the largest increase—nearly 80 percent—is shown by Falkner; the next to largest—nearly 70

TABLE 18

Index of Real Daily Wages in Manufacturing in the East, Based on Aldrich Wage Data and Hoover-Long Consumer Price Index; Compared with Indexes for Mixed Industries Computed by Other Investigators from Aldrich Data and Various Price Indexes: 1860-1890

	1860	1865	1870	1875	1880	1885	1890
Long: Manufacturing[a]	100	78	107	118	118	131	150
Mitchell: Median[b]	100	90	120	116	105	n.c.	n.c.
Mean[c]	100	86	115	120	112	n.c.	n.c.
Falkner[d]	100	64	116	123	136	167	180
Hansen[e]	100	67	125	128	135	160	168
Phelps Brown[f]	100	97	114	121	118	141	132

n.c. Not computed.

Sources and explanation: This study, Chapter 2 and Appendix Table A-1; Mitchell: *Gold, Prices, and Wages*, pp. 86, 89, 91, 169-170, 173-74, 204-206; Falkner, *Aldrich Report*, Vol. 3, Part 1, pp. 93, 176; A. H. Hansen, "Factors Affecting the Trend of Real Wages," *The American Economic Review*, Vol. xv, 1925, p. 32; E. H. Phelps Brown with Sheila V. Hopkins, "The Course of Wage-Rates in Five Countries, 1860-1939," *Oxford Economic Papers*, New Series, Vol. 2, June 1950, p. 277.

[a] Weighted mean of daily wages in 13 manufacturing industries in eastern states, deflated by Ethel D. Hoover's index of weighted mean of retail prices for 1860-80 and a new index of retail prices for 1880-90 prepared in this study. Appendix Tables B-1 and -2.

[b] Weighted median of relative wages in 21 miscellaneous industries including building, city public works, railroads and stores. Weighted median of relatives of retail prices of cost-of-living items.

[c] Weighted mean of relative wages in 21 miscellaneous industries. Weighted mean of retail prices.

[d] Mean of relative wages in 21 miscellaneous industries weighted on the industry level by census reported employment; mean of relative *wholesale* prices weighted by importance in family expenditures.

[e] Mitchell's weighted mean of relative wages from Aldrich data for 1860-80; Falkner's simple mean from Aldrich data for 1880-90. Falkner mean of relative wholesale prices weighted by importance in family expenditures.

[f] Wage index constructed from Aldrich data by weighting the relatives of occupational wages by employment in those occupations in 1870-79, then weighting the average wage of each industry by the census-reported employment in 1870. It is therefore a fixed weight index. Cost-of-living index is Mitchell's median of relative retail prices for eastern states and a "combination of indexes of cost of living and rents (Carl Snyder, *Business Cycles and Business Measurements, 1927*) for 1881-1890 based on the Russell Sage Foundation estimates."

percent—by Hansen; and the smallest—around 30 percent—by Phelps Brown. The 50 percent increase found by this study thus lies about midway. For 1860-80, also, this study shows a larger increase— 18 percent—than Mitchell's mean-wage series or his median-wage series. Why these marked differences?

In the case of the Falkner, Hansen, and Mitchell indexes, money wages rose more sharply principally because these analysts included a miscellany of nonmanufacturing industries—building, stores, city public works, and railroads—which have considerable weight in the index and which, on average, experienced relatively more increase in wages;[19] and because they averaged relative instead of dollar wages, thereby imparting an upward bias to the money wage index.

In the Hansen and Falkner investigations, the greater rise in real wages between 1860 and 1890 is also due in part to deflation in wholesale prices. Wholesale prices were more sensitive in the short run, rising more during the Civil War and falling more in the 1870's; but their trend over the whole period was somewhat more downward than that of retail prices. If the new consumer price index derived in this study had been used by Hansen and Falkner, their index of real wages, instead of rising 68 and 79 percent respectively, would have risen 61 and 71 percent. This rise, however, was still substantially greater than that of my index. Most of their greater rise in real wages is due to money wages.

In the Phelps Brown and Hopkins index, the smaller real-wage increase was due entirely to the Mitchell-Burgess cost-of-living index, rejected in this study as being strongly biased upward. Their money-wage rise is as strongly biased upward as those of the other investigations.

The Mitchell indexes based on Aldrich data were not adjusted for living cost during 1880-90 and do not offer a comparison for real wages beyond 1880. Until that year Mitchell's money-wage index was biased upward by his inclusion of nonmanufacturing wages and by his method; but his cost-of-living index was also biased for reasons already set forth.

Further comparison reveals a larger net advance in real wages up to 1880 than appears in Mitchell's series based on Weeks data (Table 19), despite his use of more industries and his construction of the index by simple medians of relative wages instead of weighted

---

[19] For these industries only a small number of firms reported to the Aldrich Committee; including them would merely prevent the construction of a wage index representative of manufacturing without allowing the construction of one that is representative of all industry or even of the industries covered.

TABLE 19

Indexes of Real Wages in Manufacturing, Based on Weeks–Bulletin 18
Wage Data and Hoover-Long Consumer Price Index; Compared with
Indexes Computed by Mitchell: United States and East and West,
1860-1890

	1860	1865	1870	1875	1880	1885	1890
		UNITED STATES					
Long: Mean[a]	100	78	103	114	122	142	154
Mitchell: Median[b]	100	83	103	103	105	n.c.	n.c.
		EAST					
Long: Mean[a]	100	79	106	118	124	149	160
Mitchell: Median[b]	100	79	105	106	105	n.c.	n.c.
		WEST					
Long: Mean[a]	100	78	99	109	120	133	144
Mitchell: Median[b]	100	89	100	100	102	n.c.	n.c.

n.c. Not computed.

Source and explanations: Chapter 2; Appendix Tables A-3, -4, and -10. Mitchell,
Gold, Prices, and Wages, pp. 86, 177, 192-193.

[a] Wage index computed by averaging dollar wages of manufacturing industries taken
from Weeks Report and Bulletin 18 and weighted at the state and industry levels by
census-reported employment; Hoover-Long cost-of-living index. See Appendix B.

[b] Wage index constructed from Weeks Report by computing simple medians of
relative wages in manufacturing industries. Cost-of-living index constructed by computing medians of relative retail prices of 35 commodities for 1860-80, weighted by importance in family expenditures. Mitchell constructed separate indexes of living cost in
the East and West, but since the retail price data are not believed good enough to
justify separate indexes, the eastern and western wages are both adjusted by means of
the retail price index for the United States.

TABLE 20

Indexes of Real Wages in Building, Based on Aldrich Report and Bulletin
18 Data and on Hoover-Long Consumer Price Index: United States,
and East, West, and South, 1860-1890

	1860	1865	1870	1875	1880	1885	1890
		ALDRICH DATA					
1860=100	100	86	128	129	115	147	162
1870=100	78	67	100	101	90	115	127
		BULLETIN 18 DATA					
United States	n.a.	n.a.	100	107	110	133	141
East	n.a.	n.a.	100	107	110	134	145
West	n.a.	n.a.	100	108	112	135	138
South	n.a.	n.a.	100	111	109	127	131

n.a. Not available.

Source: Wage data, Appendix Tables A-1 and -4; cost of living, Tables B-1 and -2.

means of dollar wages. His money-wage index rose more than mine both to 1870 and from 1860 to 1880, but his cost-of-living index rose nearly as much as his wage index and thus prevented more than a few percent rise in real wages.

This study's estimate of building wages covering the entire thirty years is based on Aldrich data, which embrace only the states east of Ohio. The Aldrich index makes a net advance of 62 percent (Table 20 and Chart 2), greater than the 50 percent for manufacturing

CHART 2

Daily Money and Real Wages in Building, Annually, 1860-1890

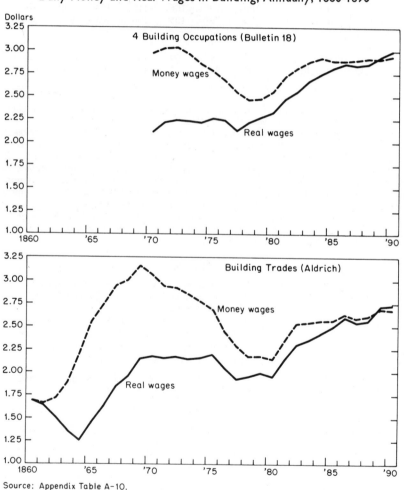

Source: Appendix Table A-10.

CHART 3

Hourly Money and Real Wages in Manufacturing, Annually, 1860-1890

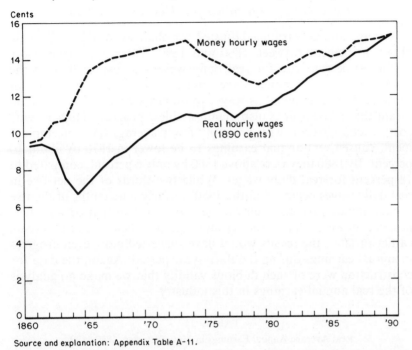

Source and explanation: Appendix Table A-11.

but well below the 84 percent for real wages in building, computed by Falkner. The difference is due partly to my cost-of-living index based on retail instead of wholesale prices, and mainly to the method of computing the money-wage index. Real wages in building declined less than those in manufacturing during the Civil War years, but fell substantially from 1875 to 1880. As with real wages in manufacturing, most of the rise occurred in last decade of the 1880's.

My other measure of building wages, based on Bulletin 18 of the Department of Labor, has some representation in all major regions—East, West, and South—but the series does not begin until 1870. Real wages rise much more by 1890 than those based on Aldrich data, in both the United States as a whole and in the eastern states. Since the living-cost index is the same, my two series for real wages in building differ entirely with respect to money wages. Money wages based on Bulletin 18 data declined only slightly between 1870 and 1890, and even rose in the East whereas the Aldrich building wages declined substantially. This difference may be due

67

to geographical and occupational coverage, since the Bulletin 18 index rests on only four skilled building occupations in large cities.

Real Annual Earnings for Decennial Years

Average annual earnings adjusted for changes in living cost rose about 46 percent between 1860 and 1890 (Table 21)—again close to the 50 percent rise for real daily wages—as expected from the similar behavior of money wages and earnings.[20] But the failure of earnings to rise as much as wages in money terms by 1870 or 1880 meant that real earnings also manifested less progress. Higher living cost, in combination with probably fewer average days of employment, caused real annual earnings to be lower in 1870 by about 10 percent. By 1880 they were above 1860 by only 6 percent, compared to 18 percent for real daily wages. While two-thirds of the net rise in real daily wages occurred in the 1880's, nearly nine-tenths of the rise in real annual earnings seems to have occurred in that decade. It is possible, however, that if the censuses had been held one or two years earlier or later, the results would have suggested more even progress in annual earnings during the thirty-year period. Again, the data for construction were of such dubious validity that we make no analysis of the real annual earnings in this industry.

TABLE 21

Real Average Annual Earnings in Manufacturing, 1860-1890

	1860	1870	1880	1890
Money annual earnings (dollars)	297	384	345	427
Consumer price index	100	144	109.5	98.5
Real annual earnings: 1860 dollars	297	267	315	434
INDEXES: 1860 = 100				
Real annual earnings	100	90	106	146
Real daily wages (Aldrich data)	100	107	118	150
Real daily wages (Weeks–Bulletin 18)	100	103	122	154

Earnings data are for years ending May 31; see text note 20.
Source: Appendix Tables A-9, B-1 and B-2; Tables 18 and 19.

[20] It should be kept in mind that the annual earnings cover the twelve months ending May 31 of each decennial year; consumer prices in some cases refer to the average for the calendar year, in some cases to June 1st, and in others to unknown dates. Therefore average annual earnings are adjusted in Table 21 to an average for living costs in 1859-60, 1869-70, 1879-80, and 1889-90. However, differences in results from deflating by means of living cost in the years 1860, 1870, 1880, and 1890 would have been small except possibly in 1870.

CHAPTER 5

Wages by Industry and Region

Wages by Industry

The daily wages paid by the various manufacturing industries differed substantially. Among the 18 industries from the Weeks Report, the highest-wage industry paid double the lowest in 1860

TABLE 22

Daily Wages for 18 Manufacturing Industries, with Relative Wages and Rankings; Weeks Report, 1860-1880

	Dollars			Rank of Dollar Wages			Relative Wages			Rank of Wage Increase
	1860	1870	1880	1860	1870	1880	1860	1870	1880	1860-1880
Stove foundries	1.78	2.30	1.90	1	5	10	100	129	107	18
Furniture	1.74	2.24	2.23	2	9	5	100	129	128	14
Flour and grist mills	1.73	2.69	2.19	3	2	6	100	155	127	15
Hardware, cutlery, etc.	1.68	2.41	2.24	4	4	4	100	143	133	13
Tin and sheet iron works	1.68	3.18	2.29	5	1	3	100	189	136	12
Saw and planing mills	1.63	2.10	2.41	6	11	1	100	129	148	3
Carriage and wagon works	1.54	1.96	1.86	7	13	11	100	127	121	16
Flint and windowglass	1.46	2.47	2.33	8	3	2	100	169	160	2
Tanneries	1.34	2.26	1.93	9	8	9	100	169	144	6
Machinery	1.33	2.13	1.96	10	10	8	100	160	147	4
Cigars and tobacco	1.32	1.58	1.48	11	15	15	100	120	112	17
Iron blast furnaces, etc.	1.29	2.27	1.83	12	7	12	100	176	142	10
Paper manufacture	1.18	1.85	1.70	13	14	13	100	157	144	5
Brickmaking	1.18	2.30	1.68	14	6	14	100	195	142	9
Clothing	1.03	1.38	1.46	15	18	16	100	134	142	8
Breweries and distilleries	1.01	1.97	2.02	16	12	7	100	195	200	1
Woolen manufactures	0.96	1.52	1.32	17	16	17	100	158	138	11
Cotton manufactures	0.90	1.42	1.29	18	17	18	100	158	143	7
Median	1.34	2.19	1.92				100	163	143	
Weighted mean	1.32	1.92	1.77				100	145	134	
Simple mean	1.38	2.11	1.90				100	153	138	
Average deviation[a]										
Dollars	0.25	0.35	0.28							
Percent of mean	18	17	15							
Highest	1.78	3.18	2.41							
Lowest	0.90	1.38	1.29							
Highest ÷ lowest	2.0	2.3	1.9							

For explanation, see Appendix Table A-3.

[a] Computed from simple mean.

TABLE 23

Daily Wages for 13 Manufacturing Industries and for the Building Trades, with Relative Wages and Rankings; Aldrich Report, 1860-1890

	Dollars				Rank of Dollar Wages				Relative Wages				Rank of Wage Increase	
	1860	1870	1880	1890	1860	1870	1880	1890	1860	1870	1880	1890	1860-1880	1860-1890
Stone	1.53	2.92	2.13	3.04	1	1	2	1	100	191	139	199	8	3
Metals	1.47	2.24	1.91	2.15	2	4	4	3	100	152	130	146	11	10
Agricultural implements	1.37	2.05	1.56	1.77	3	5	8	7	100	150	114	129	12	11
Leather	1.27	1.94	1.67	1.61	4	6	7	9	100	153	131	127	10	12
Carriages and wagons	1.22	2.27	2.44	2.44	5	3	1	2	100	186	200	200	1	2
White lead	1.19	1.81	1.32	1.49	6	7	10	10	100	152	111	125	13	13
Illuminating gas	1.18	2.38	1.92	2.06	7	2	3	5	100	202	163	175	4	4
Books and newspapers	1.12	1.80	1.52	1.75	8	8	9	8	100	161	136	156	9	8
Ale, beer, porter	1.05	1.66	1.72	2.11	9	10	5	4	100	158	164	201	2	1
Lumber	1.04	1.67	1.71	1.82	10	9	6	6	100	161	164	175	3	5
Paper	0.87	1.21	1.26	1.31	11	13	11	12	100	139	145	151	7	9
Woolen goods	0.82	1.30	1.26	1.38	12	12	12	11	100	159	154	168	5	6
Cotton goods	0.79	1.36	1.16	1.27	13	11	13	13	100	172	147	161	6	7
Median[a]	1.18	1.81	1.67	1.77					100	153	142	150		
Weighted mean	1.19	1.79	1.54	1.75					100	150	129	147		
Simple mean	1.15	1.89	1.66	1.86					100	164	144	162		
Average deviation[b]														
Dollars	0.18	0.38	0.29	0.38										
Percent of mean	16	20	17	20										
Highest	1.53	2.92	2.44	3.04										
Lowest	0.79	1.21	1.16	1.27										
Highest ÷ lowest	1.9	2.4	2.1	2.4										
Building trades	1.69	3.06	2.14	2.68	–	–	–	–	100	181	127	159		

For explanation, see Appendix Table A-1.
a In the case of the relative wages the median was computed directly from the relative wages.
b Computed from simple mean.

and almost double in 1880 (Table 22);[1] the range for the middle half of the distribution was 50 cents per day in 1860 and 70 cents in 1880. Among the 13 manufacturing industries from the Aldrich Report, the highest-wage industry paid almost double the lowest in 1860, slightly more than double in 1880, and somewhat more than double in 1890 (Table 23). In both sets the lowest-paying tended throughout to be cotton goods; but the highest-paying varied: in the Weeks data, it was foundries in 1860, tin and sheet iron in 1870, and saw and planing mills in 1880; in the Aldrich data it was stone in 1860, 1870, and 1890, carriages and wagons in 1880.

Some check on these results can be had from the decennial census of manufacturing, which reports the number of employees and total wages during the years ended May 31, 1860, 1870, 1880, and 1890, by selecting 17 industries most nearly the same as those analyzed from the Weeks Report (Table 24). Average annual earnings per worker have been computed for approximately comparable industry classifications in each decennial year. Such averages depend on the accuracy of the census enumerations and industry classifications (firms turning out more than one kind of product are classified on the basis of their principal product). They are also subject to fluctuations from industry to industry and over time—because of changes in the distribution of employed among the different wage categories and variations in the days worked by the average earner during the year. Considerable disparity might well be expected, therefore, between the industry behavior of Weeks-Aldrich daily wages and of census annual earnings. On the other hand, the census undertook to reach every establishment of more than negligible size in each industry, and if the pattern was reasonably similar to that of the wage data, this would be a heartening indication that our small samples of Weeks-Aldrich firms have some value. Census data have the advantage, moreover, of covering decennially the full period 1860-90.

The earnings differentials shown by the census were slightly greater—the highest earnings having been a little more than double the lowest during 1860-80, and a little less than triple in 1890. On the whole, the high-wage industries had high annual earnings, and the low-wage industries low earnings. But the rankings were a long way from being exactly the same. For example, saw and planing mills and flour and grist mills were fairly high in wage rates but

---

[1] Gerhard Bry has objected to my use of the ratio of highest to lowest wage on the ground that it is unstable. I have retained it because of its simplicity and because it does not appear to be very unstable in this study. However, I have not placed undue weight upon it in my analysis of wage behavior.

71

TABLE 24

Average Annual Earnings of Wage Earners in 17 Manufacturing Industries, with Relative Earnings and Rankings;
Census, 1860-1890

	Dollars				Rank of Dollar Earnings				Relative Earnings				Rank of Earnings Increases	
	1860	1870	1880	1890	1860	1870	1880	1890	1860	1870	1880	1890	1860-1880	1860-1890
Foundry and machine shop products	392	573	454	559	1	1	2	2	100	146	116	143	9	11
Carriages and wagons	362	387	411	508	2	10	4	4	100	107	114	140	10	12
Liquors, malt	358	543	465	685	3	3	1	1	100	152	130	191	2	1
Agricultural implements	342	481	388	466	4	5	7	7	100	141	113	136	11	13
Iron and steel, rolling mills	341	570	436	542	5	2	3	3	100	167	128	159	5	4
Liquors, distilled	324	394	410	467	6	9	5	6	100	122	127	144	6	9
Glass	322	496	378	465	7	4	8	8	100	154	117	144	8	10
Cigars and cigarettes	317	349	346	419	8	11	9	11	100	110	109	132	12	14
Flour and grist mills	315	249	298	383	9	15	13	12	100	79	95	122	16a	16
Leather	312	411	403	501	10	7	6	5	100	132	129	161	3	3
Lumber, sawed	298	267	215	289	11	14	15	15	100	90	72	97	17a	17a
Iron and steel, blast furnaces	285	453	304	437	12	6	11	9	100	159	107	153	13	6
Paper	254	398	349	427	13	8	10	10	100	157	137	168	1	2
Woolen goods	232	336	299	340	14	12	12	13	100	145	129	147	4	7
Cotton goods	196	288	244	302	15	13	14	14	100	147	124	154	7	5
Brick and tile	195	249	203	285	16	16	16	16	100	128	104	146	14	8
Chewing tobacco	189	239	196	233	17	17	17	17	100	126	104	123	15	15

72

Table 24, *concluded*

	Dollars				Rank of Dollar Earnings				Relative Earnings				Rank of Earnings Increases	
	1860	1870	1880	1890	1860	1870	1880	1890	1860	1870	1880	1890	1860-1880	1860-1890
The 17 manufacturing industries														
Median	315	394	346	437					100	125	110	139		
Weighted mean	277	363	325	412					100	131	117	149		
Simple mean	296	393	341	430					100	133	115	145		
Average deviation[b]														
Dollars	50	92	74	89										
Percent of mean	17	23	22	21										
Highest	392	573	465	685										
Lowest	189	239	196	233										
Highest ÷ lowest	2.1	2.4	2.4	2.9										
All manufacturing industries[c]														
Weighted Mean	297	384	345	427					100	129	116	144		

Source: Censuses of Manufactures, 1860-1890; see also Appendix Table A-9. The coverage of these industries in each year is as nearly the same as it was possible to make it.

[a] Decrease.
[b] Computed from simple mean.
[c] See Table 14.

somewhat lower in annual earnings, presumably because of fewer days worked during the year.

Industries with above-average wage levels in 1860 tended to increase less than the average. Of the nine Weeks-reported industries with above-median daily wages in 1860, six had smaller-than-median increases by 1880. Of the six Aldrich-reported industries with above-median wages in 1860, five had below-median wage increases by 1880 and four by 1890. So also with census annual earnings (Tables 22-24). These tendencies support Mitchell's findings for 1860-80: "All of the time, the highest group [males earning $2.50 or more] had the lowest relative wages."[2]

Nevertheless, there was no significant tendency for wage or earnings differentials to widen or narrow over the twenty- or thirty-year period. In general, the high-wage and -earnings industries of 1860 were also the high-wage and -earnings industries in 1880 and 1890, despite the fact that several industries shifted position rather distinctly. Three Aldrich Report industries had identical ranks in 1860 and 1890 (stone, 1; books and newspapers, 8; cotton goods, 13); three others changed one place in rank (metals, paper, and woolen goods); two others changed two or three places. Seven of the Weeks Report industries occupied the same rank in 1880 as in 1860 (hardware, tanneries, iron blast furnaces, paper, brickmaking, woolen goods, cotton goods); five others changed one to three places. Three census-reported industries held the same earnings rank in 1860 and 1890 (distilled liquors, 6; brick and tile, 16; and chewing tobacco, 17); four changed rank by one place; eight others changed rank three places or less.

Moreover, all of the three sources indicate a fairly stable average deviation of wages among industries—about 20 percent of the mean. The Aldrich and census data show a slight rise in deviation from 1860 to 1890, the Weeks data a slight decline from 1860 to 1880, both changes too small to suggest significant trends in inter-industry wage differentials for the industries and periods covered.[3]

Some industries may be primarily in high- or low-wage areas, or may be dominated by high- or low-paid occupations. Have these differences been the cause of inter-industry differentials? The effects of geographical and occupational composition will be examined later; we test here whether industry differentials persist *within* the same regions and occupations.

---

[2] *Gold, Prices, and Wages*, p. 167.

[3] The relative interquartile range was the same in 1880 as in 1860 in the Weeks and the census data. In the census data it shows a considerable drop from 1880 to 1890; in the Aldrich data, a small drop from 1860 to 1890.

One test is to compare average deviations of daily wages among ten industries from the Weeks Report for the East and West. If industry differentials are partly due to geographical location, the dispersion should be smaller for the same industries within the East or the West, than within the United States as a whole. But nothing like this is observable in Table 25. In 1860 the relative average

TABLE 25

Average Deviation of Daily Wages among Ten Industries Having Data
Separately for East and West; Weeks Report, 1860 and 1880

	United States		East		West	
	1860	1880	1860	1880	1860	1880
Median	1.31	1.85	1.34	1.76	1.58	1.98
Simple mean	1.38	1.82	1.36	1.81	1.58	2.15
Average deviation[a]						
Dollars	0.23	0.26	0.22	0.28	0.24	0.47
Percent of mean	17	14	16	16	15	22
Highest	1.54	2.41	1.82	2.41	2.33	3.12
Lowest	0.96	1.32	0.94	1.31	1.04	1.25
Highest ÷ lowest	1.6	1.8	1.9	1.8	2.2	2.5

The industries were carriages and wagons, cigars and tobacco, clothing, furniture, iron blast furnaces, machinery, paper, saw and planing mills, stove foundries, and woolens; see Appendix Table A-3.

[a] Computed from the simple mean.

deviation was slightly smaller in the East and West than in the nation as a whole; but in 1880 it was somewhat larger, and the ratios of highest- to lowest-wage industry were even a bit higher in the West than in the United States for the same industries.

A second test is to compute the same deviation of annual earnings among industries with census data for five major regions of the United States: New England, Middle Atlantic including Delaware and Maryland, Central states including Kentucky, the South, and Pacific Coast states (Table 26). Again, the within-region deviations were, if anything, higher than those within the United States as a whole. The differences were not great; for most regions and for the United States, the inter-industry deviations were roughly 20 percent; though for the South and Far West, they were 25 to 31 percent. The ratio of the highest- to lowest-earnings industries also tended to be larger in the separate regions. The paradoxically greater deviations within the regions are undoubtedly due to the greater element of

TABLE 26

Average Deviation of Annual Earnings among 17 Manufacturing Industries, in the
United States and Five Major Regions; Census, 1860 and 1890

	United States		New England		Middle Atlantic[a]		South[a]		Central[b]		Pacific	
	1860	1890	1860	1890	1860	1890	1860	1890	1860	1890	1860	1890
Median	315	437	321	487	309	434	253	315	305	458	838	620
Simple mean	296	430	320	464	296	449	270	337	298	423	796	567
Average deviation[c]												
Dollars	50	89	66	92	49	94	67	102	48	92	224	174
Percent of mean	17	21	21	20	17	21	25	30	16	22	28	31
Highest	392	685	464	745	437	755	408	581	391	614	1,667	846
Lowest	189	233	146	281	188	266	146	170	185	249	357	246
Highest ÷ lowest	2.1	2.9	3.2	2.7	2.3	2.8	2.8	3.4	2.1	2.5	4.7	3.4

Source: Censuses of Manufactures, 1860-1890; and see Appendix Table A-9. The coverage of these industries in each year is as nearly the same as it was possible to make it.
[a] Maryland, Delaware, and West Virginia included in Middle Atlantic region.
[b] Kentucky included in Central region.
[c] Computed from simple mean.

randomness among a smaller number of establishments and workers. In any case, regional location does not seem to be an important source of inter-industry wage differentials.

Were inter-industry differentials traceable to occupational composition? Data of the First Annual Report for 1885 have been classified into hourly wage rates of teamsters in 27 industries, carpenters in 22 industries, and so on, for seven occupations occurring in eight or more industries (Table 27). The report offers enough wage data by occupation, industry, and area, to minimize the element of randomness arising out of differences in the wage practices of different establishments.

The average deviation for the same occupations occurring in different industries ranged from 17 percent for teamsters to 8 percent for patternmakers, with a mean of about 12 percent for the seven occupations—compared with 20 percent for the average deviation among the 37 industries computed without regard to occupational composition. Similar results were found for occupations and industries located in a single state—New York, where observations were obtainable for a substantial number of industries.

TABLE 27

Average Deviation of Hourly Wages among Different Manufacturing
Industries for the Same Selected Occupations, First Annual Report, 1885
(wage data in dollars)

	All States[a]				New York State		
	Mean	Average Deviation			Mean	Average Deviation	
Indus-tries	Hourly Wage[b]	Dollars	Percent of Mean	Indus-tries	Hourly Wage[c]	Dollars	Percent of Mean
Teamsters	27	0.157	0.026	17	11	0.159	0.025	15
Carpenters	22	0.201	0.028	14	9	0.194	0.026	13
Patternmakers	8	0.252	0.021	8	d	d	d	d
Molders	8	0.272	0.030	11	4	0.291	0.036	12
Blacksmiths	18	0.222	0.023	10	6	0.202	0.020	10
Machinists	29	0.223	0.029	13	11	0.211	0.036	17
Laborers	34	0.134	0.016	12	11	0.120	0.017	14
Simple mean							
Six occupations[e]				13				14
The seven occu-pations				12				

[a] Not every state is represented by wage quotations.
[b] Weighted by employment.
[c] Simple mean.
[d] Less than four industries represented.
[e] Excluding patternmakers.

What part of the wage increase during 1860-90 was due to increase in wages within industries, and what part to the shift of workers from low-wage to high-wage industries? The answer can be given only from wage data that represent a substantial cross section of the nation's employment. This, the Weeks–Bulletin 18 data and the Aldrich data do not individually provide. In the former, the changing composition of employment had a slight lifting effect on average wages (at least for 1890) and in the latter a substantial depressing effect. A more reliable indication is supplied by the annual earnings data for 17 selected industries, which employed over 40 percent of the nation's factory production workers throughout the period. These data suggest that about one-fifth of the rise in average annual earnings was due to the shift of employment from lower- to higher-earnings industries (Table 28).

The relatively expanding industries were mainly those producing hard goods—durable consumer and producers' products. It was the hard goods industries that were mainly the high-wage and high-earnings industries in both 1860 and 1890, and their aggregate share grew from less than half to more than two-thirds of the total

TABLE 28

Effect of Fixed versus Current Employment Weights on Wages or Earnings
Indexes, 1860-1890

	1860	*1870*	*1880*	*1890*
Weeks–Bulletin 18 Report:[a] Daily wages, 17 industries, weighted by industrial composition of employment in:				
Current year	100	146	134	150[a]
1860	100	148	137	147[a]
Effect of changing employment	–	−2	−3	+3[a]
Aldrich Report: Daily wages, 13 industries, weighted by industrial composition of employment in:				
Current year	100	151	130	148
1860	100	162	142	160
Effect of changing employment	–	−11	−12	−12
Census: Annual earnings, 17 industries, weighted by industrial composition of employment in:				
Current year	100	131	117	149
1860	100	128	110	139
Effect of changing employment	–	+3	+7	+10

The employment weights were employment as reported by the censuses of manufactures for those states from which wage data were reported. For all states in which wage data were reported for any industry, requisite employment data by industry were available. In the Aldrich wage data, only New England and the Middle Atlantic states plus Maryland and Ohio were represented. In the census annual earnings data, all states were represented both in the earnings and the employment weights.

[a] Data by industry in the Weeks Report cover only 1860-80. The wage index for 1880-90 had to be extended by means of wages in ten manufacturing occupations reported from twelve large cities by the Department of Labor in its Bulletin 18. These wage data were weighted by occupational employment data for the states in which the cities were located, from the censuses of manufactures. In this table in 1890 wages were weighted by the occupational distribution of employment in 1880. The index of change from 1880 to 1890 was then linked to the index of change from 1860 to 1880.

employed by the 17 industries. All of the eight hard goods industries, except iron and steel blast furnaces, expanded their shares of employment; all of the nine soft goods industries, except malt liquors and cigars and cigarettes, contracted their shares. The biggest relative expansion of employment occurred for the high-wage basic metals and metal products; the biggest relative contraction for the low-wage cotton and woolen textiles.

Other data might yield other results, but we conclude from this section: that substantial wage variation did exist among different industries, the highest-wage industry having paid roughly double the lowest, and the average deviation in wage rates among the different industries having been roughly 20 percent of the mean wage; that this variation was not due to regional location of the various industries; that perhaps a third of it could have been due to differences in occupation-mix; that the rankings of industries in the national wage or earnings scale tended to maintain themselves fairly well throughout the thirty years, with a few instances, however, of an industry drastically altering its pay scale relative to other industries; and that there was no significant tendency for the wage dispersion among industries either to widen or to narrow over the three decades; and finally that about one-fifth of the rise in wages and earnings may have been due to the relative shift of workers from the low-wage soft goods industries—especially textiles—to the high-wage hard goods industries—especially basic metals and metal products.

Wages by Region

The regional structure of wages is most effectively analyzed by industries and occupations.

TABLE 29

Weighted Average Daily Wage-Rates in Manufacturing Industries for the East, West, and South; Weeks Report, 1860-1880

	1860	1865	1870	1875	1880
CURRENT DOLLARS					
East	1.23	1.71	1.84	1.78	1.68
West	1.74	2.39	2.42	2.32	2.30
South	0.99	1.07	1.07	1.15	1.17
PERCENTAGE OF WAGES IN THE EAST					
West	141	139	132	130	137
South	80	62	58	65	70

For explanation, see Appendix Table A-3.

Differentials in daily wages by industry over time may be computed from data of the Weeks Report, covering three major regions (Table 29). Inter-regional differences were substantial—with wage levels highest in the West, intermediate in the East, and lowest in the South. The alignments persisted over the twenty years to 1880, but southern and western wages rose less rapidly, so that southern wages fell relatively further below eastern wages, and western wages may have fallen somewhat toward eastern wages.

The 18 industries in the Week Report are not all represented in each region. What are the results if we compare only industries with representation in both East and West or East and South?

Ten industries offer wage data for both East and West; though the number of establishments in one or the other region is usually very small, and even in the same industry firms may produce somewhat different products in different regions.

TABLE 30

Percentage Ratio of Daily Wages in Western and Southern Establishments to Those in Eastern Establishments; Identical Industries, Weeks Report, 1860-1880

Industry	1860	1865	1870	1875	1880
WESTERN WAGES IN PERCENT OF EASTERN					
Clothing	240	253	256	244	224
Woolen goods	134	135	119	128	134
Furniture	129	93	94	85	84
Iron blast furnaces, rolling mills, etc.	127	128	130	130	127
Cigars and tobacco	119	198	198	168	185
Carriages and wagons	108	71	75	66	72
Machinery	104	102	102	81	93
Paper	88	98	59	60	73
Stove foundries	88	112	78	73	104
Saw and planing mills	84	145	132	152	155
Median percentage	114	120	111	107	116
SOUTHERN WAGES IN PERCENT OF EASTERN					
Cigars and tobacco	61	57	51	50	54
Paper	71	38	53	58	57
Saw and planing mills	65	86	79	84	84
Median ratio	65	57	53	58	57

For explanation, see Appendix Table A-3.

The wage differentials varied widely among these industries (Table 30). Wages were higher in the West for most industries in most years, but the pattern was mixed. The ratio of western to eastern wages ranged in 1860 from as high as 2.40 for clothing to 0.84 for saw mills. In four industries wages were consistently higher in the West than in the East throughout 1860-80, but in the remaining six, they were often lower—consistently lower in paper and lower in all but one or two quinquennial dates in foundries and furniture. The median of the ten industries indicates a slight rise in the ratio of western to eastern wages, though the entire change occurred during the Civil War years, and no significant trend was observable after 1865.

Only three industries had establishments in the South, but each provided wage comparisons in all three regions. These were cigars and tobacco, paper, and saw and planing mills. In all three, wages were consistently lower in the South, and in two—cigars and tobacco and saw and planing mills—lower relative to the West than to the East. Wages in the South were further below the other two regions in 1880 than in 1860, but almost the entire widening occurred between the quinquennial years 1860 and 1865; thereafter the South-East differential remained roughly constant. It would appear from our very small sample that wages tended to be lower in the East than in the West and still lower in the South, and that these differentials tended to widen during the Civil War, but not between the end of the Civil War and 1880.

Thus far, the regional wage comparisons cover only 1860-80. For 1880-90, we have two separate surveys covering large numbers of workers and establishments: the *First Annual Report of the Commissioner of Labor* for 1885 and the Dewey-Census Report for 1890.[4]

For 1885 daily wages were higher in the West and lower in the South, than in the East; but the differences were much smaller than those indicated by the Weeks Report for the earlier years: the First Annual Report shows western wages to have been 6 percent above eastern in thirteen industries with establishments in both regions, and southern wages 19 percent below eastern in five industries (Table 31). In 1890, the Dewey Report on hourly wages indicated still smaller differentials—whether for industries common to those in the First Annual Report or for a mixed list. Southern establishments paid wages equal to or higher than eastern in three industries. Only 7 out of 15 industries paid higher wages in the West than in the East.

Are we to conclude that the regional wage differentials were very high and unchanging in the years up to and including 1880, but then fell very sharply in 1885 and again, mildly, in 1890? Such a conclusion would surely be unsafe.

The Weeks Report had the virtue of enabling us to compare wages

---

[4] The Dewey Report was actually made in connection with the 1900 census, but the establishments were asked to report their wages for 1890 also.

for the same firms, occupations, and industries over time, but it was restricted to a small number of establishments. This small sample has several pitfalls. First, wages may vary widely among establishments within the same industry. Second, industries are broad classifications; a manufacturer of tobacco products in one region may produce plug tobacco, in another mainly fine-cut. Third, the occupations with wage data varied from one establishment to another as from accidents of record-keeping. The First Annual and the Dewey Reports, covering hundreds of establishments and

TABLE 31

Percentage Ratio of Wages in Manufacturing Industries in Southern and Western States to Those in Eastern States, 1885 and 1890; First Annual and Dewey Reports

	First Annual Report, Daily Wages 1885	Dewey Report, Hourly Wages 1890
WESTERN WAGES IN PERCENT OF EASTERN		
Leather	115	118
Paper	114	88
Lumber	106	100
Glass	105	111
Agricultural implements	105	107
Foundries and metal working	100	98
Woolen goods	88	117
Carriages and wagons	81	70
Median percentage: the eight industries	105	104
Median percentage: mixed list	106[a]	100[b]
SOUTHERN WAGES IN PERCENT OF EASTERN		
Cotton goods	81	95
Metals	87	100
Woolen goods	67	87
Median percentage: the three industries	81	95
Median percentage: mixed list	81[c]	90[d]

For explanation, see Chapter 2 and Appendix Tables A-7 and A-8.

[a] In addition to the above eight industries: boots and shoes 107 percent, liquors and beverages 133, machines and machinery 122, tobacco 84, brick 109.

[b] In addition to the above eight: clothing 207, cotton goods 98, breweries 80, iron and steel 107, flour mills 116, furniture 83, printing 73.

[c] In addition to the above three: tobacco 58, and lumber 107.

[d] In addition to the above three: clothing 99, glass 127, leather 79, breweries 93, lumber 80, foundries and metal working 100, flour mills 50, furniture 55, printing 67.

more than a hundred thousand workers, are less subject to the kind of variation that occurs if an abnormally high- or low-wage firm happens to represent an industry in a state or region. But all that these various data entitle us to say is, that wages in most industries were probably higher in the West and lower in the South than in the East throughout 1860-90, with the differentials varying among industries and over time, but with no net trend apparent.

This regional behavior of wage rates was broadly confirmed by average annual earnings (Table 32). Compared with the Middle Atlantic states, earnings were about the same in the Central (Middle West) states, 10-30 percent lower in the South, and much higher in the Pacific states. Again, the differentials varied widely among industries, with several having higher earnings in the South than in the Middle Atlantic states in certain years though only in the cigar and cigarette industry was this true in both initial and terminal years.[5]

Annual earnings are the only data which cover the whole nation for the entire period. In all the regions outside the Middle Atlantic, earnings tended to decline in relation to those in the Middle Atlantic, the decline being substantial in the South and enormous in the Far West (where earnings in 1860 had been extremely high). Some industries moved counter to this relative trend in all regions but in the great majority of industries earnings moved down compared with the East. For the United States as a whole, only saw mills had absolute earnings that were not higher in 1890 than in 1860. In the South, flour and grist mills, paper, and chewing tobacco had lower earnings in 1890; but eleven of the twelve Pacific Coast industries paid lower absolute dollar earnings in 1890 than thirty years before.

These declines in relative and even in absolute earnings outside the Middle Atlantic region brought the average annual earnings for New England, the Central West, and the Pacific Coast closer to those for the Middle Atlantic; but the decline for the South depressed its earnings relatively further below eastern earnings in 1890. The net effect may have been that average annual earnings showed, in general, less interstate dispersion in 1890 than in 1860 (Table 33). Thirteen industries manifested declines in relative average deviations among states, and the median declined from 21 to 17 percent. The decline, however, occurred in the last decade; most of the industries had a higher dispersion in 1880 than in 1860. Thus the census earnings confirm the Weeks wages, in showing an increase in

[5] R. A. Lester has found that the North-South wage differential varied widely in recent years. "A Range Theory of Wage Differentials," *Industrial and Labor Relations Review*, July 1952, p. 484.

TABLE 32

Percentage Ratio of Average Annual Earnings in Four Major Regions to Those in the Middle Atlantic Region, for 17 Manufacturing Industries; Census, 1860-1890

Industry	New England				South[a]				Central[a]				Pacific			
	1860	1870	1880	1890	1860	1870	1880	1890	1860	1870	1880	1890	1860	1870	1880	1890
Liquors, malt	123	85	98	99	118	75	85	77	101	77	94	81	258	92	97	112
Iron and steel, rolling mills	120	94	89	90	84	104	78	74	117	108	104	104	–	–	–	–
Leather	118	119	109	108	84	37	60	63	101	81	109	107	216	94	141	131
Carriages and wagons	113	123	115	115	97	75	73	81	98	88	94	91	266	172	151	137
Foundries and machine shops	109	98	104	99	112	104	80	88	104	92	99	92	458	207	144	141
Cotton goods	109	110	109	102	78	68	70	61	103	95	95	78	–	–	–	–
Lumber, sawed	108	99	96	108	90	84	90	101	103	101	125	106	261	163	178	172
Cigars and cigarettes	107	125	111	120	110	145	69	118	93	99	95	101	297	85	74	101
Liquors, distilled	106	135	101	91	53	52	58	42	74	119	100	84	191	113	116	55
Paper	106	106	107	103	145	100	82	74	112	98	110	94	149	167	161	145
Agricultural implements	106	94	110	103	102	67	72	79	113	101	118	97	263	127	137	159
Iron and steel, blast furnaces	106	154	99	112	75	76	68	92	112	99	84	111	–	–	–	–
Woolen goods	103	109	106	99	76	57	57	72	108	82	78	82	237	123	133	73
Glass	95	86	107	87	92	30	87	82	92	125	99	98	–	–	–	–
Flour and grist mills	93	97	112	107	78	49	54	50	109	130	117	104	281	221	179	151
Brick and tile	71	81	83	89	86	63	62	72	90	70	84	84	182	69	106	118
Chewing and smoking tobacco	–	–	–	–	75	52	43	50	89	117	85	91	–	–	–	–
Median percentage	106	103	107	103	86	68	70	74	103	99	99	94	262	125	139	134
Simple mean	106	108	104	102	91	73	70	75	101	99	99	94	255	138	136	125
Number of industries with:																
Decrease since 1860	–	6	7	10		14	15	14		12	10	11				12
Increase since 1860	–	9	8	6		3	1	3		5	7	6				0
No change	–	1	1	0		0	1	0		0	0	0				0

[a] Maryland, Delaware, and West Virginia included in Middle Atlantic region; Kentucky in Central region.

Source: Appendix Table A-9.

TABLE 33

Average Deviation of Average Annual Earnings of Employees in 17 Manufacturing Industries, among States: United States and Five Major Regions; Census, 1860-1890
(percent)

Industry	United States				New England		Middle Atlantic[a]		South[a]		Central[a]		Pacific	
	1860	1870	1880	1890	1860	1890	1860	1890	1860	1890	1860	1890	1860	1890
Brick and tile	39.9	26.7	25.1	28.1	13.4	18.5	35.9	7.0	26.0	24.8	50.8	15.9	12.8	10.5
Liquors, distilled	38.3	38.8	32.6	35.2	15.0	16.4	25.1	21.8	31.0	27.1	11.3	27.8		
Foundries and machine shops	32.4	20.9	22.6	13.6	11.6	5.6	7.1	7.0	28.1	12.1	7.5	7.9	13.3	3.5
Flour and grist mills	27.9	57.4	31.5	30.8	13.3	9.8	4.0	13.4	13.2	27.0	11.5	8.9	13.6	8.4
Cigars and cigarettes	24.6	28.4	26.5	19.1	9.8	10.1	35.5	10.6	9.6	19.5	20.7	7.6		
Woolen goods	24.1	26.2	30.7	20.2	8.7	10.5	2.1	8.9	27.4	28.1	8.3	10.2	1.8	39.8
Lumber, sawed	22.3	30.2	26.9	21.8	3.7	12.5	4.4	13.5	17.0	18.6	8.0	13.4	15.4	9.4
Leather	22.1	35.5	28.5	19.8	7.3	11.6	7.6	11.9	8.9	28.6	11.5	6.1	5.2	3.3
Chewing and smoking tobacco	21.1	44.3	53.5	51.1			16.8	9.8	19.6	62.4	11.1	26.7		
Iron and steel, rolling mills	21.1	20.7	20.1	12.7	8.2	13.9	8.9	10.0	25.9	11.5	19.9	10.1		
Carriages and wagons	20.4	32.2	30.6	17.4	12.7	10.1	4.0	8.6	19.1	15.2	6.7	9.0	22.6	8.6
Agricultural implements	19.3	26.6	22.7	14.8	8.3	9.6	8.7	6.9	15.0	17.8	8.2	11.5	12.8	17.0
Paper	18.3	19.5	22.6	11.9	6.9	3.6	8.3	6.3	36.3	15.9	12.9	8.7		
Liquors, malt	17.4	25.4	12.2	17.2	6.5	7.1	4.2	9.4	18.8	12.2	8.0	8.8		
Cotton goods	14.3	17.0	21.7	16.6	3.4	4.3	5.3	10.0	13.7	7.2	13.9	10.4		
Iron and steel, blast furnaces	14.1	39.3	32.2	16.2			8.1	13.7	18.7	15.0	8.1	13.5		
Glass	7.7	31.8	15.8	7.1			4.9	7.3			13.0	5.2		
Median deviation	21.1	28.4	26.5	17.4	8.5	10.1	7.6	9.8	18.8	18.2	11.3	10.1	13.1	9.0
Number of industries with:														
Decrease since 1860		3	5	13	–	4	–	7	–	9	–	8	–	6
Increase since 1860		14	12	4	–	10	–	10	–	7	–	9	–	2
No change		0	0	0	–	0	–	0	–	0	–	0	–	0

Source: Censuses of Manufactures, 1860-1890; see also Appendix Table A-9.

[a] Maryland, Delaware, and West Virginia included in the Middle Atlantic region; Kentucky in the Central region.

geographical dispersion of earnings by 1880, in the face of a net decrease between 1860 and 1890. In addition to a net decline in the interstate dispersion of earnings within the United States as a whole, there were also net declines within the southern, central, and Pacific regions where the states seemed to be somewhat closer, in their average earnings, in 1890 than in 1860.

Regional disparities in wages and earnings have been analyzed by industry. But the same industry may conceivably employ different combinations of occupations in different regions; say, more unskilled workers in the South and more skilled workers in the East. We now compare wages and earnings in different states and regions for the same occupation.

First we analyze the occupational wages between 1870 and 1890 reported by the Department of Labor in its Bulletin 18. This report gathered daily wages for ten occupations more or less identifiable with manufacturing, though found in other industries, and four occupations identifiable with the building trades, also found in other industries. All except laborers were skilled and all were from large cities—two in the South, five each in the East and West. None of the occupational wages were identified by establishments, but the continuity of the quotations suggests that the same occupations were reporting from one year to the next. The number of establishments was probably small.

For "manufacturing" occupations, wage rates tended actually to be higher in southern than in eastern or western cities (Table 34). Median wages for the manufacturing occupations were higher in the two southern cities than in the East and West in 1870, 1875, and 1880, and were lower only in 1885 and 1890. Wages were higher in all quinquennial years for boilermakers, cabinetmakers, and iron molders; in several quinquennial years, for compositors and stonecutters; in 1875 and 1880, even for the unskilled category laborers. For building occupations, however, southern wages were below the other regions by 10 to 20 percent in all quinquennial years.

The comparison between eastern and western wages was similarly mixed. In the manufacturing occupations, wages tended to average a few percent higher in the West (as we have already discovered from our industry data). But in two of the four building occupations, they were lower in the West. Again, in both South and West daily wages tended to decline relatively to those in the East. Wages were relatively lower in 1890 than in 1870 in seven of the ten manufacturing occupations and in three of the four building occupations; in several remaining occupations the rise was either inappreciable or nonexistent.

86

We have compared regional differentials of industry wages without regard to occupations and regional differentials of occupational wages without regard to industry. We now compare regional wage differentials for the same occupations in the same industries, relying on the First Annual Report for 1885 and the Dewey Report for 1890.

TABLE 34

Percentage Ratio of Daily Wages in Southern and Western Establishments to Those in Eastern Establishments for the Same Occupation: 10 Manufacturing and Four Building Occupations, Bulletin 18, 1870-1890

	Southern					Western				
	1870	*1875*	*1880*	*1885*	*1890*	*1870*	*1875*	*1880*	*1885*	*1890*
Manufacturing occupations										
Blacksmiths	104	94	100	98	96	107	114	107	106	104
Boilermakers	159	164	159	115	110	128	129	125	120	110
Cabinetmakers	143	152	137	128	118	102	98	108	85	90
Compositors	110	112	103	98	99	108	116	111	104	104
Iron molders	116	132	119	115	116	108	114	111	108	107
Laborers	85	108	112	97	97	99	104	105	103	102
Machinists	93	103	100	86	85	118	112	110	108	108
Patternmakers	139	129	107	105	93	101	97	98	98	90
Stonecutters	100	98	114	90	85	85	94	104	96	109
Teamsters	87	93	88	87	87	100	99	100	98	100
Median percentage	107	110	110	98	97	105	108	108	104	104
Building occupations										
Bricklayers and masons	86	84	109	93	86	96	110	126	119	112
Carpenters and joiners	87	96	83	81	81	92	97	88	88	84
Painters	80	69	75	81	63	87	87	85	86	81
Plumbers	89	96	85	71	70	107	108	107	102	103
Median percentage	87	90	84	81	76	94	103	98	95	94

For explanation, see Appendix Table A-4.

For 1885 we examine wages in selected occupations in cotton goods, woolen goods, and metal industries—using those occupations and industries with wages of substantial numbers of workers and establishments recorded in at least three major regions (Table 35). Southern establishments paid lower wages than Middle Atlantic establishments in every one of the cotton-goods and woolen-goods occupations and in five of the seven metals occupations. Again the differentials varied widely. Compared to the Middle Atlantic, southern wages ranged in cotton goods from 51 percent for teamsters to 94 percent for male weavers, in woolen goods from 35 percent for loom fixers to 68 percent for mule spinners, and in metals from 75 percent for teamsters to 121 percent for machinists.

The above comparisons are for occupations without regard to age or sex of the workers. However, since most occupations are engaged in more or less exclusively by workers of the same sex, this limitation is not serious. Nevertheless we can check our results by comparing adult-male wages in certain occupations in different regions (Table 36). In 1885, adult males invariably received lower wages in the South than in the East or West, and the same may be

TABLE 35

Percentage Ratio of Average Hourly Wages in Selected Occupations and Industries of Major Regions to Those in Middle Atlantic States, First Annual Report, 1885

	New England	*South*	*Central*	*Pacific*
Cotton goods				
Teamsters	71	51		
Carpenters	107	75		
Machinists	75	83		
Weavers, male	115	94		
Weavers, female	103	77		
Loom fixers	95	79		
Mule spinners	77			
Laborers	97	62		
Median percentage	96	77		
Woolen goods				
Teamsters	85			
Carpenters	109		105	
Machinists	77		98	
Weavers, male	95		101	111
Weavers, female	105	59	99	
Loom fixers	79	35	78	85
Mule spinners	82	68	78	
Laborers	88		109	88
Median percentage	87	59	99	88
Metals				
Teamsters		75	104	
Carpenters		96	114	171
Machinists	98	121	121	155
Patternmakers	98	98	102	
Molders	86	101	82	120
Blacksmiths	111	86	127	171
Laborers	102	95	111	
Median percentage	98	96	111	163

For explanation, see Chapter 2 above.

said for adult females. Weavers in cotton goods and packers in tobacco offer separate comparisons for males and females; in each the southern wages were below eastern wages. Western wages were below the East for three of the five metal-goods occupations, for male and female weavers in woolen goods, and for female tobacco

TABLE 36

Daily Wages of Workers of the Same Sex, in the Same Occupation and Industry: Selected Data for Southern, Eastern, and Western States; First Annual Report, 1885

	Dollars per Day			Percentage of Eastern Wages	
	South	East	West	South	West
ADULT MALES					
Cotton goods					
Weavers	0.86	1.10		78	–
Metals and metallic goods					
Heaters	3.50	4.03	4.34	87	107
Heaters' helpers	1.50	1.87	1.71	80	91
Laborers	0.92	1.19	1.17	77	98
Puddlers	2.36	3.24	3.52	73	108
Puddler's helpers	1.31	1.92	1.70	68	88
Median	1.50	1.92	1.71	77	98
Tobacco					
Foremen	2.09		2.86	–	
Laborers	0.84	1.13	1.33	74	118
Lumpmakers	1.18	1.67	1.88	71	112
Packers	0.60	2.00	2.34	30	117
Stemmers	0.60		0.93	–	
Median	0.84	1.67	1.88	71	117
Woolen goods					
Weavers		1.59	1.40	–	88
ADULT FEMALES					
Cotton goods					
Weavers	0.77	0.99		78	–
Spinners	0.65	0.73		89	–
Tobacco					
Packers	0.83	1.33	1.29	62	97
Stemmers	0.54	0.75		72	–
Woolen goods					
Weavers	0.75	1.18	0.88	64	75

Only those occupations, industries, and states were selected for which wage quotations covered a substantial number of workers.

Source: *First Annual Report of the Commissioner of Labor* (1886), pp. 151-172.

TABLE 37

Percentage Ratio of Daily Wages in Southern, Eastern, and Western Establishments to Those in Middle Atlantic Establishments; Selected Occupations, Males 16 and Older, Dewey-Census Report, 1890

	New England	South	Central	Pacific
Cotton goods				
Foremen	94	71		
Laborers	100	55		
Card hands	91	64		
Spinners	88	29		
Dyehouse hands	136			
Median percentage	93	60		
Woolen goods				
Foremen	107			
Laborers	92			
Card hands	125			
Spinners	150			
Dyehouse hands	100			
Median percentage	107			
Agricultural implements				
Foremen			85	
Laborers			117	
Machinists			100	
Molders			104	
Carpenters			133	167
Median percentage			104	
Foundries and metal working				
Foremen	103		100	140
Laborers	93	79	107	143
Blacksmiths	83	83	73	117
Blacksmith helpers		60	75	110
Machinists	88		88	
Machinists' helpers	100	75	100	147
Median percentage	93	77	94	140
Iron and steel mills				
Foremen		100	110	
Blacksmiths		91	114	
Machine hands		108	167	
Machinists		110	135	
Molders		88	104	
Median percentage		100	114	
Glass				
Laborers		77	115	
Molders			83	
Blowers		90	85	
Paper mills				
Laborers	92		92	
Machine tenders	100			

90

Table 37, *concluded*

	New England	South	Central	Pacific
Printing				
Foremen	100	95	91	
Laborers	150	100	130	
Tanners				
Laborers	145		127	164
Lumber				
Laborers		100	117	142
Machine tenders		76	94	129
Clothing				
Laborers			190	
Cutters		91		
Cigars				
Cigar makers	194	111	144	

For explanation, see Appendix Table A-8.

packers; but western wages were above eastern in the three male tobacco occupations.

For 1890 similar regional comparisons are available for homogeneous occupations and industries, but we confine this comparison entirely to males 16 and older (Table 37). Again southern wages were lower in most occupations, notably so in cotton goods, metal working, glass, and clothing. Exceptions were foremen, machine hands, and machinists in iron and steel mills, laborers in printing and lumber, and cigar makers. Wages were generally less unfavorable in the South for skilled occupations, but there were exceptions: printing foremen received 5 percent less in the South than in the Middle Atlantic, printing laborers about the same in both regions.[6] New England wages were generally mixed in relation to the Middle Atlantic, so that it would be hard to tell which were typically higher or lower.

For 1885 average deviation of wages among states was further computed for identical occupations in the same industries (Table 38). The deviations tended to be less than those in Table 33 for cotton goods and woolens, and more for metals, but on the whole the differences were not very significant. Narrowing the regional and interstate comparisons to the same occupations within the same

[6] Compare with the findings of Harry Ober, "Occupational Wage Differentials, 1907-1947" *Monthly Labor Review*, August 1948, p. 129.

TABLE 38

Average Deviation of Hourly Wages in Selected Occupations and Industries, among States within Regions, and among Regions; First Annual Report, 1885

	Number of States[a]	AVERAGE DEVIATION AS PERCENT OF AVERAGE WAGE FOR REGION[b]					DIFFERENCE BETWEEN TWO REGIONS AS PERCENT OF AVERAGE OF THE TWO REGIONS[c]					
		All States	New England	Middle Atlantic[d]	South[e]	Central[f]	South-N.E.	South-M.A.	South-Central	N.E.-M.A.	N.E.-Central	M.A.-Central
Cotton goods												
Teamsters	7	25	2	–	7		20	30	–	7	–	–
Carpenters	8	23	5	3	12		37	19	–	29	–	–
Machinists	9	15	7	11	15		10	6	–	13	–	–
Weavers, male	12	16	5	18	16		20	26	–	3	–	–
Weavers, female	13	13	8	12	1		30	24	–	6	–	–
Loom fixers	8	8	2	5	8		18	43	–	3	–	–
Laborers	11	10	10	13	20	–	40	24	–	3	–	–
Median		15	5	12	12		20	24	–	7	–	–
Woolen goods												
Teamsters	9	13	13	16			–	–	–	16	–	–
Carpenters	10	17	18	16			–	–	–	8	–	–
Machinists	12	14										
Weavers, male	14	25										
Weavers, female	15	19	9	18		24	–	–	–	6	6	1
Loom fixers	13	19	14	14						18		
Mule spinners	13	16										
Laborers	15	13										
Median	13	17										
Metals and metallic goods												
Teamsters	8	19										
Carpenters	9	19		3		7						
Machinists	13	15										
Patternmakers	7	7										
Molders	9	11										
Blacksmiths	14	23										
Laborers	14	11										
Median	9	15										

notes on following page

industry yielded results not significantly different from those computed for the industries without regard to occupational composition.

Were the wage differences between regions greater than those between states within the same region? Observing the cotton-goods occupations for 1885 (Table 38), we find that so far as South-East differentials are concerned, this was definitely so. For example, in the case of carpenters in the cotton-goods industry, the percentage difference in average hourly wages between the South and Middle Atlantic was several times the average percentage deviation among states within the Middle Atlantic and southern regions. There were exceptions—notably male weavers—but in general the greater wage differences between South and East seemed to hold for all occupations of the industry. Only cotton goods, however, offered wage data for a sufficient number of southern states to make such a comparison possible.

Hourly earnings by state, region, industry, and occupation, computed by the National Bureau of Economic Research; average deviation computed in this study. Only those occupations and industries were used here for which there were data for seven or more states.

ᵃ Number of states for which the National Bureau computed average hourly wage data by industry, occupation, and states.

ᵇ Computed by subtracting the average hourly wage for all workers and firms reported in that industry and occupation for each state, from the average for the same industry and occupation in that region, then adding these differences without regard to sign, and dividing by the number of states for which wage quotations were available. This yielded the average deviation in cents per hour, which was then expressed as a percentage of the average hourly wage for that region.

ᶜ Computed by taking the difference between the average hourly wages of the two regions and dividing by the average for the two regions.

ᵈ Includes Maryland, Delaware, and West Virginia.

ᵉ Excludes the above three states and Texas.

ᶠ Includes Kentucky.

CHAPTER 6

Wages by Occupational and Individual Characteristics

Wages by Occupation

Chapter 2 brought out that between 1860 and 1890 money wages rose roughly 50 percent. These increases were broadly confirmed in three sets of occupational classifications.

The first set consisted of five skilled occupations, rather common to a great many manufacturing industries for which data were collected in the Weeks Report: blacksmiths, carpenters, engineers, machinists, and painters (Table 39). Wages for these five were

TABLE 39

Average Daily or Hourly Wages in Five Skilled Occupations, Occurring in Various Manufacturing Establishments, Weeks and Aldrich Reports, 1860-1890
(dollars)

| | | Weeks Report, Average Daily Wages | | | | Aldrich Report, Average Hourly Wages (July) | | | |
	No. of Estab.	1860	1870	1880	No. of Estab.	1860	1870	1880	1890
Blacksmiths	26	1.64	2.68	2.31	11	0.178	0.304	0.259	0.271
Carpenters	10	1.65	2.64	2.15	2	0.182	0.410	0.276	0.322
Engineers	25	1.61	2.47	2.17	6	0.148	0.227	0.208	0.244
Machinists	15	1.61	2.67	2.45	14	0.158	0.260	0.227	0.243
Painters	9	1.62	2.67	2.21	1	0.125	0.175	0.250	0.250
Weighted mean[a]		1.62	2.61	2.26		0.163	0.275	0.238	0.257
Simple mean	85	1.63	2.63	2.26	34	0.158	0.275	0.244	0.266
Average deviation[b]									
Dollars		0.016	0.060	0.098		0.018	0.065	0.021	0.024
Percent of mean		1	2	4		11	24	9	9
Highest		1.65	2.68	2.45		0.182	0.410	0.276	0.322
Lowest		1.61	2.47	2.15		0.125	0.175	0.208	0.243
Highest ÷ lowest		1.02	1.09	1.14		1.46	2.34	1.33	1.33

[a] Weighted by number of establishments.
[b] Computed from simple mean.

40 percent higher by 1880 (a rise about 6 percent greater than that for all 18 manufacturing industries of the Weeks Report).

The second set was the same five occupations, this time from the Aldrich Report (Table 39). Their wages rose 46 percent by 1880 (compared with 40 percent for the same occupations in the Weeks Report), and 58 percent by 1890—about 10 percent more than the rise for the 13 industries of the Aldrich Report.

The third set consisted of miscellaneous occupations within four industries from the Aldrich Report (Table 40): five in books and newspapers, nineteen in metals, thirty-four in woolens, and thirty-seven male and thirty female occupations in cotton goods. The median of these rose 46 percent—close to the 48 percent indicated for the 13 industries.

In general, the spread between the highest and lowest wage seemed to be wider among occupations than among industries. Among the

TABLE 40

Median Daily Wages of Workers of all Reported Occupations, for Four Industries; Aldrich Report, 1860-1890

	Daily Wages (dollars)				Interquartile Range as Percent of Median			
	1860	1870	1880	1890	1860	1870	1880	1890
Books and newspapers[a]	1.64	2.98	2.02	2.49	71	77	82	55
Metals[b]	1.60	2.49	2.18	2.25	21	47	39	36
Cotton goods, males[c]	0.91	1.51	1.15	1.33	42	36	46	53
Cotton goods, females[d]	0.53	0.89	0.82	0.91	40	37	37	42
Woolen goods[e]	0.90	1.25	1.21	1.32	39	24	15	36
Median of the five medians	0.91	1.51	1.21	1.33	40	37	39	42
1860 = 100	100	166	133	146				

[a] Includes five occupations in four establishments, of which two were in New York, one in Connecticut, and one in Maryland.

Compositors	Press men
Folders	Printers
Press feeders	

[b] Includes nineteen occupations in nineteen establishments. Not all occupations were represented in all establishments. Those series were excluded for which more than five dates were missing between 1860 and 1891.

Blacksmiths	Engineers	Molders, iron
Boilermakers	Furnacemen	Pattern makers
Carpenters	Laborers	Teamsters
Coal wheelers	Machinists	Watchmen
Core makers	Masons	Woodworkers
Cupolamen	Millwrights	
Draughtsmen	Molders	

notes continue on following page

95

Table 40, *concluded*

^c Includes thirty-seven male occupations from four establishments, of which three were in Massachusetts and one was in New York.

Balers	Laborers	Speeders
Beam carriers	Lap carriers	Spinners, frame
Beltmen	Lapper tenders	Spinners, mule
Bobbin carriers	Openers	Stampers
Bobbin men	Pickers	Stretchers
Card grinders	Picking room hands	Third hands
Card strippers	Roller covers	Waste hands
Cloth room hands	Room hands	Weavers, 6, 7, and 8 loom
Doubler tenders	Second hands	Wipers
Drawing hands	Section hands	Warpers
Dressers	Shearers	Yarn carriers
Entrymen	Slasher tenders	
Filling carriers	Slasher tenders' helpers	

^d Includes thirty female occupations from the same four establishments.

Back hands	Holders	Spoolers
Card strippers	Room hands	Stretchers
Cloth hookers	Roving hands	Trimmers
Cloth inspectors	Servers	Warpers
Cloth room hands	Shearers	Waste pickers
Doffers	Slubber tenders	Weavers
Drawers-in	Smash piecers	Weavers, 3 and 4 loom
Drawing-frame tenders	Speeders	Weavers, 5 loom
Drawing hands	Speeder tenders	Weavers, 6, 7, and 8 loom
Dressers	Spinners, frame	Weavers, spare

^e Includes thirty-two occupations from three establishments. Not all occupations are represented in all three establishments; some occupations are represented in several.

Burlers	Finishers	Shearers
Carders	Fullers	Sorters
Card cleaners	Giggers	Spinners
Card feeders	Handers-in	Spoolers
Card tenders	Laborers, dyehouse	Twisters
Drawers-in	Loom-fixers	Warpers
Dressers	Pickers	Washers
Dyers	Pressmen	Waste sorters
Dyehouse hands	Scourers	Weavers
Filling carriers	Second hands	Yarn carriers
Filling sorters	Section hands	

fourteen occupations reported by Bulletin 18, the highest-wage occupation (usually bricklayers and masons or plumbers) paid two to two and a half to the lowest (invariably laborers). In fifteen establishments, one from each of fifteen Weeks-reported industries, the highest-wage occupation typically paid three or four times as much as the lowest in the same establishment, with wide variation in the ratio among different establishments (Table 41). In establishments (e.g., in rolling mills) employing apprentices and boys or girls, the highest wage was as much as sixteen times the lowest.

Occupational differentials showed some tendency to widen. The Bulletin 18 occupations had a higher relative average deviation in 1890 than in 1870, though the difference was too slight to be significant in itself (Table 42). Of fifteen Weeks-reported establishments selected from fifteen industries, nine had a higher relative average deviation by 1880, and only five had a smaller deviation. And of the four Aldrich-reported industries for which occupational

TABLE 41

Average Deviation of Daily Wages among Different Occupations in the Same Establishment: 15 Establishments from Each of 15 Industries, Weeks Report, 1860-1880

Industry	Establishment Location	Number of Occupations	Ratio: Highest to Lowest Occupational Wage in Same Establishment			Average Deviation as Percent of Simple Mean of Occupational Wages		
			1860	1870	1880	1860	1870	1880
Rolling mills	Troy, N.Y.	44	16.0	12.0	13.6	42	40	42
Cotton goods	Massachusetts	29	6.0	5.9	5.0	39	33	32
Iron foundries	Quincy, Ill.	16	6.0	3.5	3.5	25	22	24
Clothing	Syracuse, N.Y.	7	5.5	8.0	6.0	44	42	40
Boots and shoes	Lafayette, Ind.	25	4.0	2.8	3.1	20	15	16
Brickmaking	Philadelphia	15	4.0	10.0	7.0	28	38	30
Machinery	St. Louis	12	3.1	4.6	3.6	25	29	27
Carriages and wagons	Portland, Maine	14	2.9	4.0	3.6	18	31	29
Iron blast furnaces	Catasauqua, Pa.	11	2.8	2.7	2.5	60	60	63
Woolen goods	Indianapolis	17	2.6	4.6	4.3	20	31	29
Paper	Unionville, Conn.	21	2.6	3.8	2.8	28	32	30
Hardware, cutlery	Massachusetts	8	2.2	2.7	2.8	22	32	29
Saw and planing mill	Kentucky	10	1.8	2.0	1.8	14	10	10
Tin and sheet iron	Newark, N.J.	7	1.6	1.9	1.7	10	19	13
Furniture	New Haven	11	1.6	1.5	1.6	8	15	14
Median			2.9	3.8	3.5	25	31	29
Number of industries with:								
Decrease since 1860			–	6	5	–	6	5
Increase since 1860			–	9	8	–	8	9
No change			–	0	2	–	1	1

TABLE 42

Average Daily Wages for 14 Occupations in Large Cities, from Bulletin
18, Weighted by Census-Reported Number Attached to the Occupation
in the Respective State; 1870-1890

Occupation	Dollars per Day			Rank		
	1870	1880	1890	1870	1880	1890
Stonecutters	3.61	2.65	3.57	1	5	2
Bricklayers and masons	3.51	2.85	3.88	2	2	1
Plumbers	3.31	3.05	3.37	3	1	3
Compositors	3.10	2.84	2.88	4	3	5
Patternmakers, iron works	3.08	2.77	3.01	5	4	4
Iron molders	3.06	2.41	2.54	6	9	9
Carpenters and joiners	2.88	2.45	2.67	7	8	7
Blacksmiths	2.74	2.53	2.63	8	6	8
Machinists	2.70	2.37	2.52	9	11	10
Painters, house	2.69	2.50	2.83	10	7	6
Boilermakers	2.52	2.38	2.50	11	10	11
Cabinet makers	2.47	2.16	2.33	12	12	12
Teamsters	1.96	1.96	2.01	13	13	13
Laborers (non-street)	1.75	1.43	1.56	14	14	14
Median	2.81	2.48	2.65			
Weighted mean	2.29	1.90	2.19			
Simple mean	2.81	2.45	2.74			
Average deviation[a]						
Dollars	0.41	0.29	0.45			
Percent of mean	15	12	16			
Highest	3.61	3.05	3.88			
Lowest	1.75	1.43	1.56			
Highest ÷ lowest	2.1	2.1	2.5			

Source: Appendix Table A-4.
[a] Computed from simple mean.

data were shown above, three had a higher percentage interquartile
range toward the end of the period.

The same widening took place between wages of laborers and of
skilled occupations, covering large numbers of establishments
(Table 43). In both Weeks and Aldrich data wages of laborers fell
as a percentage of the average for the five skilled occupations. On the
whole, the data of these independent reports were in good agreement
in regard not only to the wage levels but to the differentials and the
changes in differentials.

Although inter-occupational wage differentials tended to be wide
and to become wider, the rank of occupations in the relative wage
scale tended to remain fairly stable over the period. Of the fourteen

TABLE 43

Average Wage-Rates of Laborers and of Five Skilled Occupations; Weeks
Report, 1860-1880, Aldrich Report 1860-1890,
(dollars)

	Weeks Report, Daily Wage Rates			Aldrich Report,[a] Hourly Wage Rates			
	1860	1870	1880	1860	1870	1880	1890
Laborers	1.03	1.52	1.32	0.098	0.156	0.135	0.151
5 skilled occupations: mean	1.62	2.61	2.26	0.164	0.274	0.238	0.257
Laborers' wages in percent of those of skilled occupations	63	58	58	60	57	57	59

Source and explanation: Appendix Tables A-5 and -6.

[a] The National Bureau of Economic Research converted the Aldrich wage data into hourly wage rates before computing the average.

Bulletin 18 occupations, seven had the same rank in 1890 as in 1870; five changed one place, and only two changed as much as three places (Table 42). This stability held to some extent for occupations within the same establishment over time.[1]

Two recent investigators have remarked: "It is commonly accepted that, in general, skill differentials have been narrowing for a long time."[2] But so far we have not dealt explicitly with the wage differentials between different levels of skill within the same general occupation. Fortunately, the Weeks and Aldrich Reports provide the materials for such analysis (Chart 4). Moreover it is possible to

[1] This is illustrated by the data of the following four establishments.
A woolen goods establishment in Indiana (C. E. Geisendorff), in the Weeks Report: Of 17 occupations, 8 held the same rank in 1880 as in 1860, 7 changed one place, and only 2 changed as much as two or three places.
A cotton goods establishment in Massachusetts, #39 in the Aldrich Report: Of 17 occupations, 2 held the same rank in 1890 as in 1860, 8 changed one or two places. However, 5 changed rank five places or more.
A cotton goods establishment in New York, #41 in the Aldrich Report: Of 28 occupations, 6 held the same rank in 1890 as thirty years earlier, 5 changed one place, 5 others changed two or three places. However, 4 occupations altered their rank in the wage scale by as much as ten places.
A cotton goods (ginghams) establishment in Massachusetts, #43 in the Aldrich Report: 6 held the same rank, 11 changed one place, and 2 others only two places. Only 1 changed as much as five places.

[2] K. G. J. C. Knowles and D. J. Robertson, "Differences between the Wages of Skilled and Unskilled Workers, 1880-1950," *Bulletin of the Institute of Statistics*, Oxford University, April 1951, p. 110. See also Harry Ober, who makes this finding for 1907 to 1947 and observes it in all regions. However, Ober found that the narrowing occurred mainly during World Wars I and II, and that widening occurred during the Great Depression. "Occupational Wage Differentials, 1907-1947," *Monthly Labor Review*, August 1948, p. 130.

CHART 4

Wages of Laborers and of 5 Skilled Occupations

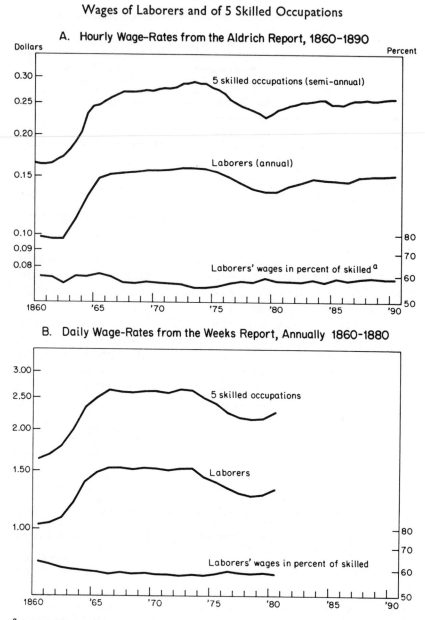

A. Hourly Wage-Rates from the Aldrich Report, 1860–1890

B. Daily Wage-Rates from the Weeks Report, Annually 1860-1880

a Computed from annual averages of semi-annual data of 5 skilled occupations

Source: Appendix Tables A-5 and −6.

Ratio scales

TABLE 44

Percentage Ratio of Daily Wages of Journeymen in Specific Occupations to Wages of Foremen or Overseers for Those Occupations, in the Same Establishment; Aldrich Report, 1860–1890

Occupation	Establishment	1860	1870	1880	1890
Pressmen	#5	83	100	100	89
Carpenters	#39	73	58	59	55
Masons	#12	64	71	61	77
	#76	80	80	75	64
Machinists	#39	80	48	58	46
	#54	46	78	–	77
	#56	37	49	58	50
	#58	62	65	45	62
	#65	67	58	59	66
	#68	55	47	38	51
Blacksmiths	#68	69	59	50	69
	#71	69	60	55	52
Boilermakers	#54	58	43	56	60
	#68	59	65	46	52
Molders	#54	60	59	55	63
	#56	62	39	43	57
Quarrymen	#79	84	75	58	68
	#80	64	75	58	68
Card strippers	#38	24	26	21	39
	#39	32	52	28	20
	#40	30	45	23	20
	#41	38	50	63	54
	#43	28	41	31	29
Spinners, Frame	#39	22	69	23	24
	#40	38	28	14	20
	#41	22	23	32	44
	#43	24	33	34	22
Weavers	#39	24	28	26	21
	#40	14	17	20	10
	#41	47	42	44	38
	#43	27	38	31	34
	#86	64	42	41	53
Card tenders	#86	31	18	19	20
	#87	26	23	23	18
Dyehouse hands	#87	41	37	44	40
Finishers	#88	53	40	49	27
Median percentage		50	48	44	50
Number of establishments with:					
Increase since 1860		–	18	11	13
Decrease since 1860		–	17	24	21
No change		–	1	0	2
Total number of establishments			36	35	36

compare wages of journeymen and foremen in identical occupations and establishments; the ratios in Table 44 reveal large differences. In 1860 quarrymen in one establishment received 84 percent as much as foremen of quarrymen, machinists in another establishment 37 percent as much as foremen of machinists, weavers in still another establishment only 14 percent as much as overseers of weavers. The same occupations often manifested wide variations among different establishments of the same industry, e.g., weavers, and overseers of weavers, in five cotton goods establishments. For all

TABLE 45

Percentage Ratio of Daily Wage-Rates of Journeymen's Helpers to Those of Journeymen in Specific Occupations, in the Same Establishment; Aldrich Report, July, 1860-1890

Occupation	Establishment	1860	1870	1880	1890
Bricklayers	#12	66	55	62	48
	#22	63	55	58	56
	#26	56	57	75	60
	#47	67	50	55	56
Carpenters	#13	63	62	70	52
	#17	61	62	76	61
	#72	50	60	79	81
Masons	#12	66	61	72	47
Machine hands	#75	75	50	54	55
Steam and gas fitters	#14	71	47	39	63
Blacksmiths	#33	55	50	58	58
	#35	69	57	72	67
Machinists	#54	68	40	56	54
	#56	63	63	60	61
Molders	#54	67	60	66	62
	#5.	70	65	65	63
	#68	61	57	63	66
Patternmakers	#74	84	55	62	53
Sidewalk layers	#77	50	76	67	67
Median percentage		66	57	63	60
Number of establishments with:					
Increase since 1860		–	4	9	5
Decrease since 1860		–	14	10	13
No change		–	1	0	1
Total number of establishments			19	19	19

comparisons, the median ratio was the same in 1890 as in 1860. But of 36 comparisons, 21 showed a decrease in the wage ratio of journeymen to foremen in charge of those journeymen, and thus a widening of the skill differential. An even larger number showed a widening by 1880.

Another comparison is between wages of journeymen and helpers, e.g., bricklayers and bricklayers' helpers within the same occupation and establishment. This reveals a substantially smaller differential between wages of journeymen and their helpers, than between

TABLE 46

Percentage Ratio of Daily Wage Rates of Helpers to Those of Journeymen in the Same
Occupation and Establishment, Weeks Report, 1860-1880

Occupation	Industry	Establishment	1860	1870	1880
		WEEKS REPORT HELPERS AND JOURNEYMEN			
Melters	Iron foundries	Quincy, Ill.	88	88	75
Machinists	Machinery	St. Louis	63	60	54
Blacksmiths	Machinery	St. Louis	63	62	60
Molders	Machinery	St. Louis	63	60	55
Keeper	Iron blast furnaces	Pennsylvania	87	92	92
Blacksmith	Iron blast furnaces	Pennsylvania	80	58	81
Rag engineer	Paper	Unionville, Conn.	61	64	68
Machine tender	Paper	Unionville, Conn.	61	61	54
Finisher	Paper	Unionville, Conn.	89	87	100
Puddler	Rolling mill	Troy, N.Y.	52	50	50
Scrupper	Rolling mill	Troy, N.Y.	31	45	40
Bar heater	Rolling mill	Troy, N.Y.	44	50	50
Blacksmith	Rolling mill	Troy, N.Y.	58	65	60
Mason	Rolling mill	Troy, N.Y.	47	46	45
Dyer	Woolen goods	Indianapolis	67	56	75
Blacksmith	Carriages and wagons	Portland, Maine	71	50	50
Keeper	Iron blast furnaces	Catasauqua, Pa.	84	87	93
Blacksmith	Iron blast furnaces	Catasauqua, Pa.	59	84	100
Median percentage			63	61	60

		ALDRICH REPORT APPRENTICES AND JOURNEYMEN				
			1860	1870	1880	1890
Compositors	Books and newspapers	#5	34	31	27	38
Boilermakers	Metals	#68	36	37	32	33
Machinists	Metals	#56	36	36	44	29
Machinists	Metals	#68	45	28	40	31
Molders	Metals	#56	39	36	39	39
Median percentage			36	36	39	33

103

journeymen and their foremen; much smaller variations in the differential from one occupation to the next; and about the same tendency for the wages of the less skilled to lag behind those of the higher skilled within the occupation, so that the skill differential tended to widen (Table 45).

Similar results derive from a further comparison, also between journeymen and their helpers, this time from the Weeks Report (Table 46). The typical ratio was again about three-fifths, and again the median ratio declined a bit between 1860 and 1880.

A final comparison—between journeymen and their apprentices in the same occupation and establishment, e.g., compositors and compositors' apprentices (Table 46)—revealed the lowest wage ratio of the less to the more skilled: scarcely more than one-third. It disclosed the same tendency for the skill differential to widen over the thirty years, though like the others the tendency was slight.

Wages by Sex and Age

The only materials for investigating wage relationships between males and females and adults and children, for a relatively large list of workers, establishments, and industries, are from the First Annual Report of the Commissioner of Labor for 1885, covering 28,671 women and 18,690 children (Table 47), and from the Dewey Report for 1890 covering 11,919 females 16 and older and 2,643 boys under 16 (Table 48). These data broadly agree in showing that the wages of adult females were somewhat less than three-fifths, and the wages of children and youths somewhat more than a third, of those of adult males. The first ratio would not have been materially different if all males, including those in industries not reporting female wages, had been used in the compilation. The Aldrich and Dewey data do not agree, however, for individual industries. In one or two industries, such as paper mills, the female-male ratios were similar; but in most industries, they were different, and in some far apart.

No systematic tendency was revealed for female wages to be differently dispersed among industries than male wages. The relative average deviation was greater for females than for males in the 1885 data, and less in the 1890 data. Somewhat the same can be said for children and youths.

For sex and age differentials over time, there are only the Weeks and Aldrich materials. The former only occasionally identified an occupation by sex; the latter included only a few industries with occupations employing females. To arrive at an average wage for

TABLE 47

Average Daily Wages of Adult Males, Adult Females, and Children and
Youths; First Annual Report, 1885

	Adult Males (dollars)	Adult Females		Children and Youths	
		Dollars	Percent of Adult-Male Wages	Dollars	Percent of Adult-Male Wages
Boots and shoes	2.05	1.24	60	0.75	37
Boxes	2.26	0.65	29	0.64	28
Carpetings	1.51	1.19	79	0.62	41
Carriages and wagons	2.00	1.15	58	0.77	39
Clocks and watches	2.00	1.60	80		–
Clothing	1.72	0.91	53	0.58	34
Cotton goods	1.26	0.87	69	0.48	38
Glass	2.98	1.85	62	0.62	21
Jute goods	1.55	0.85	55	0.58	37
Leather	1.92	1.35	70	0.70	36
Musical instruments	2.10	1.50	72	0.69	33
Paper	1.64	0.96	59	0.73	45
Print works	1.66	0.91	55	0.66	40
Rubber	1.70	1.10	65	1.04	61
Silk	2.27	1.31	58	0.87	38
Tobacco	1.33	0.85	64	0.53	40
Woolen goods	1.49	1.00	67	0.62	42
Miscellaneous	1.96	0.81	41	1.04	53
Median	1.82	1.05	61	0.66	38
Weighted average	1.71	1.00	58	0.59	35
Simple mean	1.86	1.12	60	0.70	39
Average deviation[a]					
Dollars	0.31	0.25		0.12	
Percent of mean	17	22		17	

Source: Appendix Table A-7.
[a] Computed from simple mean.

females was not possible for all manufacturing, only for the two
industries employing substantial numbers of females: cotton goods
and woolen goods (Table 49).

These differ in the ratio of female to male wages. Females earned
58 to 70 percent as much as males in cotton goods, 75 to 103 percent
as much in woolen goods. In both industries, the differential
narrowed; in both, the narrowing took place by 1880, with some
widening afterward. However, the woolen goods industry showed a
greater fluctuation in the ratio during the intervening years, with
less net change by 1890.

TABLE 48

Median Hourly Wage-Rates of Males and Females 16 and Older and of Males under 16; Dewey Report, 1890

Industry	Males 16 and Older (dollars)	Females 16 and Older		Males under 16	
		Dollars	Percent of Col. 1	Dollars	Percent of Col. 1
Carpet mills	0.15	0.09	60	0.06	40
Cotton mills	.11	.09	82		
Dyeing and finishing	.12	.10	83	.06	50
Knitting mills	.13	.08	62		
Woolen mills	.12	.10	83	.05	42
Foundries and metal working	.17	.07	41	.06	35
Iron and steel mills	.15	.08	53	.05	33
Cigars	.21	.11	52		
Clothing	.20	.07	35		
Glass	.17	.06	35	.06	35
Paper mills	.14	.08	57		
Printing	.29	.08	28	.05	17
Rubber	.15	.11	73		
Shoes	.19	.10	53		
Tanneries	.15	.06	40	.05	33
Weighted mean	.16	.09	56	.06	38
Simple mean	.16	.09	56	.06	36
Average deviation[a]					
Dollars	.033	.014		.005	
Percent of mean	21	16		8	

Source: Appendix Table A-8.
[a] Computed from simple mean.

TABLE 49

Median Daily Wage-Rates of Males and Females in Cotton and Woolen Goods Manufacturing, 1860-1890

	1860	1870	1880	1890
Cotton goods				
Males	0.89	1.52	1.14	1.33
Females				
Dollars	0.52	0.88	0.80	0.91
Percent of male wages	58	58	70	68
Woolen goods				
Males	0.96	1.29	1.20	1.62
Females				
Dollars	0.72	1.20	1.23	1.30
Percent of male wages	75	93	103	80

Source: Aldrich Report (average of January and July data).

106

So far we have been comparing wages of males and females without regard to establishments and occupations. What are the relationships between the wages of females and males who were doing—at least nominally—the same kind of work within identical establishments?

Not many establishments employ both males and females to do the same kind of job, but we do have a number of such instances in cotton goods, woolen goods, and books and newspapers (Table 50). When females did the same nominal work in the same establishment they were paid about the same wages. Indeed some occupations

TABLE 50

Daily Wage Rates of Females as a Percentage of Wages of Males in Identical Occupations and Establishments, Aldrich Report, 1860-1890

Occupation	Industry	Establishment	Percent			
			1860	1870	1880	1890
Doffers	Cotton goods	#40	107	98	97	97
Cloth room hands	Cotton goods	#40	122	104	99	66
Drawing-in hands	Cotton goods	#40	73	54	101	110
Dressers	Cotton goods	#40	114	44	55	–
Room hands	Cotton goods	#40	–	111	138	105
Roving hands	Cotton goods	#40	–	111	123	91
Spinners, frame	Cotton goods	#40	–	82	93	99
Spoolers	Cotton goods	#40	91	90	–	105
Weavers	Woolen goods	#86	100	82	118	80
Weavers	Woolen goods	#88	78	93	95	96
Press room hands	Books and news-papers	#5	192	63	84	76
Median percentage:						
All occupations			104	90	98	97
Six occupations with data for all years			104	88	98	88

Based on July data.

in some establishments paid substantially higher wages to females: for instance, in 1860, cotton goods establishment #40 in Massachusetts paid 7 to 22 percent more to female than to male doffers, cloth-room hands, and dressers; woolen goods establishment #86 paid as much to female as to male weavers; and books and newspaper establishment #5, by some curious circumstance, paid female press-room hands nearly double. In no establishment, however, did females earn more than males in the same occupation over all four decennial years. There was some tendency, obscured by counter movements in different occupations, for the female wage differential to be wider in 1890 than in 1860.

In no satisfactory instances could we compare the wages of children and adults doing the same work; but we could make a number of scattered comparisons in the Weeks data between wages of boys and laborers in the same establishment (Table 51): in cotton goods,

TABLE 51

Daily Wages of Boys as Percentages of Wages of Laborers in the Same Establishment; Weeks Report, 1860-1880

Occupation	Industry	Establishment	1860	1870	1880
Back boy	Cotton goods	Harmony Hill, N.Y.	40	40	38
Back boy	Cotton goods	Unidentified (N.Y.)	32	38	39
Back boy	Cotton goods	Unidentified (Conn.)	25	33	37
Back boy	Cotton goods	Unidentified (Mass.)	29	31	40
Back boy	Cotton goods	J. S. Brown, N. H.	25	24	24
Carder, boy	Woolen goods	S. P. Brown, Maine	50	57	60
Boy	Furniture	Unidentified (Indiana)	44	46	33
Four occupations of boys[a]	Rolling mill	Albany and Rensselaer Co., Troy, N.Y.	25	25	29
Median percentage			31	36	38

[a] Includes door boy, water boy, and two occupations identified merely as "boy." Since no occupation identifiable as laborer was given, the wages of boys were expressed as a percentage of the simple average of wages in all the forty-four occupations reported for this firm.

woolen goods, furniture, and rolling mill establishments. Percentages ranged from 25 to 60, with medians of 31 percent in 1860 and 38 percent in 1880—close to the 35 percent shown by the First Annual Report for 1885. Compared with 1860 the sex differential may have been a bit wider by 1890, and the age differential a bit narrower by 1880, but the evidence is inadequate and conflicting.

CHAPTER 7

Summary and Conclusions

DAILY wages and annual earnings in manufacturing both increased about 50 percent between 1860 and 1890. The cost of living fluctuated widely, but the long decline that began in 1865 eventually wiped out the Civil War increase and restored the buying power of the dollar to its prewar level, so that real wages and earnings in 1890 were also 50 percent higher than in 1860. Daily wages rose from slightly over $1.00 in 1860 to slightly over $1.50 in 1890—if we adjust the levels in both years to the bench marks established by the extensive wage surveys of the Department of Labor in 1885 and the Dewey-Census and a number of state labor bureau reports in 1890. Annual earnings rose from just under $300 in 1860 to just over $425 in 1890.

Wages in building rose somewhat more—perhaps 60 percent in money or real terms. Because building employed mostly adult men in skilled occupations, wages were on a higher absolute level; the average was approximately $2.75 for a ten-hour day in 1890.

The advances have been measured in daily wages, and do not for the most part take account of extra allowances, premium payments for overtime, payments in truck instead of in cash, or deductions for damages and use of tools and materials. But the Weeks Report questionnaire suggests that these factors could not have changed the picture materially—at least for the firms reporting.

The data do not take account of the shortening of the average workday. This reduction seems to have been very small—not more than 7 percent—bringing the average in 1890 down to ten hours. The net advance in hourly wages in manufacturing, money or real, was still not much more than 60 percent, or 1.6 percent compounded annually, compared with 1914-53 when the rise was over 5 percent in money terms and 2.75 percent in real terms.[1] In contrast to recent data, little or no weight was given to piece-rate earnings, which may have participated more quickly than time-rate wages in the rising productivity, or they may even have stimulated productivity increase.

Wage differentials between industries and occupations were large in the decades between 1860 and 1890; the highest-wage industry paid two or two and a half times the lowest, and the highest-wage occupation still more. Adult males typically received three-fourths

---

[1] Leo Wolman, "Wages in the United States since 1914," *Proceedings of the Sixth Annual Meeting, Industrial Relations Research Association*, 1953, pp. 44-45. The increase is still smaller compared with the increases found by Wolman for the thirty years 1914-44.

more than adult females, and two and a half to three times as much as children and youths. Between regions the differentials were not so large. Wage levels were low in the South, and high on the Pacific Coast; but the differentials between the Central states, the Middle Atlantic states, and the New England states may have been no greater than among states within these regions.

Wide variations prevailed in differentials among establishments. Although southern establishments typically paid less than northern to an adult-male worker of a given skill in a given industry, some southern establishments paid as much as northern; others more. Some firms paid more to females than to males in the same occupation.

Regional differentials may have narrowed a bit, but only outside the South, notably only on the Pacific Coast. Other differentials may have widened slightly: for occupations, skills, and the sexes. No net change in wage or earnings differentials or in average dispersion among industries was apparent, despite the tendency for many industries with below-average wage levels in 1860 to increase more, by 1890, than the average.

A fifth of the increase of wages and earnings may have been due to the relative shift of workers from low-wage soft goods industries to high-wage hard goods industries—the principal shifts having been from cotton and woolen textiles to iron and steel rolling mills and foundries and machine shop products. The data for occupations are insufficient to tell us what part of the wage increase within industry may have been due to the relative shift of workers from low-wage to high-wage occupations. As for the effect of regional movements, it is unlikely that any significant part of the wages or earnings increase was due to the more rapid growth of employment in the central and western part of the nation. The Central region, which had gained the most workers, did not pay average earnings that were significantly different in 1890 from the average of the southern, Middle Atlantic, and New England regions, which had had a relative loss of workers.

Some Concluding Questions

What were the factors responsible for the major movements of wages and earnings during these years of turbulence and growth?

To begin with, why did wages lag so far behind living costs during the Civil War—to such an extent that real wages declined more than a fourth by 1864, and were depressed below prewar levels until 1867 in building and until 1869 in manufacturing? By contrast, real wages rose in every full year of World Wars I and II, and throughout the Korean War. The relative Civil War behavior was attributable to both money wages and consumer prices. Money wages rose less than in World Wars I and II, and only slightly more than in the Korean War. Consumer prices—especially food, clothing, and rent—rose much more than in the three later conflicts.

The sluggishness of money wages may perhaps be explained partly by the fact that unions were far less significant during the Civil War; partly by the diversion of the best manpower of the nation to the armed forces, leaving a less able-bodied and less skilled wage earner which the mass-production methods of the time were not able to utilize as effectively as were those of later periods; and finally by the smaller role played by piece rates and overtime premium pay during the Civil War, perhaps because cost-plus contracts, which may place a positive incentive on the payment of premium wage rates, had not yet come into vogue. On the other hand, it must be acknowledged that the wage controls—formal or otherwise—were not the inhibiting factor in the Civil War that they came to be in the subsequent wars.

The greater rise in living costs may have been due partly to the absence of price controls, partly to the speculative fever induced by the issuance of inconvertible greenbacks, and partly to the cutting off of a large part of the southern agricultural land, thus reducing supplies of food and cotton. But an important factor in checking the inflation of later wars was lacking during the Civil War: the ability of relatively well-off wage earners' families to postpone consumption of many consumer durables, luxuries, and service items. The low real incomes at the start of the Civil War must have made it much less easy to postpone any item of consumption—since most of the outlay was on necessities. Expenditures on food, clothing, and rent were large percentages of family budgets in the Civil War years; outlays on services, house furnishings, and miscellaneous luxury items were very small percentages. The worker had to continue spending for immediate necessities—no matter how high the price—and this made the price go higher. Indeed, the erosion of real income by the Civil War inflation made workers less and less able to postpone consumption as the war progressed, thus accentuating the inflation through desperation buying. The fact that the cost of living reached its peak in 1865, and began falling immediately after the Civil War, further indicates that there was no such backlog of postponed consumer demand as existed in the three other wars, when prices continued to rise for several years after the peace.

A second question concerns the role played by productivity. The time and resources of this study do not make it possible to say anything definitive on this question. Our own tentative investigations

indicate that the net increases in real wages and earnings of manufacturing workers between 1860 and 1890 are not inconsistent with
increases in productivity—measured by manufacturing value-added
per worker in constant dollars. Estimates by Gallman disclose
that real value-added per manufacturing worker in the census year
ending May 31, 1890 was 50 percent above that of the year ending
May 31, 1860.[2] In comparison, our real annual earnings in manufacturing rose 46 percent for all industries and 49 percent for the
17 important industries.

For intermediate years, there was close decade-to-decade association between real value-added per worker in manufacturing and
mining, and real annual earnings in manufacturing from the census.
Less close was the association with real daily wages. These rose
while value-added fell in 1860-70, and rose much less than value-
added in 1880-90—thus fluctuating less from decade to decade.
On the other hand, daily wages in manufacturing moved closely
with real output per worker in manufacturing, mining, construction,
and agriculture. The similarity was especially close with the Weeks–
Bulletin 18 series. Real output per worker rose 3 percent between
1860 and 1870 compared with 3 percent for real daily wages; 21
percent between 1870 and 1880, compared with 19 percent for wages;
and 27 percent between 1880 and 1890, compared with 25 percent
for wages.

There is, of course, no necessary relation between short-run
changes in wages and productivity, either in a given industry or in
the economy as a whole. Better grounds exist for expecting that real
wages and productivity would move together in the long run and for
major movements. So large is labor's share of the national income
that any substantial disparity between productivity and real wages
would exert great impact on the other shares—either largely expro-
priating them or presenting them with huge windfalls. Long-term
associations between wages and productivity have been noted by
other observers. Even for the long run the closeness of movement
will depend upon the dates chosen for comparison. The fact that
increases of wages and productivity during these thirty years were
not inconsistent with each other is reassuring, but so imperfect are
the measures of productivity, so complex and manifold the factors
influencing productivity, and so hazy the relation of productivity
to the qualities for which labor must be rewarded economically,

[2] Robert E. Gallman, "Commodity Output, 1839-1899," *Trends in the American
Economy in the Nineteenth Century*, Studies in Income and Wealth, Vol. 24 (in press).
Both Gallman and I exclude the hand trades, building occupations, and miscellaneous
agricultural processing industries in certain years. However, Gallman includes non-
precious-metals mining.

that we leave to later investigation the question of whether the changes in wages and earnings were fully explained by changes in productivity during these decades. In any case, what labor manages to gain depends on its bargaining power. In the absence of strong unions—to a large extent even with their aid—the ability to convert rising productivity into real-wage advances will depend on the supply and demand situation in which labor finds itself.

The period 1860-90 was unquestionably one of great quantitative increase in labor supply. Total population increased 100 percent, working-age population 112 percent, and the labor force 120 percent.[3] The rise in labor force was relatively modest during the first decade because of Civil War casualties and curtailed immigration; even so, the statistics show a one-fourth increase. In each of the next two decades the increase was approximately one-third. A large share of the increment was drawn into manufacturing. For the thirty years, wage earners in manufacturing rose 265 percent, excluding construction and hand trades, and the increase was especially large during the Civil War decade. These additions to the number of workers may have had some offset in a decline in the manufacturing workweek, but we have seen that it was small.[4]

Our labor supply data are imperfect, but they do suggest that quantitative labor supply increased greatly, that it rose very heavily in manufacturing in all decades, and that much of the increase in manufacturing employment came during the Civil War decade, in contrast to a smaller percentage rise in total labor force.

If the increase in quantity of labor supply was large, what of its quality? There is no over-all measure, but some indication may be seen in its composition.[5] This information is confined to sex and broad age groups, native or foreign birth, and education.

In the labor force as a whole, the number of females seems to have increased somewhat more rapidly than the number of males. There was no breakdown by sex of the labor force for 1860, so that this appearance of a larger rise for females can apply only to the last two decades. Even for this period the differential increase for females was small compared with what has occurred since 1890. In the manufacturing and mechanical industries, females 16 and older seem to have increased somewhat less rapidly, and children under 16 much less rapidly, than males 16 and older. However, the death

[3] For population and labor force: *Historical Statistics of the United States, 1789-1945*, Bureau of the Census, 1949, p. 25; Clarence D. Long, *The Labor Force under Changing Income and Employment*, Princeton University Press for the National Bureau of Economic Research, 1958, Appendix A.

[4] Tables 14 and 13, above.

[5] Long, *op. cit.*

and crippling of half a million or more men in the Civil War, and the postwar disorganization of the southern labor force must count heavily in assessing the change in quality of the manufacturing work force between 1860 and 1870.

There remain skill, education, and immigration. No basic statistics on skill composition exist for these years; the often-repeated argument that skills were diluted by the mass production factory system should be greeted with caution since most additions to our factory labor force were surely drawn from unskilled or semiskilled farm laborers here and abroad, and the proportion of skilled workers in or out of manufacturing was probably never large to begin with. Average education evidenced some increase—judged by the proportion of persons under 20 attending school, plus the continual rise in days attended by the average student, though the increase was far less than that which took place after the 1920's.[6] As for immigration, much has been said by others about its influence on earnings, through its supposed effect in increasing the labor supply and diluting the quality of that supply. The near stopping of immigration is often cited as explaining both the narrowing of occupational differentials and the increase of wages after World War I.[7] Although immigration was relatively less important after the Civil War, it was sufficient to increase the foreign-born labor force faster than the native labor force, from a little less than one-fifth of the labor force in 1860 to a little more than one-fifth in 1890.

All in all, except during the Civil War, the large rise in labor supply during 1860-90 was not modified by changes in the average quality of worker. In view of the presumably depressing effect of the rise in labor supply, some explanation may be needed as to how increases in real wages and earnings were possible and why they were so heavily concentrated in the last decade.

For this we may turn to the quantity of capital per worker in manufacturing. Like all data of that period, these statistics, based on decennial censuses of manufactures, leave much to be desired. Conceptually, capital included the gross assets of the manufacturing establishments, embracing land, buildings, machinery, actual cash on hand, raw materials in hand or in process, finished goods on hand, and unpaid accounts for goods made or delivered. It included borrowed capital, but excluded rented capital and certain non-operating capital and intangibles such as securities and loans

[6] *Ibid.*

[7] For example, H. M. Douty, "Union Impact on Wage Structures," *Proceedings of the Sixth Annual Meeting*, Industrial Relations Research Association, 1953, p. 67. Douty merely mentions immigration as one factor, however.

representing investments in other enterprises, copyrights, trademarks, and good will.[8] The census called for valuation of capital at the amount carried on the books as of the last day of the previous year. Depreciation was not requested by the census before 1889; even as late as 1909, "The great majority of establishments make no allowances for depreciation on their books and have no definite idea as to the relation between the original cost or value of the buildings and machinery and their present value." Easterlin gives his opinion that the capital figures presented here are at book value (principally original cost) with increasing allowance for depreciation as we move forward in time." This factor would lead to downward bias in the figures for the later years of the period; on the other hand the questions addressed by the census through 1880 were vague and were believed by that agency to overlook items of capital such as goods in process. Easterlin suggests that the figures for 1870 and 1880 (and presumably 1860) were probably biased downward relative to those for subsequent years.[9] We made two adjustments to the capital data: one to exclude capital in certain nonmanufacturing industries, intermittently covered industries, and independent hand trades, the other to adjust to 1860 dollars, an operation that required some arbitrary assumptions, in view of the fact that investments were acquired at various times and prices.

These defects and assumptions keep us from saying anything final about the causes of wage and productivity increases. Nevertheless, the behavior of real capital per worker and wages and productivity were highly consistent. Between 1860 and 1890, capital per wage earner approximately doubled, with the entire increase apparently concentrated in the 1880's, the decade of the greatest rise in productivity and real wages. Thus the lag of real wages, real earnings, and productivity between 1860 and 1880 was probably due to the dilution of the capital endowment per worker during these years. Similarly, the doubling of the capital endowment per worker during the 1880's may have been responsible for so much of the rise in real wages and productivity being concentrated in that decade.

Undue emphasis should not be placed on quantity of capital. Fuller understanding is required of its industrial distribution, its quality, and the techniques by which it is used in production. At the outbreak of the Civil War, according to Clark, the United States was probably in advance of other nations in automatic machinery and interchangeable and standard parts. The Civil War

[8] Richard A. Easterlin, "Estimates of Manufacturing Activity," *Population Redistribution and Economic Growth, United States, 1870-1950*, American Philosophical Society, 1957, pp. 675-677.

[9] *Ibid.*, p. 678.

set higher standards of precision in some industries, created a demand for laborsaving machinery, and rapidly widened the use of automatic tools. Railroads were built even in the midst of hostilities. But the Civil War, Clark felt, did not create new manufactures or revolutionize industrial labor in the North, and it put a heavy burden on northern industries. In the South, it wrecked or depleted manufacturing equipment and railways, and destroyed the social organization for economic life, with the result that recovery was unexpectedly slow.[10] Thus the years of war and reconstruction were periods of quantitative rather than qualitative progress.[11] These impressions are consistent with a slow net advance between 1860 and 1870 in productivity and real wages and earnings.

In contrast, Clark regards 1873-93 as a golden age marked by the largest opening up of virgin territory and resources of any twenty-year period in our history, the linking together of transcontinental railroads, the most rapid application of scientific method to agriculture, large northern investment in southern manufacturing and railroads, the rise of new manufacturing centers in the South and West, the spread of technical education through scientific institutes, and notable improvements in steel making and railroad construction and operation.[12] Whether the qualitative advances were high compared with pre-Civil War or more recent periods is not certain, but the combination of considerable qualitative and quantitative growth is consistent with the fact that most of the real-wage advance in these thirty years of American industrial development occurred in the late 1870's and the 1880's.

The story of wage behavior during 1860-90 would be incomplete without mention of unions. The period was marked by wide fluctuations in both wages and union activity, by moderate net advance in both wages and union strength, and by the fact that the 1880's taken as a decade was the best of the three both for increase of real wages and development of lasting union organization. Can we trace connection between these developments in unionization and in wages?

The influence of unions on wages would have been hard enough to establish if the unions had been well organized and had left abundant records of their activities. Though the labor movement succeeded in gaining its first really firm foothold during the last years of this period, it was, except for the brief candescence of the Knights of Labor in the mid 1880's, a small part of the work force—typically

---

[10] Our own statistics on manufacturing employment show that the South lagged behind all the other regions in the increase between 1860 and 1880 (Appendix Table C-2).
[11] Clark, *op. cit.*, pp. 7, 18, 20, 23, 27, 61, 152.
[12] Pp. 154, 170, 182, 186.

1 or 2 percent of the total labor force—or less than 10 percent of the industrial labor force.[13]

Unions made their greatest gains and were probably strongest in skilled trades; they were surely of almost no significance for laborers. It would be interesting to investigate whether the large rise of unionization during the 1880's was associated with any greater wage gains for the skilled workers than for the unskilled laborers. Later investigation may yield a more positive result, but no differential impact of any significance could be noted in our own sketchy examination of the statistics.

As concerns manufacturing wages, any position that unionization was a significant factor must be regarded as extremely tenuous. For the first two decades we have a valuable record of the extent of union activity in the replies of manufacturing firms to a question posed by the Weeks investigation made in connection with the 1880 census: "Have strikes or lockouts been frequent in your business?" Of the 462 firms which supplied wage data, half made no reply to this question; 169 reported that they had never had a strike or lockout since 1860 or since the firm was founded, 58 said that strikes were infrequent or rare, and only 3 firms conceded that strikes had ever resulted in gains to the worker. In the 1880's, unions were undoubtedly more active in manufacturing, though they were probably never much of a factor except for some skilled occupations within some industries.

Any connection between union activity and wages is necessarily complex. Unions can influence wages, while their own activities are influenced by wage developments. Their influence can exert itself through strike activity, inspiration to unorganized workers, concessions by nonunion employers to ward off unionism, or gradual persuasion of employers that low wages are wrong or unwise. Their impact can take the form of resistance to reductions, or it can affect prices and therefore living costs.

These complexities, together with the absence of really adequate statistics of union membership for the firms and industries covered by the wage and earnings data, restrain us from trying to assess the impact of unionization in this period. We could discern no such impact in our sketchy analysis; but the final judgment on this, as on some other questions, we leave to later investigation.

[13] Trade union membership may have been as much as 14 percent of the industrial labor force in 1870-72, and it seems to have been about 7.5 percent in 1880 and 8.7 percent in 1890. For union membership, see Lloyd Ulman, *The Rise of the National Trade Union*, Harvard University Press, 1955, p. 19.

For industrial employment (including manufacturing, construction, and hand trades) see Table 14 of this study.

A Final Word

Despite the quickening in the 1880's, the pace of real wages and earnings during these three decades of almost unparalleled economic advance must, by present standards, be regarded as moderate, a walk followed by a trot, allegretto rather than allegro! This need not be surprising. A time of rapid economic development out of a mainly agricultural setting is not necessarily the best for labor. While industrial demand for labor increases apace, a great reservoir of labor supply flows into industry as a result of a simultaneously occurring agricultural revolution. This labor supply does not require as great a lure of industrial wage increases, since its flow is partly forced and is still large in relation to the industrial demand. When a large interflow of labor supply is added to a great immigration and a great natural population increase, it is an achievement even to increase the equipment per worker; qualitative standards are apt to lag.

If this perspective is sound, great quantitative growth would not necessarily be accompanied by great enhancement in the condition of labor; such gains must probably wait until the most rapid phase of quantitative growth is over. Then—when the economy can turn its strength to industrial and social improvement—can begin a golden age for labor.

APPENDIX
TABLES

TABLE A-1

Daily Wage-Rates in 13 Manufacturing Industries and in Building from the Aldrich Report, Weighted by Employment within the Establishment and by Number Gainfully Occupied Reported Attached to the Industries at the Decennial Censuses; January and July 1860-1890
(current dollars)

Industry	No. of Estab.	1860 Jan.	1860 July	1861 Jan.	1861 July	1862 Jan.	1862 July	1863 Jan.	1863 July	1864 Jan.	1864 July	1865 Jan.	1865 July	1866 Jan.	1866 July	1867 Jan.	1867 July
Weighted average, manufacturing	49	1.18	1.19	1.18	1.16	1.21	1.25	1.27	1.34	1.41	1.54	1.62	1.66	1.70	1.74	1.73	1.76
Agricultural implements	1[a]	1.36	1.37	1.40	1.39	1.35	1.23	1.34	1.38	1.53	1.85	1.93	2.02	2.06	2.12	2.07	2.16
Ale, beer, porter	1[b]	1.06	1.04	1.03	1.06	1.05	1.02	1.06	1.15	1.31	1.43	1.44	1.49	1.47	1.51	1.54	1.65
Books and newspapers	3[c]	1.07	1.16	1.07	1.07	1.14	1.12	1.20	1.27	1.40	1.43	1.42	1.51	1.50	1.63	1.54	1.61
Carriages and wagons	1[d]	1.22	1.22	1.22	1.22	2.07	2.07	2.05	2.05	2.05	2.07	2.07	2.07	2.08	2.08	2.08	2.08
Cotton manufactures	5[e]	0.78	0.79	0.79	0.82	0.80	0.86	0.85	0.88	0.95	0.99	1.07	1.14	1.22	1.26	1.29	1.32
Illuminating gas	4[f]	1.16	1.19	1.16	1.17	1.17	1.17	1.48	1.73	1.73	1.90	2.13	2.08	2.18	2.18	2.23	2.26
Leather	2[g]	1.27	1.27	1.55	1.45	1.57	1.60	1.73	1.75	1.90	1.92	1.97	2.01	1.98	1.97	1.91	1.91
Lumber	2[h]	1.03	1.05	1.06	1.06	1.04	1.10	1.15	1.25	1.32	1.38	1.44	1.44	1.42	1.43	1.50	1.54
Metals and metallic goods	19[i]	1.47	1.47	1.49	1.46	1.49	1.56	1.55	1.68	1.74	1.99	2.13	2.13	2.23	2.25	2.26	2.26
Paper	1[j]	0.88	0.86	0.84	0.83	0.70	0.72	0.82	0.82	0.86	1.06	1.15	1.22	1.13	1.16	1.16	1.19
Stone	6[k]	1.49	1.55	1.40	1.39	1.40	1.46	1.50	1.70	1.90	2.24	2.42	2.55	2.60	2.75	2.62	2.96
White lead	1[l]	1.19	1.19	1.20	1.22	1.24	1.25	1.37	1.39	1.47	1.72	1.76	1.76	1.76	1.76	1.76	1.76
Woolen manufacturers	3[m]	0.82	0.82	0.86	0.83	0.80	0.81	0.86	0.85	0.96	1.02	1.12	1.14	1.18	1.21	1.15	1.18
Building	21	1.68	1.70	1.64	1.68	1.66	1.78	1.82	1.96	2.09	2.32	2.43	2.66	2.66	2.81	2.80	3.08

table continues on following pages

Table A-1, *continued*

Industry	1868 Jan.	July	1869 Jan.	July	1870 Jan.	July	1871 Jan.	July	1872 Jan.	July	1873 Jan.	July	1874 Jan.	July	1875 Jan.	July
Weighted average	1.75	1.77	1.80	1.79	1.80	1.77	1.80	1.82	1.79	1.85	1.85	1.84	1.79	1.80	1.72	1.71
Agricultural implements	2.04	1.91	2.04	2.07	2.04	2.06	1.95	1.93	1.93	1.85	1.93	1.99	2.01	2.02	2.04	2.00
Ale, beer, porter	1.59	1.65	1.65	1.81	1.65	1.67	1.64	1.73	1.60	1.69	1.75	1.80	1.77	1.74	1.70	1.78
Books and newspapers	1.70	1.80	1.88	1.79	1.86	1.74	2.31	2.30	2.19	2.19	2.14	2.01	1.97	2.00	2.07	1.94
Carriages and wagons	2.08	2.08	2.27	2.27	2.27	2.27	2.27	2.27	2.27	2.27	2.27	2.27	2.27	2.27	2.27	2.27
Cotton manufactures	1.33	1.31	1.32	1.34	1.36	1.36	1.39	1.42	1.45	1.45	1.46	1.45	1.35	1.38	1.28	1.28
Illuminating gas	2.24	2.27	2.37	2.29	2.38	2.38	2.46	2.31	2.40	2.52	2.72	2.40	2.57	2.35	2.45	2.10
Leather	1.89	1.89	1.90	1.94	1.94	1.94	1.91	1.91	1.93	1.92	1.95	1.95	1.91	1.84	1.76	1.73
Lumber	1.55	1.53	1.59	1.64	1.66	1.68	1.67	1.66	1.67	1.72	1.71	1.72	1.72	1.78	1.74	1.79
Metals and metallic goods	2.25	2.26	2.27	2.26	2.28	2.20	2.20	2.21	2.23	2.25	2.27	2.28	2.25	2.27	2.10	2.10
Paper	1.21	1.21	1.20	1.23	1.20	1.22	1.22	1.32	1.30	1.33	1.34	1.34	1.32	1.36	1.38	1.36
Stone	2.83	3.30	3.10	3.05	2.93	2.91	2.81	3.01	2.85	3.07	2.96	2.99	2.96	2.92	2.89	2.86
White lead	1.78	1.90	1.95	1.95	1.85	1.77	1.79	1.97	1.87	1.84	1.91	1.90	1.83	1.83	1.83	1.74
Woolen manufactures	1.16	1.19	1.29	1.26	1.29	1.30	1.31	1.29	1.24	1.31	1.36	1.34	1.35	1.34	1.34	1.32
Building	2.91	3.09	3.09	3.22	3.09	3.02	2.85	3.02	2.86	2.97	2.86	2.84	2.70	2.84	2.69	2.68

Table A-1, *continued*

Industry	1876		1877		1878		1879		1880		1881		1882		1883	
	Jan.	*July*	*Jan.*	*July*	*Jan.*	*July*	*Jan.*	*July*	*Jan.*	*July*	*Jan.*	*July*	*Jan.*	*July*	*Jan.*	*July*
Weighted average	1.70	1.65	1.60	1.57	1.54	1.50	1.50	1.47	1.51	1.56	1.56	1.55	1.55	1.62	1.63	1.63
Agricultural implements	1.81	1.77	1.64	1.63	1.68	1.64	1.61	1.51	1.55	1.57	1.54	1.71	1.71	1.71	1.82	1.71
Ale, beer, porter	1.65	1.70	1.67	1.71	1.69	1.86	1.80	1.78	1.71	1.73	1.66	1.68	1.67	1.74	1.67	1.68
Books and newspapers	2.04	2.05	2.13	1.98	1.81	1.73	1.70	1.49	1.54	1.49	1.45	1.25	1.35	1.37	1.32	1.45
Carriages and wagons	2.27	2.27	2.27	2.27	2.23	2.23	2.26	2.26	2.44	2.44	2.44	2.44	2.44	2.44	2.44	2.44
Cotton manufactures	1.29	1.21	1.17	1.17	1.18	1.17	1.15	1.12	1.14	1.18	1.17	1.16	1.19	1.22	1.20	1.18
Illuminating gas	2.33	2.05	2.23	2.02	2.06	1.89	2.00	1.85	1.90	1.94	1.98	1.92	2.03	1.96	1.96	1.97
Leather	1.68	1.70	1.70	1.72	1.73	1.73	1.61	1.58	1.66	1.68	1.69	1.70	1.71	1.73	1.65	1.64
Lumber	1.78	1.78	1.83	1.77	1.78	1.80	1.80	1.68	1.71	1.70	1.75	1.73	1.68	1.65	1.67	1.68
Metals and metallic goods	2.05	2.01	1.90	1.90	1.84	1.77	1.78	1.78	1.89	1.93	1.94	1.96	1.99	2.01	2.07	2.09
Paper	1.43	1.22	1.21	1.14	1.14	1.18	1.21	1.19	1.21	1.30	1.29	1.29	1.29	1.31	1.29	1.31
Stone	2.78	2.68	2.54	2.36	2.25	2.24	2.22	2.04	2.04	2.21	2.20	2.50	2.41	2.68	2.62	2.63
White lead	1.75	1.74	1.73	1.48	1.44	1.43	1.39	1.36	1.27	1.37	1.36	1.39	1.37	1.39	1.38	1.35
Woolen manufactures	1.31	1.32	1.27	1.24	1.22	1.15	1.24	1.23	1.19	1.33	1.27	1.26	1.29	1.34	1.36	1.33
Building	2.37	2.49	2.26	2.30	2.15	2.18	2.13	2.21	2.02	2.25	2.24	2.45	2.45	2.61	2.46	2.61

table continues on following page

Table A-1, *concluded*

Industry	1884 Jan.	1884 July	1885 Jan.	1885 July	1886 Jan.	1886 July	1887 Jan.	1887 July	1888 Jan.	1888 July	1889 Jan.	1889 July	1890 Jan.	1890 July
Weighted average	1.63	1.68	1.61	1.61	1.60	1.63	1.66	1.68	1.67	1.70	1.72	1.74	1.74	1.76
Agricultural implements	1.78	1.72	1.68	1.69	1.75	1.75	1.69	1.69	1.76	1.74	1.76	1.75	1.77	1.77
Ale, beer, porter	1.62	1.68	1.65	1.68	1.66	1.69	1.65	2.09	2.08	2.18	2.11	2.12	2.10	2.12
Books and newspapers	1.57	1.50	1.56	1.48	1.59	1.54	1.66	1.78	1.54	1.65	1.65	1.79	1.81	1.69
Carriages and wagons	2.44	2.44	2.44	2.44	2.44	2.44	2.44	2.44	2.44	2.44	2.44	2.44	2.44	2.44
Cotton manufactures	1.16	1.18	1.11	1.12	1.12	1.16	1.18	1.19	1.18	1.22	1.23	1.27	1.26	1.28
Illuminating gas	1.99	1.84	1.96	2.01	1.97	2.06	2.03	2.04	1.99	1.98	2.04	1.99	2.08	2.03
Leather	1.65	1.66	1.61	1.62	1.67	1.71	1.65	1.65	1.63	1.63	1.55	1.56	1.58	1.64
Lumber	1.63	1.63	1.63	1.63	1.62	1.63	1.66	1.66	1.67	1.74	1.73	1.75	1.82	1.82
Metals and metallic goods	2.09	2.09	2.00	2.02	1.97	2.00	2.05	2.06	2.08	2.11	2.15	2.14	2.15	2.15
Paper	1.24	1.20	1.28	1.28	1.25	1.29	1.31	1.23	1.30	1.33	1.36	1.29	1.32	1.30
Stone	2.61	2.75	2.63	2.76	2.79	2.79	2.71	2.82	2.75	2.90	2.77	2.99	2.92	3.16
White lead	1.38	1.41	1.44	1.46	1.49	1.46	1.47	1.43	1.42	1.39	1.41	1.43	1.44	1.53
Woolen manufactures	1.34	1.61	1.43	1.34	1.33	1.36	1.44	1.37	1.39	1.37	1.41	1.39	1.38	1.38
Building	2.53	2.59	2.52	2.59	2.61	2.65	2.54	2.63	2.52	2.69	2.61	2.67	2.63	2.73

The only clue to the nature and coverage of these industries and their wage data is to be found in the various occupational classifications in the Aldrich Report.

For description of the method of weighting, see Chapter 2, above.

Prices are in greenback currency during the period of inconvertibility.

Source of wage data: Nelson W. Aldrich, *Wholesale Prices, Wages, and Transportation*, Report by Mr. Aldrich from the Committee on Finance, March 3, 1893, 52nd Congress, 2nd Session, Senate Report 1394, Vol. 3, Parts 1–4.

a In Massachusetts.
b New York.
c One, Connecticut; two, New York.
d New York.
e One gingham establishment, Massachusetts; three cotton goods establishments, Massachusetts; one, New York.
f Two, Massachusetts; one, New York; one, Ohio.
g Both, Massachusetts.
h One, New Hampshire; one, New York.
i Three, Connecticut; one, Maryland; four, Massachusetts; one, New Hampshire; one, New Jersey; seven, New York; two, Pennsylvania.
j Massachusetts.
k Two, Connecticut; one, Maryland; two, New York; one, Pennsylvania.
l Pennsylvania.
m One, Connecticut; one, Massachusetts; one, Rhode Island.

Daily Wage-Rates in Seven Manufacturing Industries with Establishments Reporting from Two or More States, Aldrich Report, Weighted by Employment within the Establishment; January and July 1860-1890 (current dollars)

Industry	No. of Estab.	1860		1861		1862		1863		1864		1865		1866		1867	
		Jan.	July	Jan.	July	Jan.	July	Jan.	July	Jan.	July	Jan.	July	Jan.	July	Jan.	July
Books and newspapers																	
New York	2	1.07	1.17	1.07	1.07	1.15	1.12	1.21	1.28	1.42	1.44	1.42	1.52	1.49	1.63	1.63	1.59
Connecticut	1	1.05	1.05	1.05	1.07	1.06	1.06	1.08	1.07	1.08	1.24	1.42	1.29	1.58	1.61	1.93	1.85
Cotton and ginghams																	
Massachusetts	4	0.83	0.84	0.82	0.85	0.84	0.94	0.92	0.93	0.99	1.03	1.12	1.19	1.29	1.33	1.36	1.38
New York	1	0.68	0.70	0.70	0.73	0.68	0.62	0.63	0.72	0.79	0.83	0.89	0.94	0.93	0.99	1.02	1.08
Illuminating gas																	
Massachusetts	2	0.99	1.00	1.00	1.01	1.02	1.07	1.09	1.24	1.32	1.53	1.64	1.55	1.59	1.76	1.75	1.82
New York	1	1.20	1.24	1.21	1.22	1.21	1.18	1.61	1.90	1.80	1.98	2.28	2.23	2.33	2.34	2.36	2.38
Ohio	1	1.18	1.17	1.17	1.18	1.18	1.29	1.33	1.54	1.97	2.02	2.10	2.13	2.27	1.98	2.27	2.27
Lumber																	
New Hampshire	1	0.49	0.50	0.49	0.50	0.64	0.61	0.88	0.89	0.93	0.96	0.98	0.99	0.99	1.00	1.01	0.97
New York	1	1.09	1.12	1.13	1.13	1.09	1.16	1.18	1.29	1.36	1.43	1.49	1.49	1.47	1.48	1.55	1.60
Metals																	
Connecticut	3	1.46	1.50	1.48	1.47	1.46	1.50	1.53	1.62	1.67	1.94	2.01	2.06	2.09	2.22	2.25	2.30
Maryland	1	1.50	1.50	1.53	1.22	1.34	1.42	1.60	1.74	1.87	2.15	2.33	2.35	2.54	2.46	2.46	2.41
Massachusetts	4	1.54	1.53	1.58	1.52	1.61	1.72	1.55	1.90	1.85	2.06	2.27	2.32	2.40	2.39	2.40	2.43
New Hampshire	1	1.42	1.46	1.44	1.43	1.50	1.46	1.51	1.56	1.65	1.78	1.87	1.72	1.88	1.88	1.86	1.84
New Jersey	1	2.11	2.06	2.01	1.97	1.92	1.96	1.83	1.95	1.96	2.24	2.31	2.36	2.49	2.49	2.53	2.52
New York	7	1.29	1.32	1.32	1.34	1.32	1.39	1.42	1.52	1.61	1.90	2.02	2.04	2.11	2.14	2.16	2.15
Pennsylvania	2	1.47	1.46	1.50	1.48	1.52	1.57	1.63	1.67	1.77	1.99	2.14	2.08	2.22	2.23	2.22	2.20
Stone																	
Connecticut	2	0.83	1.20	1.14	1.10	0.99	1.08	0.99	1.37	1.21	1.61	1.30	1.82	1.45	1.90	1.47	1.95
Maryland	1	1.47	1.57	1.47	1.45	1.54	1.58	1.48	1.63	1.66	2.07	2.24	2.20	2.24	2.24	2.23	2.32
New York	2	1.60	1.55	1.42	1.31	1.42	1.41	1.45	1.66	1.87	2.35	2.45	2.57	2.64	2.77	2.67	3.06
Pennsylvania	1	1.38	1.63	1.42	1.65	1.42	1.68	1.75	1.92	2.20	2.56	2.69	2.79	2.90	3.03	2.90	3.13
Woolens																	
Connecticut	1	0.94	0.93	1.03	1.00	0.96	1.03	1.20	0.98	1.11	1.21	1.46	1.43	1.43	1.52	1.43	1.47
Massachusetts	1	0.72	0.72	0.80	0.75	0.70	0.70	0.78	0.83	0.92	0.99	1.19	1.23	1.27	1.29	1.21	1.24
Rhode Island	1	0.88	0.89	0.89	0.89	0.90	0.90	0.95	0.95	1.02	1.05	1.06	1.09	1.11	1.15	1.18	1.16

125

table continues on following pages

Table A-2, *continued*

Industry	No. of Estab.	1868 Jan.	1868 July	1869 Jan.	1869 July	1870 Jan.	1870 July	1871 Jan.	1871 July	1872 Jan.	1872 July	1873 Jan.	1873 July	1874 Jan.	1874 July	1875 Jan.	1875 July
Books and newspapers																	
New York	2	1.70	1.80	1.87	1.78	1.86	1.74	2.34	2.32	2.21	2.20	2.15	2.02	1.96	2.00	2.08	1.94
Connecticut	1	1.76	1.78	2.07	1.95	1.86	1.82	1.88	1.91	1.94	1.95	1.96	1.93	2.07	2.06	1.97	1.96
Cotton and ginghams																	
Massachusetts	4	1.39	1.37	1.37	1.40	1.43	1.43	1.46	1.50	1.52	1.52	1.53	1.52	1.42	1.45	1.33	1.33
New York	1	1.08	1.08	1.11	1.09	1.06	1.09	1.09	1.09	1.10	1.13	1.11	1.11	1.00	1.04	1.04	1.04
Illuminating gas																	
Massachusetts	2	1.79	1.80	1.85	1.83	1.91	1.86	1.91	1.87	1.89	2.09	2.14	2.15	2.15	1.93	1.95	1.76
New York	1	2.36	2.41	2.55	2.44	2.56	2.57	2.64	2.44	2.60	2.71	3.05	2.52	2.80	2.52	2.70	2.18
Ohio	1	2.26	2.26	2.26	2.26	2.25	2.25	2.43	2.32	2.32	2.39	2.37	2.30	2.35	2.30	2.29	2.19
Lumber																	
New Hampshire	1	1.00	0.97	1.02	1.02	1.00	1.02	1.00	1.00	0.99	0.98	1.00	1.02	1.09	1.01	0.98	0.99
New York	1	1.61	1.59	1.65	1.71	1.73	1.75	1.75	1.74	1.76	1.82	1.82	1.82	1.82	1.91	1.88	1.93
Metals																	
Connecticut	3	2.33	2.30	2.30	2.34	2.44	2.39	2.39	2.34	2.37	2.40	2.48	2.39	2.48	2.45	2.40	2.22
Maryland	1	2.47	2.39	2.48	2.42	2.42	2.42	2.44	2.40	2.42	2.34	2.47	2.47	2.47	2.49	2.28	2.27
Massachusetts	4	2.47	2.40	2.42	2.49	2.51	2.46	2.46	2.55	2.52	2.46	2.51	2.61	2.42	2.44	2.17	2.19
New Hampshire	1	1.75	1.89	2.00	2.04	2.26	1.92	1.87	1.86	1.97	1.74	1.68	1.73	1.82	1.84	1.85	1.68
New Jersey	1	2.56	2.57	2.60	2.60	2.61	2.62	2.62	2.52	2.50	2.46	2.53	2.59	2.60	2.76	2.67	2.72
New York	7	2.13	2.17	2.17	2.18	2.19	2.18	2.20	2.22	2.25	2.28	2.24	2.23	2.14	2.15	2.16	2.07
Pennsylvania	2	2.17	2.21	2.19	2.14	2.12	1.94	1.91	1.93	1.97	2.05	2.09	2.08	2.13	2.13	1.96	1.94
Stone																	
Connecticut	2	1.49	2.12	1.65	2.52	1.66	2.49	1.57	2.45	1.64	2.48	1.52	2.44	1.51	2.17	1.65	1.87
Maryland	1	2.28	2.29	2.31	2.26	2.26	2.26	2.29	2.29	2.30	2.30	2.25	2.25	2.19	2.19	2.23	2.23
New York	2	2.83	3.48	3.25	3.41	3.15	2.90	2.89	3.00	2.87	2.98	2.95	2.86	2.96	2.77	2.88	2.74
Pennsylvania	1	3.30	3.38	3.30	2.45	2.88	3.19	3.08	3.32	3.25	3.60	3.53	3.61	3.50	3.64	3.35	3.53
Woolens																	
Connecticut	1	1.30	1.39	1.46	1.36	1.41	1.37	1.36	1.40	1.15	1.34	1.35	1.37	1.35	1.35	1.31	1.38
Massachusetts	1	1.22	1.25	1.28	1.24	1.28	1.30	1.32	1.28	1.27	1.32	1.40	1.35	1.42	1.38	1.38	1.32
Rhode Island	1	1.16	1.16	1.18	1.22	1.22	1.23	1.23	1.24	1.24	1.24	1.24	1.26	1.16	1.23	1.25	1.25

126

Table A-2, continued

Industry	No. of Estab.	1876 Jan.	1876 July	1877 Jan.	1877 July	1878 Jan.	1878 July	1879 Jan.	1879 July	1880 Jan.	1880 July	1881 Jan.	1881 July	1882 Jan.	1882 July	1883 Jan.	1883 July
Books and newspapers																	
New York	2	2.05	2.06	2.15	1.99	1.80	1.72	1.70	1.48	1.54	1.49	1.44	1.23	1.32	1.35	1.29	1.43
Connecticut	1	1.91	1.85	1.88	1.88	1.90	1.87	1.65	1.66	1.57	1.60	1.73	1.65	1.80	1.79	1.75	1.74
Cotton and ginghams																	
Massachusetts	4	1.35	1.27	1.22	1.22	1.24	1.23	1.20	1.17	1.20	1.22	1.21	1.19	1.22	1.27	1.26	1.22
New York	1	0.94	0.89	0.87	0.90	0.86	0.85	0.88	0.81	0.87	0.99	0.97	0.99	1.02	0.95	0.90	0.96
Illuminating gas																	
Massachusetts	2	1.82	1.65	1.70	1.55	1.56	1.56	1.58	1.59	1.57	1.54	1.53	1.58	1.71	1.73	1.74	1.67
New York	1	2.57	2.15	2.46	2.24	2.32	2.00	2.19	1.89	1.98	2.03	2.11	1.99	2.14	2.01	2.09	2.05
Ohio	1	2.19	2.15	2.15	1.90	1.90	1.90	1.93	1.97	1.97	2.06	2.05	2.05	2.05	2.04	1.87	2.03
Lumber																	
New Hampshire	1	1.00	0.99	0.98	0.93	1.03	1.01	1.02	0.98	0.99	0.96	0.92	0.92	0.93	0.93	0.93	0.93
New York	1	1.93	1.93	2.01	1.95	1.95	1.98	1.98	1.85	1.90	1.89	1.95	1.93	1.86	1.83	1.83	1.85
Metals																	
Connecticut	3	2.30	2.19	2.12	2.08	2.07	1.99	2.00	1.86	2.11	2.16	2.10	2.18	2.23	2.25	2.36	2.36
Maryland	1	2.24	2.09	2.05	2.00	2.04	2.04	1.99	2.00	2.03	2.12	2.30	2.29	2.25	2.30	2.30	2.32
Massachusetts	4	2.21	2.16	1.96	1.96	1.92	1.87	1.89	1.84	1.86	1.86	1.95	1.95	1.93	1.97	1.97	1.98
New Hampshire	1	1.39	1.69	1.60	1.52	1.46	1.39	1.32	1.32	1.34	1.33	1.39	1.34	1.38	1.34	1.35	1.35
New Jersey	1	2.74	2.74	2.82	2.82	2.82	2.82	2.67	2.67	2.69	2.69	2.64	2.64	2.54	2.59	2.74	2.86
New York	7	2.02	1.97	1.86	1.87	1.82	1.62	1.81	1.76	1.80	1.95	1.93	2.00	2.02	2.04	2.07	2.08
Pennsylvania	2	1.82	1.78	1.73	1.67	1.62	1.64	1.62	1.70	1.71	1.74	1.75	1.76	1.83	1.84	1.91	1.93
Stone																	
Connecticut	2	1.45	1.63	1.14	1.54	1.13	1.56	1.04	1.50	1.03	1.43	1.04	1.68	1.14	1.85	1.16	1.83
Maryland	1	2.22	2.22	2.02	2.00	1.90	1.88	1.66	1.70	1.62	1.62	1.66	1.73	1.80	1.99	1.99	2.00
New York	2	2.69	2.66	2.46	2.33	2.31	2.28	2.26	2.11	2.18	2.25	2.30	2.60	2.51	2.68	2.67	2.55
Pennsylvania	1	3.45	3.10	3.17	2.71	2.44	2.39	2.51	2.07	2.03	2.44	2.36	2.64	2.60	2.99	2.97	3.09
Woolens																	
Connecticut	1	1.27	1.26	1.22	1.28	1.27	1.29	1.23	1.25	1.26	1.27	1.30	1.25	1.32	1.41	1.51	1.47
Massachusetts	1	1.35	1.38	1.31	1.25	1.21	1.10	1.25	1.23	1.18	1.41	1.29	1.30	1.31	1.39	1.39	1.35
Rhode Island	1	1.24	1.19	1.19	1.19	1.20	1.19	1.20	1.20	1.19	1.19	1.19	1.19	1.20	1.19	1.22	1.22

table continues on following page

127

Table A-2, concluded

Industry	No. of Estab.	1884 Jan.	1884 July	1885 Jan.	1885 July	1886 Jan.	1886 July	1887 Jan.	1887 July	1888 Jan.	1888 July	1889 Jan.	1889 July	1890 Jan.	1890 July
Books and newspapers															
New York	2	1.56	1.48	1.55	1.46	1.58	1.51	1.64	1.77	1.52	1.63	1.64	1.79	1.80	1.67
Connecticut	1	1.75	1.76	1.68	1.78	1.84	1.81	1.86	1.88	1.83	1.92	1.87	1.84	1.94	1.84
Cotton and ginghams															
Massachusetts	4	1.20	1.21	1.16	1.16	1.16	1.21	1.24	1.23	1.22	1.26	1.27	1.30	1.28	1.31
New York	1	0.97	0.97	0.87	0.92	0.88	0.88	0.88	0.92	0.95	0.99	1.01	1.04	1.08	1.11
Illuminating gas															
Massachusetts	2	1.69	1.59	1.66	1.64	1.65	1.59	1.64	1.60	1.63	1.56	1.66	1.62	1.65	1.68
New York	1	2.15	2.08	2.09	2.19	2.12	2.32	2.24	2.27	2.18	2.19	2.25	2.19	2.35	2.26
Ohio	1	1.93	1.55	1.93	1.93	1.92	1.92	1.91	1.91	1.91	1.91	1.91	1.91	1.93	1.83
Lumber															
New Hampshire	1	0.92	0.91	0.94	0.93	0.93	0.93	0.92	0.91	0.94	0.93	0.93	0.93	0.93	0.94
New York	1	1.79	1.79	1.79	1.79	1.76	1.77	1.81	1.81	1.82	1.90	1.89	1.91	1.98	1.98
Metals															
Connecticut	3	2.34	2.30	2.23	2.38	2.38	2.55	2.61	2.56	2.58	2.58	2.51	2.47	2.57	2.53
Maryland	1	2.33	2.31	2.33	2.22	2.22	2.22	2.26	2.27	2.24	2.26	2.28	2.28	2.29	2.30
Massachusetts	4	1.98	2.04	2.01	1.91	1.88	1.95	1.98	1.96	1.93	1.97	2.05	2.01	2.04	1.98
New Hampshire	1	1.43	1.44	1.49	1.53	1.47	1.56	1.57	1.51	1.41	1.42	1.50	1.53	1.54	1.62
New Jersey	1	2.80	2.82	2.80	2.79	2.73	2.73	2.73	2.75	2.91	2.91	2.91	2.91	2.91	2.91
New York	7	2.07	2.06	2.01	1.96	1.95	2.02	2.02	2.07	2.09	2.09	2.10	2.06	2.09	2.12
Pennsylvania	2	1.96	1.95	1.79	1.88	1.77	1.76	1.86	1.85	1.88	1.95	2.00	2.02	2.00	2.02
Stone															
Connecticut	2	1.16	1.81	1.15	1.79	1.16	1.94	1.15	1.91	1.16	1.96	1.18	1.94	1.17	2.01
Maryland	1	2.04	2.04	2.05	2.04	2.05	1.99	1.99	2.02	2.12	2.12	2.05	2.07	2.02	2.02
New York	2	2.60	2.77	2.66	2.84	2.88	2.92	2.91	2.98	2.95	3.03	2.97	3.14	3.22	3.53
Pennsylvania	1	3.06	3.06	2.99	2.97	3.13	2.91	2.85	2.88	2.87	3.02	2.91	2.96	2.99	3.03
Woolens															
Connecticut	1	1.45	1.32	1.41	1.37	1.39	1.44	1.62	1.41	1.47	1.45	1.50	1.50	1.58	1.47
Massachusetts	1	1.35	1.85	1.52	1.39	1.37	1.39	1.48	1.41	1.44	1.41	1.46	1.43	1.38	1.41
Rhode Island	1	1.24	1.25	1.24	1.24	1.24	1.25	1.24	1.24	1.24	1.24	1.27	1.26	1.25	1.26

TABLE A-3

Daily Wage-Rates in 18 Manufacturing Industries from the Weeks Report, Weighted by Number of Gainfully Occupied Reported Attached to These Industries at the Decennial Censuses; United States, by Regions, Annually 1860-1880
(current dollars)

Industry	No. of Estab.	1860	1861	1862	1863	1864	1865	1866	1867	1868	1869
					UNITED STATES						
Weighted average	67	1.32	1.36	1.53	1.51	1.72	1.82	1.90	1.94	1.92	1.93
Breweries and distilleries[a]	1	1.01	1.01	1.20	1.39	1.73	1.73	2.02	2.02	2.02	1.97
Brickmaking[b]	2	1.18	1.16	1.18	1.33	1.41	1.73	1.96	2.15	2.36	2.24
Carriage and wagon works[c]	2	1.54	1.55	1.45	1.49	1.67	1.85	1.86	1.93	1.95	1.96
Cigars and tobacco[d]	4	1.32	1.26	1.46	1.54	1.61	1.58	1.61	1.61	1.59	1.59
Clothing[e]	3	1.03	1.16	1.29	1.36	1.43	1.46	1.46	1.44	1.40	1.39
Cotton manufactures[f]	5	0.90	0.91	0.91	0.90	1.03	1.18	1.36	1.42	1.38	1.39
Flint and window glass[g]	2	1.46	1.46	1.45	1.63	1.76	1.75	2.49	2.41	2.41	2.42
Flour and grist mills[h]	4	1.73	1.70	1.84	2.14	2.45	2.56	2.69	2.72	2.71	2.68
Furniture[i]	8	1.74	1.74	1.77	1.79	2.19	2.21	2.22	2.23	2.24	2.25
Hardware, cutlery, etc.[j]	4	1.68	1.69	1.74	1.97	2.15	2.23	2.36	2.37	2.35	2.40
Iron blast furnaces, etc.[k]	7	1.29	1.26	1.33	1.60	2.09	2.27	2.20	2.19	2.19	2.27
Machinery[l]	3	1.33	1.42	1.43	1.57	2.02	2.02	2.10	2.17	2.17	2.13
Paper manufactures[m]	7	1.18	1.38	1.40	1.52	1.66	1.48	1.71	1.75	1.76	1.78
Saw and planing mills[n]	7	1.63	1.59	1.60	1.72	1.84	1.99	2.01	2.01	2.02	2.33
Stove foundries, etc.[o]	2	1.78	1.81	1.86	1.64	1.81	2.03	2.26	2.22	2.25	2.20
Tanneries[p]	1	1.34	1.40	1.29	1.53	1.98	2.08	2.19	2.23	2.27	2.26
Tin and sheet iron works[q]	1	1.68	1.93	2.07	2.61	2.86	3.29	3.29	3.39	3.39	3.39
Woolen manufacturers[r]	4	0.96	0.96	1.00	0.98	1.16	1.42	1.50	1.44	1.44	1.46

Examination of the establishment reports suggests that the wages for most of these industries would not have been significantly different if they had been adjusted to take account, on the one hand, of overtime earnings and allowances (in the form of free housing, pasture land, fuel, free merchandise) or, on the other hand, of the cost to the worker of furnishing his own tools and materials or of making payments possibly to helpers and underhands. Some exceptions are indicated in the notes to the following industries: hardware, etc.; saw and planing mills; machinery; blast furnaces, etc.; brick making; cotton manufacturing.

Nearly all payments were in cash; payments in kind or in store orders were very exceptional. These exceptions are indicated in the notes to the following industries: tin and sheet iron; saw and planing mills; boots and shoes; cigars and tobacco; and blast furnaces, etc. However, according to the Weeks Report, "the small proportion of works paying in truck probably arises from the fact that the establishments from which wage schedules were received were selected establishments. If reports had been received from all establishments in the states named, it is probable that a larger proportion of truck payment would have been shown in some industries than appears in the reports."

Source: *Report on the Statistics of Wages in Manufacturing Industries...*, by Joseph D. Weeks, 1880 Census, Vol. xx, p. xxiii.

The typical workday was 10 hours, though there were many deviations. Some industries had a longer day in summer than in winter; others had an irregular workday, the worker being expected to stay until his job was finished; others worked less than 10 hours, while still others worked a 12-hour shift, seven days a week. These departures from a 10-hour day are indicated in the notes to the following industries: furniture; flour and grist mills; saw and planing mills; flint and window glass; iron blast furnaces, etc.; breweries and distilleries; woolen manufacturing; and cotton manufacturing. However, there was very little reduction in length of workday over the twenty years 1860-80.

For description of the method of weighting see Chapter 2, above.

Industry	1870	1871	1872	1873	1874	1875	1876	1877	1878	1879	1880
Weighted average	1.92	1.95	1.95	1.97	1.87	1.84	1.79	1.75	1.72	1.72	1.77
Breweries and distilleries	1.97	1.82	1.82	1.73	1.73	1.73	1.82	1.82	1.82	2.02	2.02
Brickmaking	2.30	2.27	2.23	2.17	2.09	1.95	1.84	1.73	1.64	1.53	1.68
Carriage and wagon works	1.96	1.95	1.94	1.92	1.79	1.70	1.67	1.66	1.64	1.80	1.86
Cigars and tobacco	1.58	1.57	1.53	1.50	1.49	1.47	1.46	1.46	1.46	1.46	1.48
Clothing	1.38	1.35	1.33	1.37	1.37	1.37	1.42	1.45	1.48	1.47	1.46
Cotton manufactures	1.42	1.49	1.49	1.51	1.48	1.41	1.37	1.32	1.30	1.24	1.29
Flint and window glass	2.47	2.47	2.48	2.48	2.48	2.48	2.48	2.49	2.33	2.33	2.33
Flour and grist mills	2.69	2.68	2.63	2.62	2.46	2.49	2.34	2.30	2.19	2.20	2.19
Furniture	2.24	2.25	2.25	2.24	2.21	2.24	2.23	2.21	2.21	2.22	2.23
Hardware, cutlery, etc.	2.41	2.41	2.42	2.35	2.20	2.21	2.17	2.12	2.12	2.12	2.24
Iron blast furnaces, etc.	2.27	2.23	2.35	2.32	2.01	1.87	1.70	1.63	1.58	1.58	1.83
Machinery	2.13	2.26	2.27	2.26	2.24	2.21	2.13	2.01	1.95	1.87	1.96
Paper manufactures	1.85	1.90	1.95	1.96	1.95	1.81	1.91	1.90	1.83	1.84	1.70
Saw and planing mills	2.10	2.32	2.31	2.47	2.43	2.38	2.38	2.34	2.32	2.30	2.41
Stove foundries, etc.	2.30	2.25	2.25	2.23	2.19	2.18	1.96	1.82	1.54	1.80	1.90
Tanneries	2.26	2.25	2.27	2.27	2.19	2.18	2.04	2.00	2.00	1.96	1.93
Tin and sheet iron works	3.18	3.18	3.18	3.46	2.25	2.25	2.25	2.25	2.43	2.29	2.29
Woolen manufactures	1.52	1.51	1.53	1.52	1.45	1.43	1.35	1.31	1.29	1.29	1.32

[a] None of the great establishments of the country returned their schedules. Workday ranged from 12 to 15½ hours in breweries, 12 hours in distilleries. There were no reports of any hours changed during 1860-80, but the workweek could scarcely have been much longer in 1860 than it was at the time of the report, in 1880. (P. 23.)

[b] Frequent opportunities for extra earnings ("without exception"); estimates of manufacturers on extra earnings for overtime vary from 10 to 25 or 50 percent; overtime was paid at regular price. Hours vary from summer to winter and also vary widely even among employees of the same establishments; the average for non-pieceworkers was 10 per day. Nothing was said about any hour reductions during 1860-80. (Pp. 27-34.)

[c] Includes manufacture of all grades of carriages and wagons. The usual hours were 10 per day, some establishments reporting shorter hours in winter, longer hours during spring and summer. The few firms giving historical information on hours reported no change since 1860 or since reports began. (Pp. 410-426.)

[d] Includes manufacture of cigarettes and smoking and plug tobacco. No allowances except free tobacco and cigars. Wages generally paid in cash, but in one southern firm employing colored labor, a large portion of wages were paid in provisions, firewood, etc. When paid in kind, rates were much higher. Hours ranged from 8 to 10 in cigar shops, averaged 10 in fine cut and plug tobacco. The three firms giving historical information on hours reported no change in normal hours during 1860-80. (Pp. 39-40.)

[e] Based on very few returns, since most firms seemed disinclined to give information on wages because their rates were so low. Hours varied between 10 and 13 depending on occupation, establishment, or time of year. The one firm giving information on hours changes over time indicated no change in hours during 1860-80. (Pp. 51-53.)

[f] "Very satisfactory" returns of wages, including returns from some of the oldest and best known mills in the nation. Includes manufacture of sheetings, shirtings, ginghams, dress goods, cretonnes, jeans, tickings, sacks, quilts, thread, yarn, etc. Opportunities for extra earnings were seldom available to strictly cotton-mill employees—because of the expense of operating mills with only a few hands—but they were often available to cloth room or repair work employees or to others during peak season demand. Many firms provided housing or board at reduced rates; some gave free garden land or pasture. The overwhelming majority of firms reported hours unchanged at 11 per day throughout 1860-80, but there was some reduction in the number working more than 11 hours and a substantial increase in the number working fewer than 11 hours. (Pp. 327-328.)

TABLE A-3, *continued*

Industry	No. of Estab.	1860	1861	1862	1863	1864	1865	1866	1867	1868	1869
					WESTERN STATES						
Weighted average	25	1.74	1.85	1.93	2.11	2.29	2.39	2.42	2.44	2.43	2.43
Breweries and distilleries	1	1.01	1.01	1.20	1.39	1.73	2.02	2.02	2.02	2.02	1.97
Carriage and wagon works	1	1.56	1.56	1.40	1.35	1.46	1.67	1.67	1.75	1.77	1.77
Cigars and tobacco	2	1.60	1.59	2.21	2.56	2.87	2.89	3.04	3.16	3.18	3.26
Clothing	1	2.33	2.86	3.10	3.41	3.41	3.41	3.31	3.23	3.23	3.23
Flour and grist mills	4	1.73	1.70	1.84	2.14	2.45	2.56	2.69	2.72	2.71	2.68
Furniture	6	2.00	2.00	2.04	2.09	2.10	2.12	2.14	2.16	2.16	2.17
Iron blast furnaces, etc.	1	1.60	1.60	1.60	1.89	2.74	2.76	2.73	2.56	2.61	2.72
Machinery	2	1.38	1.48	1.53	1.77	1.95	2.06	2.17	2.13	2.08	2.08
Paper	1	1.04	1.04	1.04	1.27	1.39	1.46	1.54	1.54	1.40	1.22
Saw and planing mills	3	1.45	1.46	1.48	1.76	2.02	2.31	2.34	2.32	2.33	2.32
Stove foundries, etc.	1	1.59	1.78	1.97	2.06	2.17	2.19	2.19	2.06	1.97	1.94
Tanneries	1	1.34	1.40	1.29	1.53	1.98	2.08	2.19	2.23	2.27	2.26
Woolen manufactures	1	1.26	1.33	1.49	1.53	1.76	1.88	1.91	1.92	1.79	1.78

Industry	1870	1871	1872	1873	1874	1875	1876	1877	1878	1879	1880
Weighted average	2.42	2.45	2.45	2.48	2.32	2.32	2.29	2.26	2.25	2.27	2.03
Breweries and distilleries	1.97	1.82	1.82	1.73	1.73	1.73	1.82	1.82	1.82	2.02	2.02
Carriage and wagon works	1.77	1.77	1.77	1.77	1.60	1.50	1.48	1.48	1.52	1.73	1.73
Cigars and tobacco	3.24	3.20	3.03	2.91	2.88	2.80	2.78	2.82	2.80	2.80	2.85
Clothing	3.23	3.12	3.12	3.12	3.12	3.12	3.12	3.12	3.12	3.12	3.12
Flour and grist mills	2.69	2.68	2.63	2.62	2.46	2.49	2.34	2.30	2.19	2.20	2.19
Furniture	2.16	2.18	2.17	2.15	2.08	2.05	2.04	1.99	1.99	2.02	2.02
Iron blast furnaces, etc.	2.76	2.63	2.85	2.83	2.31	2.27	2.05	1.91	1.90	1.79	2.19
Machinery	2.18	2.19	2.19	2.19	1.97	1.86	1.78	1.76	1.73	1.72	1.85
Paper	1.09	1.09	1.09	1.09	1.09	1.09	1.11	1.11	1.24	1.24	1.25
Saw and planing mills	2.31	2.64	2.63	2.88	2.79	2.71	2.73	2.66	2.64	2.60	2.76
Stove foundries, etc.	1.92	1.94	1.95	1.95	1.81	1.78	1.78	1.78	1.92	1.94	1.94
Tanneries	2.26	2.25	2.27	2.27	2.19	2.18	2.04	2.00	1.99	1.96	1.93
Woolen manufactures	1.79	1.79	1.86	1.82	1.82	1.82	1.75	1.75	1.75	1.75	1.76

g Includes manufacture of lamp chimneys, and druggists' and chemists' flint ware; does not include the re-working of glass. Production restricted by the trade unions. In window glass, since the men were paid by quality of glass produced, it was not possible to tell how much they made until glass had been inspected. During the delay, sometimes consuming several weeks, the men were advanced market money, and final settlements were made at end of the "fire"—usually in June. A few plants report payment by workers to underhands. Hours typically 10 per day, varying from 9 to 12. Those few firms giving historical information on hours reported little or no change in length of normal workday during 1860-80. (Pp. 78-102.)

h Some schedules gave wages for one year and stated that these rates had been paid for many years without change. Hours vary with supply of water and kind of work, ranging generally between 10 and 12. Two 12-hour shifts were reported in many mills, except wheat and flour. The few firms giving historical information on hours reported little or no change in length of workday during 1860-80. (Pp. 54-56.)

TABLE A-3, *continued*

Industry	No. of Estab.	1860	1861	1862	1863	1864	1865	1866	1867	1868	1869
				EASTERN	STATES						
Weighted average	37	1.23	1.28	1.32	1.39	1.62	1.71	1.80	1.82	1.83	1.83
Brickmaking	2	1.18	1.16	1.18	1.33	1.41	1.73	1.96	2.15	2.36	2.24
Carriage and wagon works	1	1.44	1.49	1.63	1.99	2.33	2.35	2.35	2.35	2.35	2.35
Cigars and tobacco	1	1.35	1.35	1.35	1.35	1.46	1.46	1.58	1.58	1.60	1.60
Clothing	2	0.97	1.08	1.20	1.25	1.33	1.35	1.35	1.34	1.29	1.27
Cotton manufactures	5	0.90	0.91	0.91	0.90	1.03	1.18	1.36	1.42	1.38	1.39
Flint and window glass	2	1.46	1.46	1.45	1.63	1.76	1.75	2.49	2.41	2.41	2.42
Furniture	2	1.55	1.55	1.56	1.56	2.27	2.27	2.28	2.28	2.30	2.30
Hardware, cutlery	4	1.68	1.69	1.74	1.97	2.15	2.23	2.36	2.37	2.35	2.40
Iron blast furnaces, etc.	6	1.26	1.20	1.28	1.54	1.94	2.15	2.07	2.09	2.08	2.15
Machinery	1	1.33	1.40	1.41	1.54	2.03	2.01	2.08	2.18	2.19	2.14
Paper	5	1.19	1.38	1.41	1.52	1.66	1.49	1.73	1.76	1.77	1.79
Saw and planing mills	1	1.73	1.73	1.73	1.68	1.59	1.59	1.59	1.59	1.75	1.75
Stove foundries, etc.	1	1.82	1.82	1.82	1.46	1.64	1.96	2.30	2.30	2.39	2.38
Tin and sheet iron	1	1.68	1.93	2.07	2.61	2.86	3.29	3.29	3.39	3.39	3.39
Woolen manufactures	3	0.94	0.94	0.97	0.95	1.13	1.39	1.48	1.41	1.43	1.44

	1870	1871	1872	1873	1874	1875	1876	1877	1878	1879	1880
Weighted average	1.84	1.87	1.88	1.88	1.81	1.78	1.73	1.68	1.66	1.62	1.68
Brickmaking	2.30	2.27	2.23	2.17	2.09	1.95	1.84	1.73	1.64	1.53	1.68
Carriage and wagon works	2.36	2.36	2.34	2.30	2.30	2.29	2.27	2.27	2.08	2.08	2.41
Cigars and tobacco	1.64	1.64	1.67	1.67	1.67	1.67	1.58	1.54	1.54	1.54	1.54
Clothing	1.26	1.24	1.22	1.27	1.28	1.28	1.33	1.37	1.40	1.39	1.39
Cotton manufactures	1.42	1.49	1.49	1.51	1.48	1.41	1.37	1.32	1.30	1.24	1.29
Flint and window glass	2.47	2.47	2.48	2.48	2.48	2.48	2.48	2.49	2.33	2.33	2.33
Furniture	2.30	2.30	2.32	2.31	2.30	2.39	2.39	2.39	2.39	2.39	2.40
Hardware, cutlery	2.41	2.41	2.42	2.35	2.20	2.21	2.17	2.12	2.12	2.12	2.24
Iron blast furnaces, etc.	2.13	2.11	2.22	2.18	1.93	1.75	1.61	1.55	1.49	1.53	1.73
Machinery	2.13	2.27	2.29	2.27	2.31	2.31	2.24	2.09	2.02	1.92	2.00
Paper	1.86	1.92	1.98	1.99	1.97	1.82	1.94	1.93	1.86	1.87	1.71
Saw and planing mills	1.75	1.75	1.75	1.75	1.78	1.78	1.75	1.78	1.78	1.75	1.78
Stove foundries, etc.	2.48	2.42	2.42	2.40	2.43	2.45	2.09	1.85	1.82	1.68	1.87
Tin and sheet iron	3.18	3.18	3.18	3.46	2.25	2.25	2.25	2.25	2.43	2.29	2.29
Woolen manufactures	1.51	1.49	1.51	1.50	1.43	1.42	1.34	1.29	1.28	1.27	1.31

[i] Includes furniture of all kinds, cabinetwork, and wooden ware. A great deal of this was piece-work. Shorter in winter than in summer. A frequency distribution on length of workday revealed that the overwhelming majority of firms kept hours unchanged at 10 per day during 1860-80, but there was a small increase in the number reporting less than 10 hours. (Pp. 433-434.)

[j] Includes manufacture of building and marine hardware, hammers, saws, cutlery. Some extra earnings for overtime at certain seasons; no allowances except where houses and gardens are provided cheaper than going rates; few expenses for furnishing own tools or for spoiling work. Over the entire period 1860-80, hours of labor were remarkably uniform—at 10 hours in all but two establishments. (Pp. 154-155.)

[k] Also rolling mills and nail factories. Iron blast furnaces include furnaces using anthracite, bituminous or charcoal fuel. Most of wage rates quoted were for furnace labor. Rolling mills and

TABLE A-3 *continued*

Industry	No. of Estab.	1860	1861	1862	1863	1864	1865	1866	1867	1868	1869
				SOUTHERN STATES							
Weighted average	5	0.99					1.07	0.98	0.98	0.98	0.98
Cigars and tobacco	1	0.83					0.83	0.83	0.83	0.83	0.83
Paper	1	0.85					0.57	0.92	0.92	0.99	0.95
Saw and planing mills	2	1.13					1.37	1.17	1.17	1.17	1.17

	1870	1871	1872	1873	1874	1875	1876	1877	1878	1879	1880
Weighted average	1.07	1.08	1.08	1.09	1.14	1.15	1.15	1.16	1.14	1.15	1.17
Cigars and tobacco	0.83	0.83	0.83	0.83	0.83	0.83	0.83	0.83	0.83	0.83	0.83
Paper	0.98	1.06	1.07	1.10	0.98	1.05	1.02	1.00	0.89	0.88	0.97
Saw and planing mills	1.38	1.38	1.38	1.38	1.50	1.49	1.49	1.49	1.47	1.47	1.50

nail factories include mills which convert pig iron into various forms of wrought iron. At some furnaces a system of bounties was paid when output was over a certain number of tons per day. At many furnaces in remote areas and in some rolling mills and nail factories, free housing, free fuel, and free land for gardening was allowed. Among charcoal furnaces quite a number of deductions were made for tools, power, and lights. Among rolling mills and nail factories, much of the skilled work was paid for at a certain contract price per ton, out of which the head workman paid his assistant; for instance, puddlers and heaters pay their helpers, rollers their assistants, nailers their machine feeders. These tonnage or keg rates have a very interesting history, for in many sections of the country a sliding scale system prevailed through much of the period. Under this system the rate rose and fell in accordance with the selling price of iron—though there was a certain minimum below which the rate was not supposed to fall. The arrangement was subject to frequent breakdown as a result of failure to agree on the proper rate. These quotations were not proportionally numerous when the wages of all rolling mill labor are considered, and have been omitted from the averages of daily wages. Cash payments were the rule, but many blast furnaces and rolling mills in remote areas maintained stores and permitted workers to trade on credit of their earnings—some as an accommodation to workers, others as a profit-making device. Many firms reported they had abandoned payment in store-orders as they were too bothersome. Hours were 12 per day at blast furnaces; hours per day at rolling mills were very irregular—where stated they tended to be 10 hours. The wages for some trades, e.g. blast engineers, were quoted on a weekly basis; where this was done they were converted to a daily basis on the assumption of a 7-day week. Only two firms gave information on whether hours had changed in the past. One indicated no change, the other a drop from 10 to 9 hours in 1876. (Pp. 110-111; 197-204.)

[1] Includes machine shops and manufacture of locomotives, engines, woodworking machines, machine tools, and sewing machines. Frequent overtime earnings, some at time and a quarter or time and a half. The 10-hour day was almost universal in this industry in 1880. Two firms reported 9 hours in winter. A number of firms gave information on the history of hours, two firms reporting a temporary reduction to 7½ hours during part of the depression of the 1870's, but the great majority reported no change. (Pp. 168-196.)

[m] Includes manufacture of many grades of book, news, writing, envelope, wall, colored, wrapping, and manila papers; also of straw-, leather-, and cardboard. Tour men normally work 12 hours a day; day men usually 10 hours. In several establishments giving hours of labor for 1845 and 1850 hours worked were unchanged up to 1880. (Pp. 264-265.)

[n] Includes also working of lumber into house, bridge, and car building materials, boxes, barrels, and staves. Some establishments are only saw mills. Widely varying opportunities for overtime, on the whole these were not very great. Allowances depend on locality; include free homes, gardens, and, in rural localities, board. Cost to men of furnishing own tools was not more than 1 percent of wages paid; some instances of payment in kind in South and West. Typical hours 10-12 in summer, 8-10 in winter. Several firms reported reduction of hours during 1860-80; one reported an increase. (Pp. 460-461.)

TABLE A-3 *concluded*

[o] Includes stove, car wheel, and general foundries. Little or no extra allowances were mentioned except for a 5 percent year-end bonus in the case of one stove foundry firm and some occasional "prize money" for working full time. Ten hours was the normal workday in all establishments, but there was a shorter workday in winter and a longer one in summer in some establishments. The three establishments giving historical information on hours reported no appreciable change in average workday during the periods covered by this report. (Pp. 135-136, 139-140, 149.)

[p] Includes manufacture of sole, harness, and belting leather, with some kip, calf, glove, and buck. A frequency distribution of normal hours worked per day in firms at five-year intervals indicates no change during 1860-80, with the overwhelming majority of firms reporting a 10-hour day during that period. (Pp. 307-308).

[q] Includes canning tin, copper, sheet iron work; plumbing and gas fittings; pump, refrigerator and filter manufacturing. (Pp. 233-234.)

[r] "Very complete" wage tabulations, covering small and large establishments. Opportunities for extra earnings through overtime existed for some classes of employees at mills with seasonal output, but little overtime as a rule prevailed at the large establishments. Low rents on housing and cheap boarding rates were allowed at many mills and may have a material effect on wage comparisons. No payments were made to underhands or for tools. Hours were typically 10-11 per day. A frequency distribution of hours worked at quinquennial dates for 1860 to 1880 showed that nearly half of all firms reported 11 hours throughout 1860-80, and another very large group reported 10 hours during this period. However, the proportion of firms reporting more than 11 hours tended to decline and the proportion reporting less than 11 hours increased substantially during the twenty year period. (Pp. 374-376.)

TABLE A-4

Daily Wage-Rates in 10 "Manufacturing" Occupations and 4 "Building" Occupations from Bulletin 18 of the Department of Labor, Weighted by Number Reported Attached to the Occupations at the Decennial Censuses; United States, by Regions, Annually 1870-1880
(current dollars)

Occupation	1870	1871	1872	1873	1874	1875	1876	1877	1878	1879	1880
				UNITED STATES							
Weighted average, 10 manufacturing occupations	2.05	2.01	2.04	2.04	1.97	1.93	1.90	1.77	1.71	1.69	1.72
Blacksmiths	2.74	2.81	2.82	2.81	2.77	2.70	2.64	2.58	2.55	2.51	2.53
Boilermakers	2.52	2.49	2.51	2.54	2.50	2.44	2.45	2.42	2.34	2.40	2.38
Compositors	3.10	3.11	3.09	3.11	3.05	3.04	3.09	3.00	2.83	2.82	2.84
Cabinetmakers	2.47	2.37	2.36	2.32	2.30	2.23	2.19	2.15	2.11	2.12	2.16
Iron molders	3.06	2.96	2.97	2.94	2.71	2.57	2.41	2.35	2.32	2.23	2.41
Laborers	1.75	1.70	1.73	1.74	1.68	1.66	1.64	1.47	1.41	1.41	1.43
Machinists	2.70	2.62	2.62	2.66	2.63	2.54	2.45	2.43	2.35	2.31	2.37
Stonecutters	3.61	3.59	4.12	3.86	3.44	3.22	2.92	2.66	2.64	2.54	2.65
Patternmakers, iron works	3.08	3.03	3.04	3.09	3.09	3.05	2.99	2.94	3.19	2.91	2.77
Teamsters	1.96	1.97	1.99	1.98	1.99	1.97	1.98	1.96	1.95	1.93	1.96
Weighted average, 4 building occupations	2.97	3.02	3.03	2.96	2.85	2.78	2.67	2.54	2.46	2.47	2.55
Bricklayers and masons	3.51	3.72	3.83	3.64	3.31	3.31	3.11	2.87	2.76	2.83	2.85
Carpenters and joiners	2.88	2.91	2.88	2.86	2.78	2.67	2.59	2.45	2.35	2.37	2.45
Painters, house	2.69	2.68	2.77	2.64	2.53	2.57	2.48	2.44	2.42	2.36	2.50
Plumbers	3.31	3.29	3.13	3.11	3.08	3.13	3.11	3.08	3.06	2.93	3.05
Weighted average, 14 occupations	2.29	2.27	2.28	2.26	2.17	2.13	2.07	1.94	1.87	1.86	1.90

table continues on following pages

135

Table A-4, continued

Occupation	1881	1882	1883	1884	1885	1886	1887	1888	1889	1890
Weighted average, 10 manufacturing occupations	1.80	1.87	1.89	1.90	1.87	1.89	1.92	1.92	1.91	1.93
Blacksmiths	2.59	2.60	2.62	2.67	2.58	2.62	2.70	2.68	2.63	2.63
Boilermakers	2.37	2.60	2.55	2.55	2.45	2.45	2.48	2.53	2.51	2.50
Compositors	2.85	2.85	2.84	2.93	2.92	2.89	2.90	2.89	2.88	2.88
Cabinetmakers	2.31	2.30	2.30	2.29	2.28	2.33	2.30	2.33	2.33	2.33
Iron molders	2.62	2.52	2.59	2.59	2.48	2.51	2.57	2.55	2.51	2.54
Laborers	1.49	1.57	1.59	1.58	1.56	1.56	1.57	1.56	1.56	1.56
Machinists	2.43	2.55	2.49	2.58	2.47	2.49	2.54	2.54	2.54	2.52
Stonecutters	3.03	3.10	3.22	3.34	3.18	3.28	3.35	3.43	3.48	3.57
Patternmakers, iron works	2.83	2.89	2.89	2.99	2.84	2.90	2.96	3.00	2.93	3.01
Teamsters	1.95	1.96	1.98	1.92	1.95	1.98	1.98	1.99	1.93	2.01
Weighted average, 4 building occupations	2.72	2.81	2.88	2.92	2.89	2.89	2.90	2.92	2.91	2.94
Bricklayers and masons	3.24	3.46	3.51	3.63	3.63	3.61	3.71	3.68	3.72	3.88
Carpenters and joiners	2.60	2.67	2.70	2.73	2.68	2.67	2.65	2.67	2.66	2.67
Painters, house	2.59	2.64	2.81	2.81	2.79	2.82	2.86	2.87	2.83	2.83
Plumbers	3.10	3.06	3.22	3.24	3.26	3.31	3.38	3.38	3.39	3.37
Weighted average, 14 occupations	2.00	2.07	2.11	2.13	2.11	2.13	2.16	2.17	2.17	2.19

Table A-4, continued

Occupation	1870	1871	1872	1873	1874	1875	1876	1877	1878	1879	1880
			WESTERN CITIES								
Weighted average, 10 manufacturing occupations	2.06	2.06	2.12	2.15	2.01	1.98	1.93	1.86	1.81	1.79	1.83
Blacksmiths	2.85	2.82	2.86	2.89	2.86	2.92	2.80	2.71	2.70	2.66	2.64
Boilermakers	2.91	2.88	2.90	2.98	2.96	2.87	2.80	2.74	2.79	2.75	2.75
Compositors	3.24	3.31	3.29	3.32	3.30	3.35	3.32	3.29	3.02	3.04	3.05
Cabinetmakers	2.50	2.30	2.21	2.29	2.29	2.19	2.22	2.29	2.26	2.14	2.26
Iron molders	3.24	3.28	3.27	3.25	2.89	2.78	2.64	2.48	2.46	2.38	2.56
Laborers	1.75	1.75	1.83	1.87	1.73	1.69	1.64	1.59	1.54	1.52	1.56
Machinists	3.00	3.00	2.96	2.97	2.81	2.76	2.64	2.54	2.50	2.44	2.53
Stonecutters	3.30	3.33	4.29	3.53	3.22	3.11	2.99	2.68	2.58	2.59	2.70
Patternmakers, iron works	3.09	3.14	3.14	3.13	2.99	2.98	2.91	2.79	2.74	2.79	2.73
Teamsters	1.98	2.00	2.03	2.05	1.95	1.96	2.00	2.00	1.95	1.94	1.97
Weighted average, 4 building occupations	2.83	3.00	3.01	2.90	2.71	2.67	2.68	2.64	2.54	2.49	2.47
Bricklayers and masons	3.42	3.99	4.05	3.64	3.31	3.15	3.42	3.15	3.21	3.22	3.30
Carpenters and joiners	2.77	2.88	2.85	2.84	2.65	2.63	2.63	2.60	2.42	2.37	2.30
Painters, house	2.47	2.48	2.67	2.46	2.37	2.33	2.33	2.33	2.29	2.20	2.26
Plumbers	3.50	3.44	3.11	3.18	3.32	3.35	3.27	3.30	3.30	3.27	3.23
Weighted average, 14 occupations	2.25	2.29	2.33	2.32	2.17	2.13	2.10	2.03	1.96	1.93	1.96

Table A-4, continued

Occupation	1881	1882	1883	1884	1885	1886	1887	1888	1889	1890
Weighted average, 10 manufacturing occupations	1.89	1.92	1.93	1.92	1.90	1.92	1.94	1.95	1.96	1.96
Blacksmiths	2.74	2.73	2.69	2.71	2.67	2.67	2.68	2.70	2.71	2.70
Boilermakers	2.71	2.80	2.76	2.79	2.77	2.60	2.59	2.66	2.65	2.65
Compositors	3.00	3.01	2.99	2.99	2.99	2.97	2.97	2.95	2.95	2.96
Cabinetmakers	2.20	2.18	2.09	2.06	2.06	2.23	2.16	2.17	2.17	2.19
Iron molders	2.70	2.71	2.74	2.73	2.61	2.59	2.73	2.74	2.61	2.65
Laborers	1.60	1.63	1.64	1.61	1.59	1.59	1.59	1.58	1.59	1.58
Machinists	2.61	2.64	2.66	2.66	2.61	2.60	2.66	2.66	2.68	2.66
Stonecutters	2.99	3.14	3.25	3.23	3.12	3.42	3.50	3.61	3.61	3.79
Patternmakers, iron works	2.83	2.84	2.83	2.83	2.81	2.82	2.75	2.80	2.76	2.82
Teamsters	1.98	1.97	1.94	1.95	1.93	2.00	2.01	2.01	2.01	2.02
Weighted average, 4 building occupations	2.67	2.72	2.80	2.81	2.78	2.76	2.78	2.78	2.75	2.74
Bricklayers and masons	3.70	3.74	3.93	3.93	4.07	3.95	4.14	4.09	4.18	4.20
Carpenters and joiners	2.47	2.51	2.56	2.60	2.52	2.51	2.49	2.49	2.43	2.42
Painters, house	2.40	2.53	2.58	2.56	2.54	2.53	2.53	2.57	2.55	2.49
Plumbers	3.36	3.08	3.35	3.34	3.33	3.45	3.48	3.45	3.45	3.46
Weighted average, 14 occupations	2.05	2.10	2.12	2.13	2.11	2.12	2.15	2.16	2.16	2.16

Table A-4, *continued*

EASTERN CITIES

Occupation	1870	1871	1872	1873	1874	1875	1876	1877	1878	1879	1880
Weighted average, 10 manufacturing occupations	2.07	2.00	2.00	1.99	1.96	1.91	1.88	1.71	1.65	1.63	1.66
Blacksmiths	2.65	2.81	2.79	2.76	2.73	2.58	2.55	2.51	2.45	2.40	2.46
Boilermakers	2.27	2.25	2.29	2.29	2.26	2.21	2.26	2.25	2.12	2.23	2.20
Compositors	3.03	3.01	3.00	3.00	2.92	2.88	2.99	2.86	2.73	2.71	2.74
Cabinetmakers	2.44	2.40	2.41	2.32	2.30	2.24	2.15	2.07	2.02	2.09	2.09
Iron molders	2.97	2.81	2.81	2.79	2.61	2.46	2.29	2.27	2.23	2.14	2.31
Laborers	1.77	1.68	1.68	1.67	1.66	1.63	1.62	1.39	1.32	1.32	1.33
Machinists	2.63	2.50	2.51	2.56	2.57	2.47	2.38	2.39	2.29	2.26	2.31
Stonecutters	3.90	3.82	3.98	4.16	3.68	3.31	2.84	2.63	2.68	2.47	2.59
Patternmakers, iron works	3.07	2.99	2.99	3.07	3.11	3.06	3.02	2.99	3.34	2.94	2.78
Teamsters	1.97	1.96	1.98	1.95	2.03	1.98	1.98	1.95	1.96	1.94	1.96
Weighted average, 4 building occupations	3.07	3.06	3.06	3.00	2.92	2.86	2.67	2.50	2.43	2.47	2.63
Bricklayers and masons	3.58	3.61	3.74	3.66	3.33	3.43	2.97	2.73	2.52	2.62	2.60
Carpenters and joiners	2.98	2.95	2.92	2.88	2.89	2.71	2.57	2.37	2.32	2.39	2.59
Painters, house	2.83	2.81	2.84	2.75	2.66	2.73	2.59	2.52	2.52	2.48	2.67
Plumbers	3.27	3.26	3.14	3.10	3.01	3.07	3.06	3.03	2.99	2.83	3.01
Weighted average, 14 occupations	2.33	2.27	2.27	2.24	2.19	2.13	2.06	1.89	1.82	1.81	1.86

Table A-4, continued

Occupation	1881	1882	1883	1884	1885	1886	1887	1888	1889	1890
Weighted average, 10 manufacturing occupations	1.75	1.84	1.84	1.90	1.87	1.88	1.90	1.90	1.90	1.92
Blacksmiths	2.50	2.51	2.58	2.66	2.52	2.60	2.74	2.68	2.58	2.58
Boilermakers	2.22	2.35	2.45	2.42	2.30	2.38	2.43	2.46	2.43	2.40
Compositors	2.77	2.76	2.77	2.90	2.88	2.85	2.87	2.86	2.84	2.83
Cabinetmakers	2.36	2.37	2.42	2.42	2.40	2.39	2.38	2.42	2.44	2.41
Iron molders	2.57	2.41	2.49	2.51	2.40	2.47	2.46	2.42	2.45	2.47
Laborers	1.40	1.54	1.56	1.56	1.55	1.54	1.54	1.53	1.52	1.55
Machinists	2.36	2.52	2.43	2.56	2.41	2.44	2.50	2.49	2.48	2.46
Stonecutters	3.07	3.07	3.20	3.46	3.25	3.19	3.25	3.32	3.41	3.43
Patternmakers, iron works	2.82	2.91	2.91	3.07	2.86	2.94	3.07	3.10	3.02	3.11
Teamsters	1.94	1.98	2.02	1.92	1.97	1.98	1.97	1.99	2.01	2.02
Weighted average, 4 building occupations	2.79	2.91	2.98	3.03	3.00	3.01	3.04	3.05	3.06	3.11
Bricklayers and masons	3.00	3.33	3.30	3.50	3.40	3.44	3.51	3.49	3.49	3.73
Carpenters and joiners	2.72	2.83	2.85	2.88	2.85	2.84	2.82	2.85	2.88	2.89
Painters, house	2.72	2.74	2.99	2.98	2.97	3.03	3.10	3.10	3.06	3.10
Plumbers	3.02	3.07	3.19	3.23	3.26	3.27	3.35	3.38	3.39	3.35
Weighted average, 14 occupations	1.97	2.08	2.11	2.16	2.14	2.16	2.18	2.19	2.19	2.23

Table A-4, *continued*

SOUTHERN CITIES

Occupation	1870	1871	1872	1873	1874	1875	1876	1877	1878	1879	1880
Weighted average, 10 manufacturing occupations	1.82	1.81	1.79	1.78	1.74	1.91	1.89	1.70	1.68	1.67	1.67
Blacksmiths	2.77	2.77	2.77	2.77	2.58	2.45	2.45	2.45	2.45	2.45	2.45
Boilermakers	3.63	3.64	3.61	3.63	3.63	3.61	3.65	3.63	3.64	3.60	3.50
Compositors	3.33	3.29	3.27	3.25	3.23	3.22	2.79	3.05	2.81	2.81	2.82
Cabinetmakers	3.50	3.00	3.33	3.00	3.25	3.38	3.38	3.33	3.08	3.08	2.88
Iron molders	3.44	3.25	3.30	3.25	3.42	3.25	2.88	2.88	2.87	2.75	2.75
Laborers	1.50	1.50	1.50	1.50	1.50	1.75	1.75	1.51	1.50	1.50	1.50
Machinists	2.40	2.89	2.83	2.72	2.63	2.54	2.29	2.32	2.34	2.29	2.30
Stonecutters	3.91	3.87	3.83	3.79	3.40	3.24	3.16	2.90	2.91	2.92	2.93
Patternmakers, iron works	4.25	3.83	3.88	4.00	4.00	4.00	3.00	3.00	3.00	2.92	3.00
Teamsters	1.71	1.83	1.84	1.83	1.80	1.83	1.80	1.80	1.76	1.73	1.73
Weighted average, 4 building occupations	2.64	2.68	2.79	2.77	2.53	2.56	2.52	2.36	2.30	2.24	2.24
Bricklayers and masons	3.08	3.38	3.42	3.40	2.92	2.88	2.84	2.84	2.84	2.73	2.84
Carpenters and joiners	2.60	2.60	2.69	2.70	2.55	2.60	2.55	2.31	2.23	2.19	2.15
Painters, house	2.27	2.27	2.54	2.41	1.88	1.88	1.88	2.00	2.00	1.87	2.00
Plumbers	2.91	2.89	2.92	2.91	2.94	2.94	2.91	2.93	2.89	2.93	2.57
Weighted average, 14 occupations	2.06	2.06	2.06	2.04	1.94	2.06	2.03	1.84	1.81	1.79	1.78

141

Table A-4, *concluded*

Occupation	1881	1882	1883	1884	1885	1886	1887	1888	1889	1890
					SOUTHERN CITIES					
Weighted average, 10 manufacturing occupations	1.67	1.67	1.68	1.68	1.69	1.70	1.89	1.90	1.89	1.73
Blacksmiths	2.45	2.45	2.46	2.46	2.46	2.47	2.47	2.48	2.48	2.48
Boilermakers	3.00	3.00	3.00	3.00	2.63	2.63	2.64	2.60	2.64	2.63
Compositors	2.82	2.82	2.82	2.82	2.82	2.82	2.82	2.82	2.81	2.81
Cabinetmakers	2.88	2.88	2.55	2.88	3.06	2.75	2.53	2.67	2.63	2.83
Iron molders	2.75	2.80	2.88	2.80	2.75	2.57	2.88	2.88	2.88	2.88
Laborers	1.50	1.50	1.50	1.50	1.50	1.50	1.75	1.75	1.75	1.50
Machinists	2.29	2.04	2.04	2.07	2.08	2.08	2.06	2.08	2.08	2.08
Stonecutters	2.96	3.00	2.96	2.93	2.93	2.93	2.93	2.93	2.93	2.93
Patternmakers, iron works	3.00	3.00	3.00	3.00	3.00	2.88	3.00	3.00	3.00	2.88
Teamsters	1.71	1.69	1.71	1.72	1.72	1.82	1.86	1.87	1.76	1.75
Weighted average, 4 building occupations	2.33	2.35	2.40	2.45	2.44	2.33	2.28	2.34	2.33	2.42
Bricklayers and masons	2.96	2.99	3.17	3.17	3.18	3.20	2.98	2.99	3.07	3.22
Carpenters and joiners	2.25	2.27	2.32	2.31	2.29	2.14	2.17	2.25	2.22	2.35
Painters, house	2.00	2.00	2.00	2.39	2.39	2.39	2.11	2.10	2.10	1.95
Plumbers	2.64	2.60	2.32	2.34	2.33	2.33	2.31	2.26	2.35	2.34
Weighted average, 14 occupations	1.81	1.82	1.84	1.86	1.87	1.86	1.99	2.02	2.01	1.93

Based on the data of twelve large United States cities comprising: *eastern cities*, Baltimore, Boston, New York, Philadelphia, Pittsburgh; *western cities*, Chicago, Cincinnati, St. Louis, St. Paul, San Francisco; *southern cities*, Richmond, New Orleans. For explanation of the method of weighting, see Chapter 2, above.

Data for the greenback period up to 1879 were converted in this study into greenback currency, as originally reported by the establishment. The Department of Labor had converted these into gold on the basis of the currency value of gold given in the *American Almanac* and published in Bulletin 18. These conversion rates were used to reconvert the data into the currency value of wages.

Source of wage data: *Bulletin of the Department of Labor*, No. 18, September 1898, ed. Carroll D. Wright, pp. 665–682.

TABLE A-5

Hourly Wages of Five Skilled Occupations and of Laborers, Various Manufacturing Establishments, Aldrich Report, January and July 1860-1890 (current dollars)

Occupation	No. of Estab.	1860 Jan.	1860 July	1861 Jan.	1861 July	1862 Jan.	1862 July	1863 Jan.	1863 July	1864 Jan.	1864 July	1865 Jan.	1865 July	1866 Jan.	1866 July	1867 Jan.	1867 July	1868 Jan.	1868 July	1869 Jan.	1869 July
Blacksmiths	11	0.180	0.178	0.176	0.174	0.189	0.195	0.206	0.224	0.239	0.269	0.281	0.280	0.288	0.290	0.298	0.303	0.303	0.302	0.303	0.306
Carpenters	2	.182	.182	.184	.181	.185	.185	.203	.216	.249	.266	.281	.292	.297	.314	.319	.356	.330	.355	.355	.358
Engineers	6	.148	.148	.147	.149	.149	.150	.158	.165	.167	.187	.203	.204	.204	.214	.215	.220	.221	.225	.225	.228
Machinists	14	.158	.158	.160	.162	.159	.161	.169	.174	.189	.221	.231	.233	.245	.251	.259	.261	.263	.258	.260	.260
Painters	1	.125	.125	.125	.125	.175	.175	.175	.175	.175	.175	.175	.175	.175	.175	.175	.175	.175	.175	.175	.175
Average[a]	34	.164	.163	.163	.164	.169	.172	.181	.191	.204	.232	.244	.245	.253	.259	.265	.270	.270	.270	.271	.273
Laborers[b]		.098		.097		.097		.111		.130		.148		.152		.153		.154		.156	

Occupation	1870 Jan.	1870 July	1871 Jan.	1871 July	1872 Jan.	1872 July	1873 Jan.	1873 July	1874 Jan.	1874 July	1875 Jan.	1875 July	1876 Jan.	1876 July	1877 Jan.	1877 July	1878 Jan.	1878 July	1879 Jan.	1879 July
Blacksmiths	.298	.304	.306	.307	.308	.317	.324	.326	.324	.322	.314	.312	.306	.287	.283	.276	.275	.264	.260	.253
Carpenters	.361	.410	.413	.413	.416	.415	.414	.412	.400	.400	.400	.383	.385	.314	.315	.300	.286	.275	.273	.272
Engineers	.232	.227	.231	.231	.234	.249	.250	.254	.250	.250	.243	.243	.239	.232	.235	.229	.224	.217	.207	.200
Machinists	.264	.260	.261	.259	.261	.266	.260	.268	.264	.264	.254	.249	.240	.243	.226	.223	.219	.223	.219	.213
Painters	.175	.175	.175	.175	.175	.175	.175	.175	.175	.175	.175	.175	.175	.175	.175	.175	.175	.175	.175	.175
Average[a]	.272	.275	.277	.276	.278	.286	.286	.290	.286	.286	.278	.274	.268	.257	.250	.244	.241	.237	.232	.226
Laborers[b]	.156		.157		.159		.159		.158		.154		.149		.142		.137		.135	

Occupation	1880 Jan.	1880 July	1881 Jan.	1881 July	1882 Jan.	1882 July	1883 Jan.	1883 July	1884 Jan.	1884 July	1885 Jan.	1885 July	1886 Jan.	1886 July	1887 Jan.	1887 July	1888 Jan.	1888 July	1889 Jan.	1889 July	1890 Jan.	1890 July
Blacksmiths	.254	.259	.266	.269	.270	.269	.268	.274	.275	.276	.267	.268	.264	.269	.276	.277	.274	.275	.273	.273	.271	.271
Carpenters	.267	.276	.275	.279	.279	.320	.316	.316	.313	.313	.305	.305	.301	.340	.348	.348	.350	.320	.320	.320	.325	.322
Engineers	.201	.208	.208	.209	.209	.218	.219	.219	.226	.227	.221	.221	.227	.231	.232	.232	.234	.234	.234	.244	.244	.244
Machinists	.216	.227	.230	.236	.241	.242	.242	.243	.244	.242	.235	.239	.233	.233	.232	.233	.236	.237	.239	.239	.243	.244
Painters	.250	.250	.250	.250	.250	.250	.250	.250	.250	.250	.250	.250	.250	.250	.250	.250	.250	.250	.250	.250	.250	.250
Average[a]	.230	.238	.241	.245	.247	.251	.251	.253	.255	.255	.247	.247	.246	.251	.254	.254	.255	.256	.254	.256	.257	.257
Laborers[b]	.135		.140		.143		.147		.146		.145		.144		.149		.150		.150		.151	

Source: Compiled by the National Bureau of Economic Research, from the Aldrich Report.
[a] Weighted by number of establishments; unweighted within each occupation.
[b] Laborers in twenty establishments excluding those engaged in public works.

143

TABLE A-6

Daily Wages of Five Skilled Occupations and of Laborers, Occurring in Various Manufacturing Establishments, Weeks Report, Annually 1860-1880
(current dollars)

Occupation	No. of Estab.	1860	1861	1862	1863	1864	1865	1866	1867	1868	1869	
Blacksmiths	26	1.64	1.65	1.77	2.07	2.42	2.61	2.74	2.69	2.73	2.73	
Carpenters	10	1.65	1.80	1.97	2.09	2.58	2.68	2.77	2.75	2.67	2.68	
Engineers	25	1.61	1.65	1.72	1.87	2.19	2.33	2.44	2.38	2.35	2.40	
Machinists	15	1.61	1.66	1.77	2.05	2.28	2.56	2.73	2.73	2.66	2.66	
Painters	9	1.62	1.64	1.76	2.02	2.25	2.31	2.40	2.47	2.52	2.61	
Average[a]	85	1.62	1.67	1.78	2.00	2.33	2.50	2.62	2.59	2.58	2.60	
Laborers[b]		1.03	1.04	1.08	1.20	1.39	1.48	1.53	1.53	1.51	1.53	
		1870	1871	1872	1873	1874	1875	1876	1877	1878	1879	1880
Blacksmiths		2.68	2.66	2.69	2.70	2.52	2.41	2.32	2.27	2.23	2.21	2.31
Carpenters		2.64	2.57	2.59	2.52	2.42	2.42	2.12	2.06	2.03	2.05	2.15
Engineers		2.47	2.38	2.53	2.50	2.40	2.33	2.17	2.11	2.06	2.08	2.17
Machinists		2.67	2.72	2.72	2.73	2.53	2.47	2.34	2.29	2.29	2.35	2.45
Painters		2.67	2.67	2.70	2.68	2.60	2.35	2.20	2.09	2.04	2.08	2.21
Average[a]		2.61	2.58	2.64	2.62	2.48	2.39	2.24	2.18	2.15	2.16	2.26
Laborers[b]		1.52	1.50	1.52	1.52	1.43	1.39	1.33	1.28	1.26	1.27	1.32

Source: Compiled by the National Bureau of Economic Research, from the Weeks Report.
[a] Weighted by number of establishments; unweighted within each occupation.
[b] Laborers in seventy-eight establishments.

TABLE A-7

Daily and Hourly Wage-Rates by Sex, Age, Industry, and Number of Employees,
First Annual Report, 1885
(wage rates in current dollars)

| Industry | AVERAGE DAILY WAGE-RATES | | | | AVERAGE HOURLY WAGE-RATES | | | | Average Hours Per Day |
	Adult Males	Adult Females	Children and Youths	Total	Adult Males	Adult Females	Children and Youths	Total	
Agricultural implements	1.86		0.69	1.84	0.187		0.069	0.185	9.95
Arms and ammunition	2.02			2.02	0.202			0.202	10.00
Artisans' tools	1.59		1.12	1.55	0.159		0.112	0.155	10.00
Boots and shoes	2.05	1.24	0.75	1.71	0.206	0.125	0.076	0.172	9.93
Boxes	2.26	0.65	0.64	1.07	0.226	0.065	0.064	0.107	10.00
Bricks	1.49		0.50	1.47	0.149		0.050	0.147	10.00
Brooms	1.47			1.47	0.147			0.147	10.00
Carpetings	1.51	1.19	0.62	1.27	0.150	0.118	0.061	0.126	10.10
Carriages and wagons	2.00	1.15	0.77	1.95	0.200	0.115	0.077	0.195	10.00
Clocks and watches	2.00	1.60		1.87	0.200	0.160		0.187	10.00
Clothing	1.72	0.91	0.58	1.18	0.169	0.090	0.057	0.116	10.15
Cooking and heating apparatus	2.28		0.72	1.92	0.228		0.072	0.192	10.00
Cotton compressing	1.70			1.70	0.170			0.170	10.00
Cotton goods	1.26	0.87	0.48	0.88	0.115	0.079	0.044	0.080	10.97
Engraving and printing	3.36			3.36	0.305			0.305	11.00
Food preparations	1.86		0.77	1.80	0.158		0.066	0.153	11.75
Furniture	1.59		0.58	1.50	0.161		0.059	0.152	9.88
Glass	2.98	1.85	0.62	2.18	0.307	0.191	0.064	0.225	9.70
Jute goods	1.55	0.85	0.58	0.93	0.152	0.084	0.057	0.091	10.17
Leather	1.92	1.35	0.70	1.84	0.189	0.133	0.069	0.181	10.17
Liquors and beverages	2.01			2.01	0.173			0.173	11.63
Lumber	1.58			1.58	0.150			0.150	10.50
Machines and machinery	2.12		0.69	2.01	0.212		0.069	0.201	10.00
Metals and metallic goods	1.80		0.74	1.76	0.168		0.069	0.164	10.70
Musical instruments and materials	2.10	1.50	0.69	1.98	0.210	0.150	0.069	0.198	10.00
Oils and illuminating fluids	1.55			1.55	0.155			0.155	10.00
Paper	1.64	0.96	0.73	1.43	0.140	0.082	0.062	0.122	11.75

table continues on following pages

TABLE A-7, *continued*

Industry	AVERAGE DAILY WAGE-RATES				AVERAGE HOURLY WAGE-RATES				Average Hours Per Day
	Adult Males	Adult Females	Children and Youths	Total	Adult Males	Adult Females	Children and Youths	Total	
Print works	1.66	0.91	0.66	1.30	0.163	0.090	0.065	0.128	10.17
Railroad construction	1.68		0.61	1.62	0.168		0.061	0.162	10.00
Rubber	1.70	1.10	1.04	1.41	0.170	0.110	0.104	0.141	10.00
Silk	2.27	1.31	0.87	1.52	0.220	0.127	0.084	0.147	10.33
Stone	2.18			2.18	0.218			0.218	10.00
Tobacco	1.33	0.85	0.53	0.97	0.135	0.086	0.054	0.099	9.83
Vessels	1.77		0.70	1.74	0.177		0.070	0.174	10.00
Wooden goods	1.90		0.74	1.64	0.190		0.074	0.164	10.00
Woolen goods	1.49	1.00	0.62	1.21	0.140	0.094	0.058	0.113	10.67
Miscellaneous	1.96	0.81	1.04	1.49	0.193	0.080	0.102	0.147	10.15
Weighted averages[a]									
All manufacturing	1.79			1.44	0.174			0.140	
Industries with females	1.71	1.00			0.168	0.096		0.161	
Industries with children	1.79		0.59		0.174		0.057		
Industries represented in Aldrich Report	1.70			1.37				0.129	10.62

146

TABLE A-7, *concluded*

Industry	NUMBER OF ESTABLISHMENTS	NUMBER OF EMPLOYEES			
		Adult Males	Adult Females	Children and Youths	Total
Agricultural implements	20	5,843		84	5,927
Arms and ammunition	1	437			437
Artisans' tools	1	91		8	99
Boots and shoes	48	4,900	2,567	517	7,984
Boxes	3	112	287	31	430
Bricks	5	461		8	469
Brooms	5	359			359
Carpetings	10	6,213	4,404	1,674	12,291
Carriages and wagons	12	1,404	45	27	1,476
Clocks and watches	2	781	395		1,176
Clothing	21	1,289	1,299	551	3,139
Cooking and heating apparatus	25	4,736		1,407	6,143
Cotton compressing	1	26			26
Cotton goods	48	7,211	12,056	6,596	25,863
Engraving and printing	1	77			77
Food preparations	28	1,543		94	1,637
Furniture	8	1,332		127	1,459
Glass	29	2,580	27	1,327	3,934
Jute goods	3	161	301	213	675
Leather	12	869	28	52	949
Liquors and beverages	11	493			493
Lumber	7	834			834
Machines and machinery	15	2,357		203	2,560
Metals and metallic goods	66	20,026		736	20,762
Muscial instruments and materials	7	1,802	18	159	1,979
Oils and illuminating fluids	3	193			193
Paper	16	1,220	500	32	1,752
Print works	6	1,355	176	670	2,201
Railroad construction	5	559		31	590
Rubber	4	1,169	944	118	2,231
Silk	6	419	1,138	107	1,664
Stone	1	194			194
Tobacco	36	3,005	1,751	2,035	6,791
Vessels	5	2,576		62	2,638
Wooden goods	3	283		81	364
Woolen goods	38	4,933	2,379	1,564	8,876
Miscellaneous	7	694	356	176	1,226
Total	519	82,537	28,671	18,690	129,898
Industries with females		40,117	28,671		
Industries with children		79,143		18,690	
Industries in Aldrich Report		46,246			71,394

Source: *The First Annual Report of the Commissioner of Labor* (March 1886), p. 226.
a Computed in this study.

TABLE A-8

Hourly Wage-Rates by Sex, Age, Industry, and Number of Employees,
Dewey Report, 1890

Industry	Males 16 and over	Females 16 and over	Males Under 16	Females Under 16	Total Males	Total Females	Total
			Median Hourly Wages (current dollars)				
Agricultural implements	0.160		0.050		0.159		0.159
Breweries	.210		a		.210a	0.060	.200a
Candy					.130	.050	.080
Car and railroad shops	.200				.200		.200
Carpet mills	.150	0.090	.060	.050	.137	.081	.120
Chemicals	.140				.140		.140
Cigars	.210	.110			.210	.110	.180
Clothing	.200	.070		a	.200	.070a	.120a
Collars and cuffs		.080		.050		.072	.070
Cotton mills	.110	.090	a	a	.110a	.090a	.100a
Distilleries	.150				.150		.150
Dyeing and finishing	.120	.100	.060		.118	.100	.120
Flour mills	.200				.200		.200
Foundries and metal working	.170	.070	.060		.168	.070	.160
Furniture	.160		a		.160a		.160a
Glass	.170	.060	.060		.135	.060	.130
Iron and steel mills	.150	.080	.050		.149	.080	.150
Knitting mills	.130	.080		.050	.130	.075	.100
Lumber and planing mills	.140		.070		.138		.138
Paper mills	.140	.080			.140	.080	.130
Pianos	.160		a		.160a		.160a
Potteries and brickyards	.210				.212	.090	.190
Printing	.290	.080	.050		.280	.080	.260
Rubber	.150	.110			.150	.110	.150
Shipyards	.210				.210		.210
Shoes	.190	.100	a	a	.190a	.100a	.170a
Slaughtering	.170				.170		.170
Tanneries	.150	.060	.050		.149	.060	.150
Tobacco	.090		a		.090a	.050	.080a
Wagons and carriages	.160		.050		.158		.158
Woolen mills	.120	.100	.050	.050	.115	.094	.100
Weighted averages of medians							
All industries	.167			.050a	.165a	.084a	.153a
Industries with females	.163	.090					
Industries with male children	.163		.058a				

table continues on following page

TABLE A-8, *concluded*

Industry	Males 16 and over	Females 16 and over	Males Under 16	Females Under 16	Total Males	Total Females	Total
Agricultural implements	4,093		41		4,134		4,134
Breweries	3,123		24[a]		3,123[a]	311	3,434[a]
Candy					375	573	948
Car and railroad shops	6,131				6,131		6,131
Carpet mills	763	272	126	80	889	352	1,241
Chemicals	3,307				3,307		3,307
Cigars	697	254			697	254	951
Clothing	737	1,263		160[a]	737	1,263[a]	2,000[a]
Collars and cuffs		198		73		271	271
Cotton mills	2,880	3,877	392[a]	231[a]	2,880[a]	3,877[a]	6,757[a]
Distilleries	123				123		123
Dyeing and finishing	1,777	213	63		1,840	213	2,053
Flour mills	1,026				1,026		1,026
Foundries and metal working	23,170	617	479		23,649	617	24,266
Furniture	2,936		106[a]		2,936[a]		2,936[a]
Glass	2,774	188	1,271		4,045	188	4,233
Iron and steel mills	16,835	37	97		16,932	37	16,969
Knitting mills	280	284		57	280	341	621
Lumber and planing mills	2,227		80		2,307		2,307
Paper mills	897	224			897	224	1,121
Pianos	825		21[a]		825[a]		825[a]
Potteries and brickyards	691				691	137	828
Printing	3,082	374	131		3,213	374	3,587
Rubber	995	99			995	99	1,094
Shipyards	4,691				4,691		4,691
Shoes	1,372	362	139[a]	90[a]	1,372[a]	362[a]	1,734[a]
Slaughtering	9,076				9,076		9,076
Tanneries	2,546	18	17		2,563	18	2,581
Tobacco	1,232		215[a]		1,232[a]	278	1,510[a]
Wagons and carriages	2,056		42		2,098		2,098
Woolen mills	3,585	3,639	296	475	3,881	4,114	7,995
Total	103,927	11,919	2,643[a]	685[a]	106,945[a]	13,903[a]	120,848[a]

Source: Census of 1900, *Employees and Wages*, by Davis R. Dewey.

[a] Where median wage was less than five cents per hour, the median was not reported and the number employed at that wage was not included in totals and averages.

TABLE A-9

Average Annual Earnings of Manufacturing Wage Earners in 17 Industries; United States, by Regions; Census, Decennial Years Ending May 31, 1860-1890
(current dollars)

Industry	United States				New England				Middle Atlantic[a]			
	1860	1870	1880	1890	1860	1870	1880	1890	1860	1870	1880	1890
Foundry and machine shop production	392	573	454	559	395	565	468	569	364	575	451	572
Carriages and wagons	362	387	411	508	392	488	481	603	347	398	420	525
Liquors, malt	358	543	465	685	407	527	472	745	331	622	480	755
Agricultural implements	342	481	388	466	338	457	411	488	320	485	372	475
Iron and steel, rolling mills	341	570	436	542	402	530	394	490	334	561	442	542
Liquors, distilled	324	394	410	467	464	492	424	512	437	364	420	565
Glass	322	496	378	465	308	429	405	405	325	497	380	467
Cigars and cigarettes	317	349	346	419	334	420	407	486	312	337	366	404
Flour and grist mills	315	249	298	383	286	240	341	437	309	248	303	410
Leather	312	411	403	501	357	510	428	526	302	430	393	488
Lumber sawed	298	267	215	289	289	263	184	287	268	265	192	266
Iron and Steel, blast furnaces	285	453	304	437	301	714	338	488	284	465	342	434
Paper	254	398	349	427	254	413	354	442	240	390	332	428
Woolen goods	232	336	299	340	240	360	314	333	234	331	295	337
Cotton goods	196	288	244	302	205	303	253	325	188	276	233	320
Brick and tile	195	249	203	285	146	241	193	281	206	296	232	314
Chewing and smoking tobacco	189	239	196	233	–	–	–	–	238	280	298	338
The 17 Industries:												
Median	315	394	349	437	321	448	400	487	309	364	366	434
Weighted mean	277	363	325	412	251	359	308	393	286	399	357	464
Simple mean	296	393	341	430	320	435	367	464	296	401	350	449
All manufacturing (excluding men's clothing, and boots and shoes)	297	384	345	427								

table continues on following page

TABLE A-9, *concluded*

Industry	South[a]				Central[b]				Pacific			
	1860	1870	1880	1890	1860	1870	1880	1890	1860	1870	1880	1890
Foundry and machine shop production	408	600	360	504	378	529	445	529	1,667	1,188	650	807
Carriages and wagons	336	300	306	427	341	351	394	478	924	684	634	721
Liquors, malt	392	464	406	581	335	481	451	614	854	572	468	846
Agricultural implements	326	327	266	377	361	488	440	461	842	615	508	757
Iron and steel, rolling mills	281	584	343	407	391	606	458	564	–	–	–	–
Liquors, distilled	232	190	243	236	322	432	422	475	833	413	486	310
Glass	300	147	330[c]	384	298	621	376	458	–	–	–	–
Cigars and cigarettes	342	488	251	478	289	332	349	408	928	287	270	410
Flour and grist mills	240	122	163	204	336	322	356	425	867	549	543	619
Leather	253	160	236	308	305	349	429	521	653	404	554	641
Lumber, sawed	242	222	173	269	276	268	240	283	700	433	341	458
Iron and steel, blast furnaces	212	353	231	401	318	459	287	482	–	–	–	–
Paper	348	389	273	315	270	382	365	403	357	650	533	621
Woolen goods	179	189	169	242	253	273	231	275	555	408	393	246
Cotton goods	146	188	164	194	194	261	222	249	–	–	–	–
Brick and tile	177	185	144	226	185	207	194	264	375	205	246	372
Chewing and smoking tobacco	178	146	127	170	212	327	254	307	–	–	–	–
Median	253	222	243	315	305	351	365	458	838	491	496	620
Weighted mean, all manufacturing	233	223	183	280	304	358	335	409	790	475	448	528
Simple mean	270	297	246	337	298	393	348	423	796	534	469	567

Source: Censuses of Manufactures, 1860-1890. The coverage of the industries in each year is as nearly the same as it was possible to make it.

[a] Delaware, Maryland, and West Virginia are included in the Middle Atlantic states.

[b] Kentucky is included in the Central states.

[c] Data on wage earners in glass manufactures not given separately for the southern states in 1890; estimated on the basis of the 1890 country-wide ratio between wages of wage earners and of all employees in glass manufacturing.

TABLE A-10

Manufacturing and Building Wages Adjusted for Changes in Living Cost; Annually
1860-1890

| | | MANUFACTURING | | | | | | BUILDING | | | |
| | | Aldrich | | Weeks | | Bulletin 18 | | Aldrich | | Bulletin 18 | |
	Cost of Living 1860=100	Current Dollars	1860 Dollars	Current Dollars	1860 Dollars	Current Dollars	1860 Dollars	Current Dollars	1860 Dollars	Current Dollars	1860 Dollar
1860	100	1.19	1.19	1.32	1.32			1.69	1.69		
1861	101	1.17	1.16	1.36	1.35			1.66	1.64		
1862	114	1.23	1.08	1.53	1.34			1.72	1.51		
1863	140	1.31	.94	1.51	1.08			1.89	1.35		
1864	177	1.48	.84	1.72	.97			2.21	1.25		
1865	176	1.64	.93	1.82	1.03			2.55	1.45		
1866	168	1.72	1.02	1.90	1.13			2.74	1.63		
1867	159	1.75	1.10	1.94	1.22			2.94	1.85		
1868	154	1.76	1.14	1.92	1.25			3.00	1.95		
1869	147	1.80	1.22	1.93	1.31			3.16	2.15		
1870	141	1.79	1.27	1.92	1.36	2.05	1.45	3.06	2.17	2.97	2.11
1871	136	1.81	1.33	1.95	1.43	2.01	1.48	2.93	2.15	3.02	2.22
1872	135	1.82	1.35	1.95	1.44	2.04	1.51	2.92	2.16	3.03	2.24
1873	133	1.85	1.39	1.97	1.48	2.04	1.53	2.85	2.14	2.96	2.23
1874	129	1.80	1.40	1.87	1.45	1.97	1.53	2.77	2.15	2.85	2.21
1875	123	1.72	1.40	1.84	1.50	1.93	1.57	2.69	2.19	2.78	2.26
1876	119	1.68	1.41	1.79	1.50	1.90	1.60	2.43	2.04	2.67	2.24
1877	119	1.59	1.34	1.75	1.47	1.77	1.49	2.28	1.92	2.54	2.13
1878	111	1.52	1.37	1.72	1.55	1.71	1.54	2.17	1.95	2.46	2.22
1879	109	1.49	1.37	1.72	1.58	1.69	1.55	2.17	1.99	2.47	2.27
1880	110	1.54	1.40	1.77	1.61	1.72	1.56	2.14	1.95	2.55	2.32
1881	110	1.56	1.42			1.80	1.64	2.35	2.14	2.72	2.47
1882	110	1.59	1.45			1.87	1.70	2.53	2.30	2.81	2.55
1883	108	1.63	1.51			1.89	1.75	2.54	2.35	2.88	2.67
1884	106	1.66	1.57			1.90	1.79	2.56	2.42	2.92	2.75
1885	103	1.61	1.56			1.87	1.82	2.56	2.49	2.89	2.81
1886	101	1.62	1.60			1.89	1.87	2.63	2.60	2.89	2.86
1887	102	1.67	1.64			1.92	1.88	2.59	2.54	2.90	2.84
1888	102	1.69	1.66			1.92	1.88	2.61	2.56	2.92	2.86
1889	99	1.73	1.75			1.91	1.93	2.69	2.72	2.91	2.94
1890	98	1.75	1.79			1.93	1.97	2.68	2.73	2.94	3.00

Source: Wage data, Tables A-1 through A-4; cost of living, Tables B-1, -2.

TABLE A-11

Average Hourly Wages in Manufacturing Adjusted for Changes in Living
Cost; Annually 1860-1890

	Money Hourly Wages, Cents	Cost of Living, 1890=100	Real Hourly Wages 1890 Cents		Money Hourly Wages, Cents	Cost of Living, 1890=100	Real Hourly Wages 1890 Cents
1860	9.5	102	9.3	1875	14.0	126	11.1
1861	9.7	103	9.4	1876	13.7	121	11.3
1862	10.6	116	9.1	1877	13.2	121	10.9
1863	10.7	143	7.5	1878	12.8	113	11.3
1864	12.2	181	6.7	1879	12.6	111	11.4
1865	13.4	180	7.4	1880	13.0	112	11.6
1866	13.8	171	8.1	1881	13.5	112	12.1
1867	14.1	162	8.7	1882	13.8	112	12.3
1868	14.2	157	9.0	1883	14.2	110	12.9
1869	14.4	150	9.6	1884	14.4	108	13.3
1870	14.5	144	10.1	1885	14.1	105	13.4
1871	14.7	139	10.6	1886	14.3	103	13.9
1872	14.8	138	10.7	1887	14.9	104	14.3
1873	15.0	136	11.0	1888	15.0	104	14.4
1874	14.4	132	10.9	1889	15.1	101	15.0
				1890	15.3	100	15.3

Source: Tables 13, A-8, A-10, B-1, and B-2.
Method: The Aldrich and Weeks–Bulletin 18 series on daily wages were averaged
and adjusted to the level of average daily wages in 1890 in the Dewey Report. These
were divided by the Aldrich series on average daily hours of work for 13 industries.

TABLE A-12

Wages of Skilled and Laboring Occupations Adjusted for Changes in Living Cost;
Annually 1860-1890

	FIVE SKILLED OCCUPATIONS				LABORERS			
	Aldrich Data		Weeks Data		Aldrich Data		Weeks Data	
	Current Dollars	1860 Dollars	Current Dollars	1860 Dollars	Current Dollars	1860 Dollars	Current Dollars	1860 Dollars
1860	0.164	0.164	1.62	1.62	0.098	0.098	1.03	1.03
1861	0.164	0.162	1.67	1.65	0.097	0.096	1.04	1.03
1862	0.171	0.150	1.78	1.56	0.097	0.085	1.08	0.95
1863	0.186	0.133	2.00	1.43	0.111	0.079	1.20	0.86
1864	0.218	0.123	2.33	1.32	0.130	0.073	1.39	0.79
1865	0.245	0.139	2.50	1.42	0.148	0.084	1.48	0.84
1866	0.256	0.152	2.62	1.56	0.152	0.090	1.53	0.91
1867	0.268	0.169	2.59	1.63	0.153	0.096	1.53	0.96
1868	0.270	0.175	2.58	1.68	0.154	1.000	1.51	0.98
1869	0.272	0.185	2.60	1.77	0.156	1.061	1.53	1.04
1870	0.274	0.194	2.61	1.85	0.156	1.106	1.52	1.08
1871	0.277	0.204	2.58	1.90	0.157	1.154	1.50	1.10
1872	0.282	0.209	2.64	1.96	0.159	1.177	1.52	1.13
1873	0.288	0.217	2.62	1.97	0.159	1.195	1.52	1.14
1874	0.286	0.222	2.48	1.92	0.158	1.225	1.43	1.11
1875	0.276	0.224	2.39	1.94	0.154	1.252	1.39	1.13
1876	0.263	0.221	2.24	1.88	0.149	1.252	1.33	1.12
1877	0.247	0.208	2.18	1.83	0.142	1.193	1.28	1.08
1878	0.239	0.215	2.15	1.94	0.137	1.234	1.26	1.14
1879	0.228	0.209	2.16	1.98	0.135	1.239	1.27	1.17
1880	0.234	0.213	2.26	2.05	0.135	1.227	1.32	1.20
1881	0.243	0.221			0.140	1.272		
1882	0.249	0.226			0.143	1.300		
1883	0.252	0.233			0.147	1.360		
1884	0.255	0.241			0.146	1.377		
1885	0.247	0.240			0.145	1.407		
1886	0.249	0.247			0.144	1.426		
1887	0.254	0.249			0.149	1.460		
1888	0.255	0.250			0.150	1.470		
1889	0.255	0.258			0.150	1.515		
1890	0.257	0.262			0.151	1.540		

TABLE A-13

Annual Earnings of Factory Wage Earners (Census), Adjusted for Changes in Living Cost; United States, by Industry and Region, Decennial Years Ending May 31, 1860-1890
(1860 dollars)

	1860	1870	1880	1890
Cost of living[a]	100	144	109.5	98.5
Foundry and machine shop	392	398	415	567
Carriages and wagons	362	269	375	516
Liquors, malt	358	377	425	695
Agricultural implements	342	334	354	473
Iron and steel, rolling mills	341	396	398	550
Liquors, distilled	324	274	374	474
Glass	322	344	345	472
Cigars and cigarettes	317	242	316	425
Flour and grist mills	315	173	272	389
Leather	312	285	368	509
Lumber, sawed	298	185	196	293
Iron and steel, blast furnaces	285	315	278	444
Paper	254	276	319	433
Woolen goods	232	233	273	345
Cotton goods	196	200	223	307
Brick and tile	195	173	185	289
Chewing and smoking tobacco	189	166	179	236
Weighted means, 17 industries:				
United States	277	252	297	418
New England	251	249	281	399
Middle Atlantic	286	277	326	471
South	233	155	167	284
Central	304	249	306	415
Pacific	790	330	409	536
United States: all manufacturing	297	267	315	433

[a] Since the decennial years covered the twelve months ending May 31, the cost of living index for each decennial year was the average of that year and the preceding year.

TABLE B-1

The Hoover Consumer Price Index for the United States during 1860-1880
(1860=100)

	All Items	Food	Clothing	Rent	Fuel and Light	Other
Weight	100.0	54.8	18.0	16.9	7.9	2.4
1860	100	100	100	100	100	100
1861	101	99	110	95	103	102
1862	114	108	143	101	112	105
1863	140	131	197	113	136	115
1864	177	168	261	130	155	141
1865	176	172	238	134	159	147
1866	168	172	194	138	152	146
1867	159	167	166	135	140	144
1968	154	165	148	138	133	144
1869	147	152	148	141	132	145
1870	141	143	141	142	126	143
1871	136	138	128	144	125	142
1872	135	138	126	144	122	141
1873	133	136	122	139	120	142
1874	129	135	115	133	114	141
1875	123	129	105	129	110	140
1876	119	124	104	123	106	138
1877	119	127	99	123	98	138
1878	111	114	95	124	93	135
1879	109	111	94	122	92	134
1880	110	111	94	127	95	133

Source: Ethel D. Hoover, "Prices in the Nineteenth Century," *Trends in the American Economy in the Nineteenth Century*, Studies in Income and Wealth, Vol. 24 (in press).

TABLE B-2

A new Consumer Price Index for the United States during 1880-1890,
Prepared in This Study for Linkage with the Hoover Index

	1880=100,	*1860=100*					
	All Items	*All Items*	*Food*	*Clothing*	*Rent*	*Fuel and Light*	*Other*[a]
Weights		100.0	42.5	14.0	13.0	5.3	25.2
1880	100	110	111	94	127	95	133
1881	100	110	111	95	127	93	132
1882	100	110	111	93	127	93	133
1883	98	108	110	91	126	89	130
1884	96	106	105	88	126	89	128
1885	94	103	103	86	126	86	125
1886	92	101	102	85	126	86	121
1887	93	102	102	85	124	91	121
1888	93	102	102	86	124	92	121
1889	90	99	98	84	124	92	120
1890	89	98	99	82	124	88	114

Source and method: Chapter 4, above, and Appendix Table B-3.
[a] Combines housefurnishings and miscellaneous.

TABLE B-3

A New Consumer Price Index Constructed from Retail Price Data for Food, Clothing, Housing, Fuel and Light, and Other Cost of Living Items, 1880-1890

	Unit	Number of Unit Quotations	Percent of Family Expense	1880 Price	Index (1880=100)										
					1880	1881	1882	1883	1884	1885	1886	1887	1888	1889	1890
Food			42.50		100	100	100	99	95	93	92	92	92	88	89
Beef, roasting	lb.	7	3.95	0.129	100	97	104	107	103	94	97	101			93
Beef, steak	lb.	5	3.95	0.144	100					105					102
Pork, fresh	lb.	5	2.18	0.100	100					105					97
Pork, bacon	lb.	5	0.38	0.114	100					102					104
Pork, corned	lb.	3	0.38	0.100	100					100					97
Pork, ham	lb.	6	0.38	0.152	100	97	106	109	103	99	91	93	97	97	94
Codfish, dried	lb.	7	0.57	0.098	100	103	98	97	109	96	97	89	88	93	91
Eggs	doz.	6	1.60	0.297	100	97	100	103	97	90	88	88	89	85	83
Milk	qt.	5	2.89	0.068	100	100	103	96	94	91	90	93	85	79	85
Butter	lb.	6	5.60	0.360	100	100	101	102	94	93	93	96	92	89	82
Cheese	lb.	8	0.34	0.166	100	101	106	101	96	95	92	92	93	93	92
Lard	lb.	7	1.02	0.120	100	108	93	90	100	87	86	84	92	87	83
Tea, Oolong	lb.	7	0.87	0.684	100	96	96	94	89	88	89	81	82	80	79
Coffee, Rio roasted	lb.	9	1.35	0.300	100	100	98	98	94	91	91	101	100	100	103
Coffee, Rio green	lb.	4	1.35	0.212	100	100	96	92	94	94	91	94	97	94	92
Sugar, granulated	lb.	9	1.61	0.107	100	97	100	97	83	79	74	75	78	77	71
Sugar, coffee	lb.	5	1.61	0.086	100	98	98	97	89	89	85	87	86	81	78
Molasses, New Orleans	gal.	8	0.09	0.644	100	99	102	98	93	93	88	89	88	88	87
Molasses, Puerto Rico	gal.	6	0.09	0.497	100	99	99	98	98	92	89	90	90	88	91
Syrup	gal.	8	0.09	0.551	100	99	96	94	89	90	89	90	90	84	83
Flour: wheat, superfine	lb.	7	2.95	0.051	100	96	92	100	88	87	83	82	85	75	77
Flour: wheat, family	lb.	5	2.95	0.045	100	92	100	96	81	81	79	79	86	73	77
Rye	lb.	6	0.74	0.041	100	100	96	87	98	90	90	89	88	86	86
Corn meal	lb.	7	0.74	0.030	100	96	93	96	86	95	85	85	90	84	80
Rice	lb.	8	0.11	0.085	100	97	98	98	96	92	93	89	90	88	88
Beans	lb.	6	2.41	0.107	100	108	100	97	97	89	90	95	91	90	89
Potatoes	bu.	5	2.30	0.800	100	106	101	97	101	95	92	101	95	93	117

table continues on following pages

Table B-3, *continued*

	Unit	Number of Quotations	Percent of Family Expense	1880 Price	Index (1880=100)										
					1880	1881	1882	1883	1884	1885	1886	1887	1888	1889	1890
Clothing															
Men's suits	pair	1	14.00	12.92	100	101	99	97	94	91	90	90	91	89	87
Overalls	pair	1	1.41	0.70	100	97	117	108	113	99	102	101	106	111	96
			1.41		100	106	100	97	100	99	99	100	110	99	99
Dresses, cloth for															
Gingham	yard	7	0.84	0.111	100	108	100	90	86	82	79	79	79	77	77
Shirting checks	yard	8	0.84	0.161	100	95	96	91	90	86	86	87	87	86	84
Boots and shoes															
Leather boots	pair	2	0.70	3.44	100	100	101	95	87	93	90	91	89	90	76
Gum boots	pair	2	0.14	3.35	100	96	96	94	93	85	82	82	81	81	72
Shoes	pair	1	0.70	1.59	100	101	107	108	109	107	104	108	109	106	103
Shoe repair	pair	1	0.70	0.65	100	100	100	100	89	100	100	100	100	100	108
Miscellaneous															
Flannel cloth	yard	12	3.63	0.156	100	99	102	99	95	93	90	89	89	89	90
Denim cloth	yard	7	3.63	0.193	100	101	87	91	84	81	79	81	78	76	76
Rent															
Four rooms	room	4	13.00	2.73	100	100	100	99	99	99	99	98	98	98	98
Six rooms	room	4	6.50	2.62											
	room		6.50	2.84											
Fuel and light															
Coal	bu.	3	5.30	2.83	100	98	98	94	94	91	90	96	97	97	93
			2.40		100	98	100	92	94	92	88	100	100	100	88
Wood	cord	5	2.40	6.10	100	99	98	97	95	93	95	97	99	101	103
Kerosene	gal.	6	0.50	0.195	100	96	88	88	85	78	76	72	69	68	67
House furnishings															
Woolen blankets	blanket	3	3.40	6.17	100	98	97	95	94	88	85	85	84	84	84
			1.13		100	100	100	100	99	95	95	93	92	91	88
Carpets, ingrain	yard	11	1.13	1.25	100	96	91	91	93	85	79	76	78	74	78
Sheeting, 4-4	yard	8	0.57	0.101	100	102	101	95	90	85	84	88	79	89	88
Sheeting, 9-4	yard	8	0.57	0.300	100	95	101	94	90	84	80	81	84	83	84

159

Table B-3, concluded

	Unit	Number of Quotations	Percent of Family Expense	1880 Price	Index (1880 = 100)										
					1880	1881	1882	1883	1884	1885	1886	1887	1888	1889	1890
Miscellaneous			21.80												
Tobacco	lb.	1	2.68	0.52	100	99	100	99	96	95	92	92	92	91	86
Insurance, fire	$1000	1	0.80	2.17	100	98	109	100	94	96	84	81	83	84	77
Newspapers	daily paper	8	2.50	0.031	100	91	73	95	69	75	82	108	94	97	98
Stamps	oz.	3	0.57	0.05	100	100	104	92	88	88	86	84	88	76	74
Soap	bar	6	2.28	0.058	100	100	100	82	82	45	45	45	45	45	45
Starch	lb.	5	2.28	0.080	100	100	100	103	103	97	97	93	93	90	90
R. R. fares	pass. mile	1	2.28	0.030	100	98	98	98	93	93	83	80	83	85	83
Physicians' fees	office call	1	8.41	0.62	100	100	100	100	100	100	100	100	100	100	100

Source: Retail Prices:

Retail grocers in New York City and Brooklyn, *Tenth Annual Report of the Bureau of Statistics of Labor of the State of New York* (for 1892), I, pp. 277-284. (Only two stores specified the month to which prices referred.) Country stores in central Pennsylvania and in Chester County—groceries, kerosene, cloth, and boots—from *Annual Report of the Secretary of Internal Affairs of the Commonwealth of Pennsylvania* (for 1890), Part III, "Industrial Statistics," XVIII, A-44 to -47. Prices quoted from January, April, July, and October of each year. Also for groceries, clothing, miscellaneous items, T. M. Adams, *Prices Paid by Vermont Farmers for Goods and Services . . .*, Bulletin 507—Supplement (University of Vermont and State Agricultural College), February 1944, pp. 41-66.

Rents, Leavenworth (Kansas), Boston, and St. Louis: For 1880, all from the Weeks Report on retail prices, pp. 104-107. Leavenworth, 1889, from *Seventh Annual Report*, Kansas Bureau of Labor Statistics, p. 198. Boston, 1890, from Massachusetts *Report on the Statistics of Labor*, 1890, pp. 481, 491. St. Louis, 1890, from Missouri Bureau of Labor Statistics *Twelfth Annual Report . . .* for the year ending November 5, 1890, pp. 414-515. Meat prices for 1880, 1885, and 1890: *Thirty-first Annual Report of the Massachusetts Bureau of Statistics of Labor*, March 1901, pp. 529-547 and passim; *Eighteenth Annual Report of the Commissioner of Labor* (for 1903), II, pp. 667-686 and passim.

Newspapers in eight cities: *Baltimore American, Boston Morning Journal, Charleston (S. C.) News-Courier, Memphis Ledger, Hartford Courant, New York Herald, Chicago Tribune,* and *Philadelphia Inquirer* (from files of the Library of Congress).

Postage rate *per ounce* for first class letters: Average of nonlocal letters and carrier office drop letters, with additional weight given to postal cards, *United States Domestic Postage Rates, 1789-1956,* Post Office Department, Publication 15, pp. 22-23.

Expenditure Weights:

Eighteenth Annual Report of the Commissioner of Labor, Cost of Living and Retail Prices of Food, p. 648; Nelson W. Aldrich, *Retail Prices and Wages,* Report by Mr. Aldrich from the Committee on Finance, July 19, 1892, 52nd Congress, 1st Session, Senate Report 986, Parts I and III, pp. xlii-xliii, 2090-2097.

TABLE C-1

Employment in 13 Manufacturing Industries from the Aldrich Report, January and July 1860-1890
(number of persons)

Industry	1860 Jan.	1860 July	1861 Jan.	1861 July	1862 Jan.	1862 July	1863 Jan.	1863 July	1864 Jan.	1864 July	1865 Jan.	1865 July	1866 Jan.	1866 July
Agricultural implements	9	8	8	7	7	8	7	12	13	12	13	17	21	17
Ale, beer, porter	39	40	44	44	37	43	36	39	40	40	33	28	41	32
Books and newspapers	116	98	121	119	113	116	112	121	124	143	160	159	153	158
Carriages and wagons	14	14	14	14	14	14	15	15	15	14	14	14	20	20
Cotton manufactures	1,351	1,338	1,297	1,216	1,149	969	895	912	1,071	1,153	1,128	1,310	1,497	1,446
Illuminating gas	460	477	510	496	501	459	365	341	440	363	337	320	338	326
Leather	46	46	46	45	41	41	41	41	44	44	47	47	42	42
Lumber	35	34	43	46	35	34	29	29	33	33	37	44	41	39
Metals and metallic goods	846	891	830	964	977	916	873	966	1,121	1,239	1,188	1,117	1,185	1,214
Paper	41	41	39	39	38	38	37	37	34	35	35	35	35	34
Stone	228	445	214	273	160	269	80	459	350	458	300	463	481	593
White lead	17	19	20	19	19	18	13	13	11	8	5	9	12	11
Woolen manufactures	178	182	169	181	207	237	225	244	246	227	235	227	250	273
The 13 manufacturing industries	3,380	3,633	3,355	3,463	3,298	3,162	2,728	3,229	3,542	3,769	3,532	3,790	4,116	4,205

table continues on following pages

161

Table C-1, *continued*

Industry	1867		1868		1869		1870		1871		1872		1873		1874	
	Jan.	July	Jan.	July	Jan.	July	Jan.	July	Jan.	July	Jan.	July	Jan.	July	Jan.	July
Agricultural implements	20	13	19	21	18	22	27	25	28	32	33	37	34	34	31	27
Ale, beer, porter	36	26	33	28	32	29	39	30	32	36	38	44	52	45	50	47
Books and newspapers	170	177	178	203	166	178	182	152	150	188	186	203	167	142	149	142
Carriages and wagons	20	20	20	20	24	24	24	24	24	24	24	24	24	24	24	24
Cotton manufactures	1,534	1,543	1,550	1,593	1,590	1,573	1,665	1,613	1,699	1,743	1,677	1,733	1,754	1,692	1,615	1,629
Illuminating gas	363	335	382	354	434	414	515	461	509	563	588	546	398	355	449	396
Leather	41	41	52	52	55	56	76	76	68	68	67	67	76	76	77	77
Lumber	42	38	37	36	43	45	40	43	40	41	42	36	38	38	36	31
Metals and metallic goods	1,252	1,163	1,054	1,096	1,074	1,148	1,117	1,105	1,075	1,142	1,199	1,260	1,183	1,210	1,098	1,079
Paper	33	34	31	33	33	33	33	33	33	32	31	31	31	31	31	31
Stone	902	552	509	552	601	826	860	642	659	759	216	809	575	682	449	563
White lead	10	11	9	10	10	10	9	10	10	10	8	8	7	8	12	12
Woolen manufactures	257	251	244	253	245	255	293	297	307	311	340	315	310	311	335	325
The 13 manufacturing industries	4,680	4,204	4,118	4,251	4,325	4,613	4,880	4,511	4,634	4,949	4,449	5,113	4,649	4,648	4,356	4,383

Table C-1, *continued*

Industry	1875 Jan.	1875 July	1876 Jan.	1876 July	1877 Jan.	1877 July	1878 Jan.	1878 July	1879 Jan.	1879 July	1880 Jan.	1880 July	1881 Jan.	1881 July	1882 Jan.	1882 July
Agricultural implements	27	28	27	24	22	24	23	24	22	24	33	32	44	34	36	41
Ale, beer, porter	56	51	52	46	53	48	49	51	62	53	58	55	54	48	57	46
Books and newspapers	158	148	149	160	184	180	187	177	197	184	199	193	204	191	192	183
Carriages and wagons	24	24	24	24	24	24	30	30	34	34	40	40	40	40	40	40
Cotton manufactures	1,621	1,634	1,625	1,767	1,721	1,740	1,744	1,803	1,835	1,869	1,847	1,888	1,960	2,007	2,166	2,143
Illuminating gas	435	402	357	281	320	287	302	274	303	274	315	294	353	333	376	349
Leather	72	72	76	76	75	75	79	80	81	81	84	84	93	93	91	91
Lumber	30	24	27	31	25	25	29	23	20	26	22	22	26	26	30	29
Metals and metallic goods	998	1,026	980	955	962	938	1,043	976	962	1,040	1,167	1,527	1,688	1,776	1,849	1,804
Paper	31	31	29	29	29	29	28	29	28	27	29	28	27	25	25	25
Stone	513	514	216	533	472	563	329	539	409	644	555	697	526	732	624	767
White lead	12	12	11	12	13	12	14	15	19	25	26	20	23	22	31	31
Woolen manufactures	331	345	322	341	353	367	357	379	342	329	342	364	358	355	350	370
The 13 manufacturing industries	4,308	4,311	3,895	4,279	4,253	4,312	4,214	4,400	4,314	4,610	4,717	5,244	5,396	5,682	5,867	5,919

table continues on following page

Table C-1, *concluded*

Industry	1883		1884		1885		1886		1887		1887		1889		1890	
	Jan.	*July*	*Jan.*	*July*	*Jan.*	*July*	*Jan.*	*July*	*Jan.*	*July*	*Jan.*	*July*	*Jan.*	*July*	*Jan.*	*July*
Agricultural implements	36	55	44	51	35	36	35	36	42	40	26	27	40	39	40	32
Ale, beer, porter	52	55	68	58	68	58	65	59	67	46	59	39	52	48	52	52
Books and newspapers	196	171	198	166	172	171	190	165	207	188	168	163	197	158	177	157
Carriages and wagons	40	40	40	40	40	40	40	40	40	40	40	40	40	40	40	40
Cotton manufactures	2,058	2,076	1,987	1,988	1,960	2,003	1,999	2,033	2,099	2,251	2,301	2,249	2,311	2,300	2,232	2,325
Illuminating gas	458	356	424	270	437	366	427	348	415	354	441	403	420	373	432	395
Leather	95	95	92	92	71	71	74	74	92	92	87	87	83	83	68	68
Lumber	28	28	29	30	32	31	30	30	30	28	24	26	26	26	23	23
Metals and metallic goods	1,839	1,589	1,661	1,537	1,500	1,259	1,355	1,450	1,519	1,542	1,488	1,384	1,459	1,517	1,571	1,652
Paper	27	27	29	31	28	26	29	28	27	30	27	25	25	26	25	27
Stone	634	755	587	708	572	646	470	839	629	555	588	579	569	568	507	689
White lead	31	38	28	26	23	19	17	18	22	23	23	29	25	23	25	17
Woolen manufactures	389	376	388	367	371	376	390	435	421	433	421	426	429	449	445	441
The 13 manufacturing industries	5,883	5,661	5,575	5,364	5,309	5,102	5,121	5,555	5,610	5,622	5,693	5,477	5,676	5,650	5,637	5,918

TABLE C-2

Employment of Manufacturing Wage Earners in 17 Industries; United States, by Regions, Decennial Years Ending May 31, 1860-1890
(thousands of persons)

Industry	United States				New England				Middle Atlantic[a]			
	1860	1870	1880	1890	1860	1870	1880	1890	1860	1870	1880	1890
Foundry and machine shop production	41.2	83.5	145.4	231.6	9.9	18.9	29.9	43.4	17.4	36.0	67.9	95.4
Carriages and wagons	37.1	54.9	52.9	132.3	7.7	8.0	6.4	15.1	14.0	18.7	14.4	37.6
Liquors, malt	6.4	12.4	26.2	30.3	0.2	0.4	1.7	1.1	3.1	5.4	12.2	12.3
Agricultural implements	14.8	25.3	39.6	38.8	1.6	1.9	2.4	1.6	5.1	8.0	9.8	7.7
Iron and steel, rolling mills	20.0	47.1	96.1	134.9	1.3	3.2	7.8	5.7	13.9	33.1	60.1	91.9
Liquors, distilled	5.6	5.1	6.5	4.7	0.1	0.1	0.2	0.1	1.4	1.1	0.7	0.6
Glass	9.0	15.8	24.2	45.0	2.0	2.4	1.0	0.5	6.4	11.8	18.0	30.2
Cigars and cigarettes	8.0	26.0	53.3	87.1	1.4	2.1	2.3	3.7	4.8	13.6	28.9	49.6
Flour and grist mills	27.7	58.5	58.4	47.3	1.5	3.0	2.1	1.6	8.6	15.1	11.6	8.6
Leather	26.1	35.2	34.9	42.6	5.5	8.3	9.6	9.6	13.6	17.5	16.0	22.2
Lumber, sawed	75.9	150.0	148.0	266.7	8.9	18.1	15.1	22.1	19.4	37.1	31.0	35.8
Iron and steel, blast furnaces	15.9	27.6	41.7	32.9	0.8	0.6	0.9	0.1	9.4	14.5	19.5	18.5
Paper	10.9	18.8	24.4	28.4	5.4	7.3	11.0	11.4	4.0	8.0	7.6	8.7
Woolen goods	41.4	80.1	86.5	76.9	25.6	42.9	47.9	40.3	11.6	23.7	28.1	23.5
Cotton goods	122.0	135.4	172.5	218.9	81.4	94.5	127.2	147.4	29.1	29.0	28.4	31.8
Brick and tile	21.4	43.5	66.4	104.2	2.1	5.3	4.6	6.8	10.4	19.6	22.2	31.6
Chewing and smoking tobacco	18.9	21.8	32.8	29.8	–	–	–	–	1.4	5.6	7.1	3.1
The 17 industries[d]												
Total	502.3	841.0	1,109.8	1,552.4	155.4	217.3	270.1	310.5	173.6	297.8	383.5	509.1
1860=100	100	167	221	309	100	140	174	200	100	172	221	293
All manufacturing (excluding men's clothing, and boots and shoes)	884.7	1,617.2	2,268.2	3,245.5								
All manufacturing	1,122.5	1,861.2	2,562.8	3,613.5								

table continues on following page

Table C-2, concluded

Industry	South[a]				Central[b]				Pacific			
	1860	1870	1880	1890	1860	1870	1880	1890	1860	1870	1880	1890
Foundry and machine shop production	4.4	3.7	5.2	9.0	9.0	23.4	38.8	74.6	0.4	1.1	2.9	4.2
Carriages and wagons	5.8	3.7	3.1	7.6	8.7	23.5	27.8	68.7	0.5	0.7	0.7	2.1
Liquors, malt	0.1	0.2	0.2	1.0	2.6	5.7	10.3	14.4	0.2	0.9	1.3	1.0
Agricultural implements	1.0	0.6	1.4	1.5	7.1	14.6	25.3	27.4	e	–	–	0.6
Iron and steel, rolling mills	2.0	1.3	3.0	3.9	2.8	9.3	24.6	32.3	–	0.1	0.3	1.1
Liquors, distilled	0.6	0.4	0.3	0.4	3.2	3.2	5.1	3.4	e	0.1	0.1	e
Glass	0.2	–	–	–	0.3	1.6	4.8	13.3	–	e	–	–
Cigars and cigarettes	0.2	0.8	3.9	10.8	1.6	7.7	14.4	19.9	e	1.8	3.6	2.6
Flour and grist mills	5.0	15.4	14.4	10.1	11.0	23.7	28.2	25.1	0.5	0.9	1.2	1.3
Leather	2.9	2.5	1.8	1.5	3.7	6.2	6.4	7.5	0.1	0.3	0.9	1.1
Lumber, sawed	16.1	18.4	23.2	56.5	28.4	67.9	69.1	134.8	3.0	5.2	4.5	15.0
Iron and steel, blast furnaces	1.7	2.7	5.1	6.6	4.0	9.7	15.8	7.7	e	–	0.3	–
Paper	0.4	0.4	0.4	0.3	1.1	3.0	5.3	7.0	e	e	0.2	0.2
Woolen goods	1.7	1.8	1.3	3.2	2.3	10.6	7.7	8.0	0.1	0.8	1.1	1.6
Cotton goods	9.7	9.6	17.8	34.3	1.6	1.7	2.6	3.6	–	–	–	–
Brick and tile	2.8	2.9	8.6	13.7	5.7	15.0	28.8	43.8	0.4	0.7	1.0	3.8
Chewing and smoking tobacco	13.6	9.2	17.8	16.5	3.8	6.7	7.1	9.6	–	e	e	e
Total	68.8	73.6	107.5	176.9	96.9	233.5	322.1	501.1	5.2	12.6	18.1	34.6
The 17 industries[d] 1860=100	100	107	156	257	100	241	332	517	100	242	348	665

Source: Censuses of Manufactures, 1860-1890; see notes to Table A-9, above.

[a] Delaware, Maryland, and West Virginia are included in the Middle Atlantic states.
[b] Kentucky is included in the Central states.

e Less than fifty workers.
[d] Employment totals for regions will not add exactly to total for the United States, because of very small amount of manufacturing in Mountain states which were excluded. Employment for industries may not add to the total for all 17, because of rounding error.

INDEX

INDEX